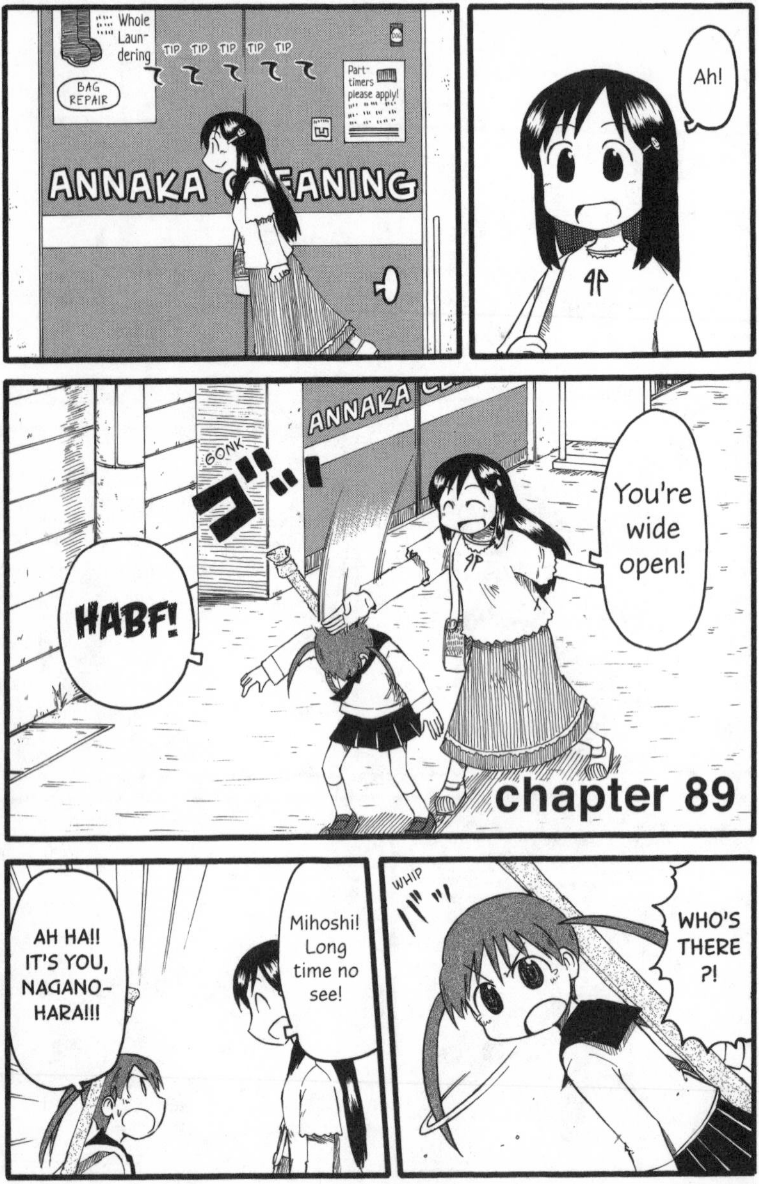
Ah!
Whole Laundering
TIP TIP TIP TIP TIP
BAG REPAIR
Part-timers please apply!
ANNAKA C EANING
ANNAKA C
GONK
You're wide open!
HABF!
chapter 89
WHIP
WHO'S THERE ?!
Mihoshi! Long time no see!
AH HA!! IT'S YOU, NAGANO-HARA!!!

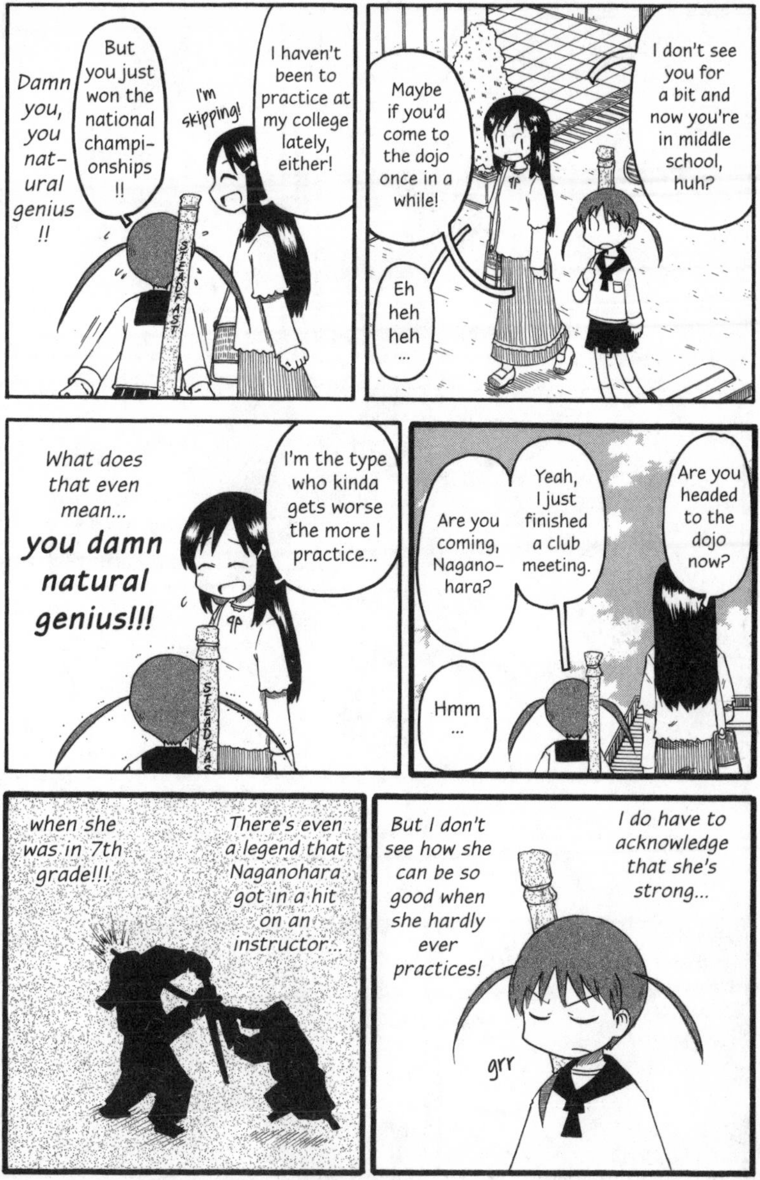
I don't see you for a bit and now you're in middle school, huh?
Maybe if you'd come to the dojo once in a while!
Eh heh heh ...
I haven't been to practice at my college lately, either!
I'm skipping!
But you just won the national champi-onships !!
Damn you, you nat-ural genius !!
STEADFAST
Are you headed to the dojo now?
Yeah, I just finished a club meeting.
Are you coming, Nagano-hara?
Hmm ...
I'm the type who kinda gets worse the more I practice...
What does that even mean... **you damn natural genius!!!**
STEADFAST
I do have to acknowledge that she's strong...
But I don't see how she can be so good when she hardly ever practices!
grr
There's even a legend that Naganohara got in a hit on an instructor...
when she was in 7th grade!!!

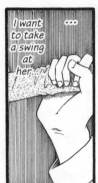

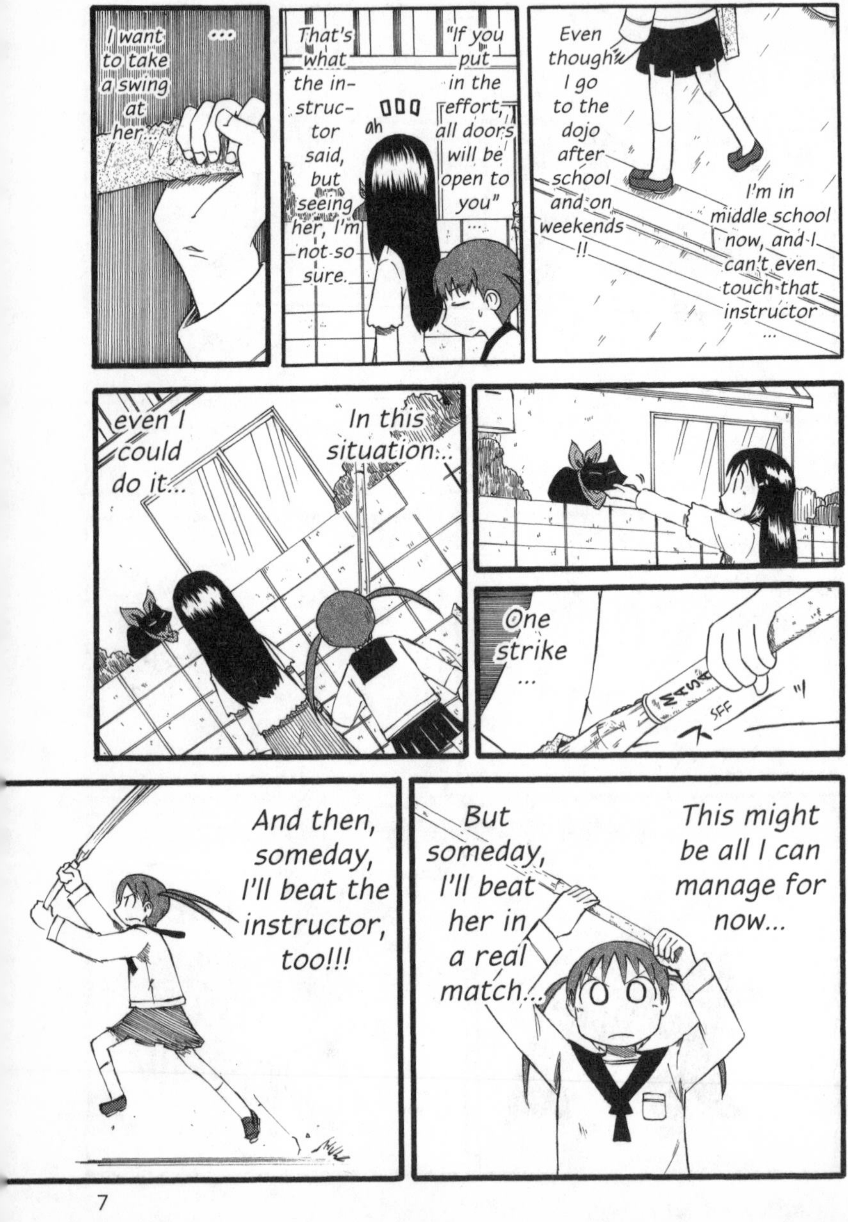
I'm in middle school now, and I can't even touch that instructor ...
Even though I go to the dojo after school and on weekends !!
"If you put in the effort, all doors will be open to you" ...
That's what the instructor said, but seeing her, I'm not so sure.
ah
...
I want to take a swing at her...
One strike ...
SFF
In this situation...
even I could do it...
This might be all I can manage for now...
But someday, I'll beat her in a real match...
And then, someday, I'll beat the instructor, too!!!

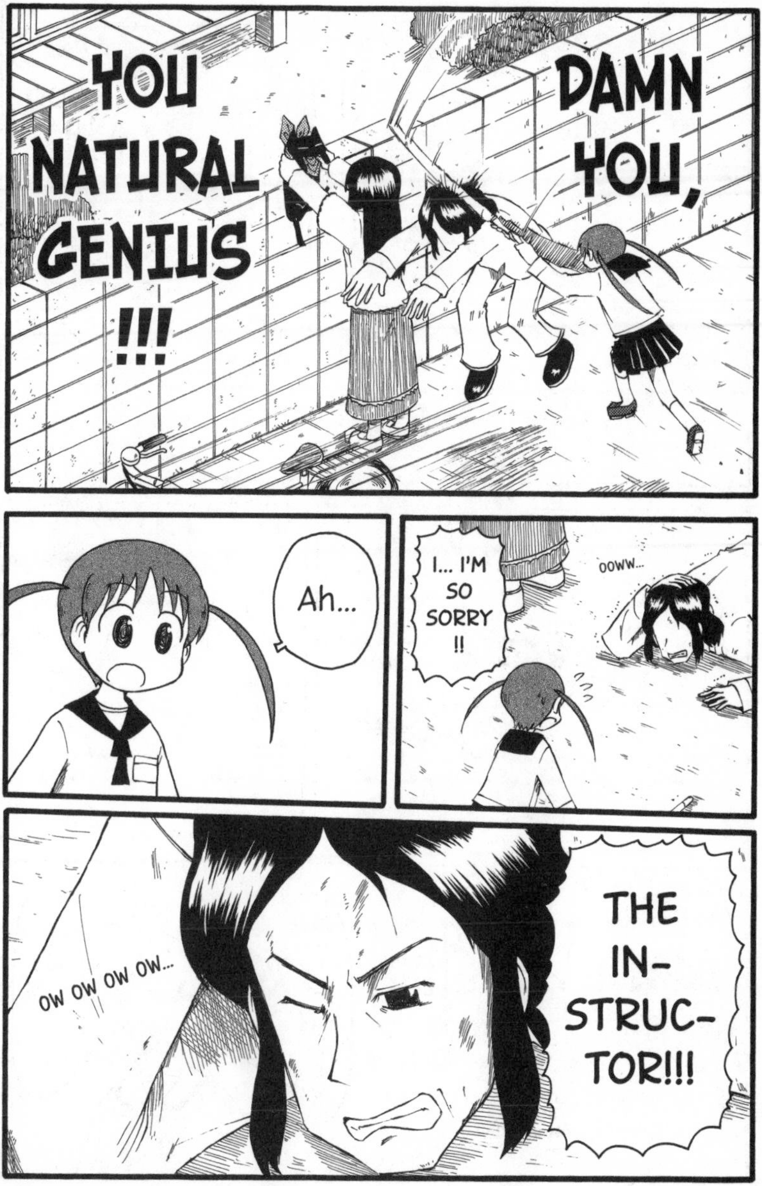
DAMN YOU,
YOU NATURAL GENIUS !!!
I... I'M SO SORRY !!
OOWW...
Ah...
THE IN-STRUC-TOR!!!
OW OW OW OW...

chapter 89: end

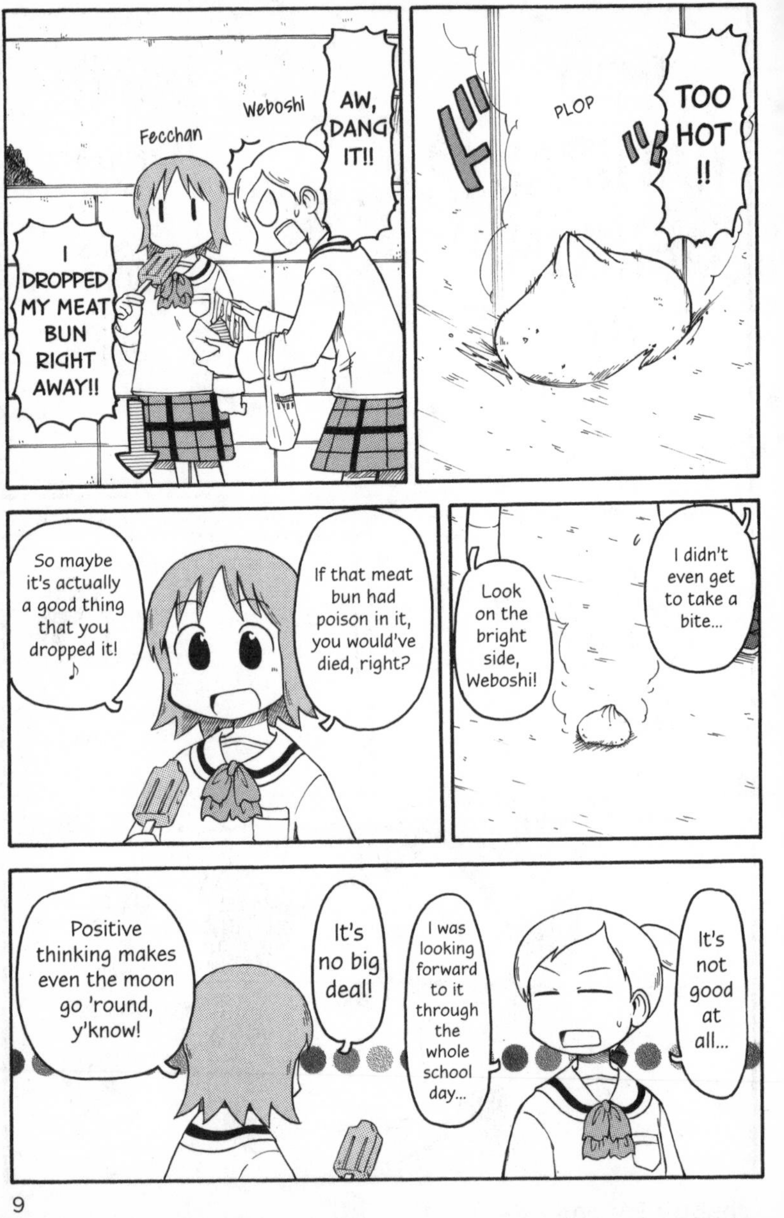
TOO HOT !!
PLOP
AW, DANG IT!!
Weboshi
Fecchan
I DROPPED MY MEAT BUN RIGHT AWAY!!
I didn't even get to take a bite...
Look on the bright side, Weboshi!
If that meat bun had poison in it, you would've died, right?
So maybe it's actually a good thing that you dropped it! ♪
It's not good at all...
I was looking forward to it through the whole school day...
It's no big deal!
Positive thinking makes even the moon go 'round, y'know!

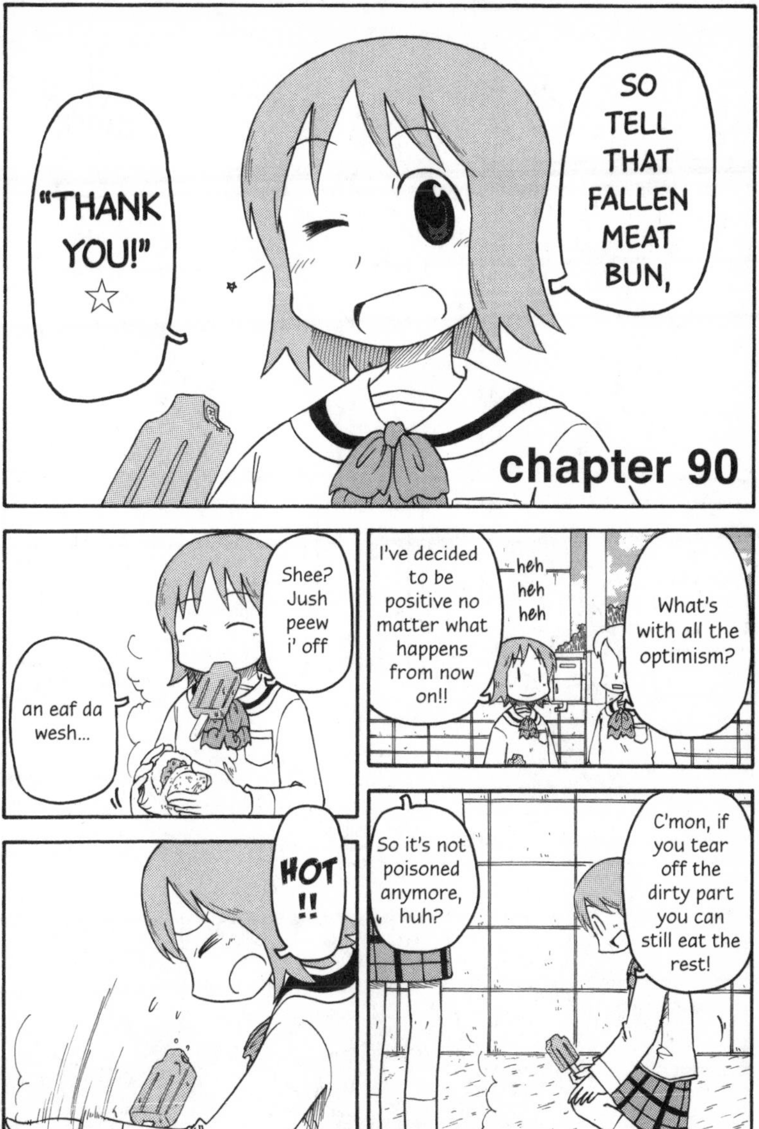
SO TELL THAT FALLEN MEAT BUN,
"THANK YOU!" ☆
chapter 90
What's with all the optimism?
heh heh heh
I've decided to be positive no matter what happens from now on!!
Shee? Jush peew i' off
an eaf da wesh...
C'mon, if you tear off the dirty part you can still eat the rest!
So it's not poisoned anymore, huh?
HOT !!

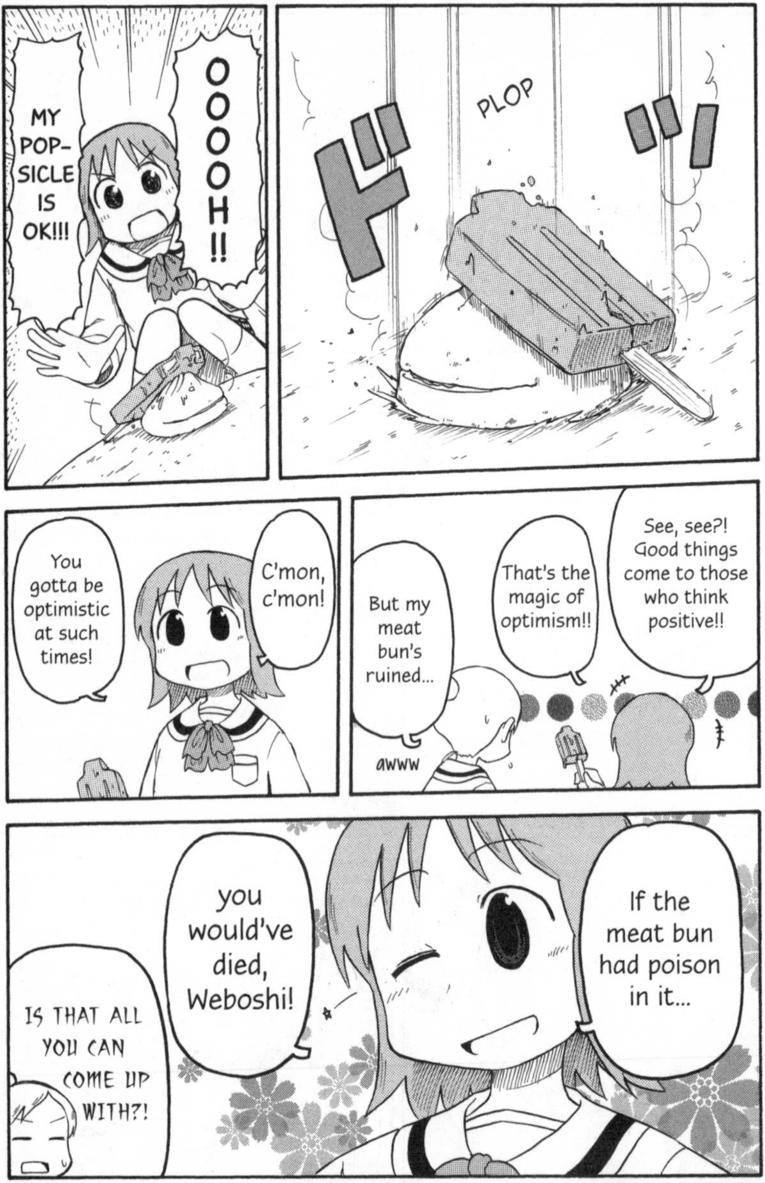
PLOP
OOOOOH!!
MY POP-SICLE IS OK!!!
See, see?! Good things come to those who think positive!!
That's the magic of optimism!!
But my meat bun's ruined...
awww
C'mon, c'mon!
You gotta be optimistic at such times!
If the meat bun had poison in it...
you would've died, Weboshi!
IS THAT ALL YOU CAN COME UP WITH?!

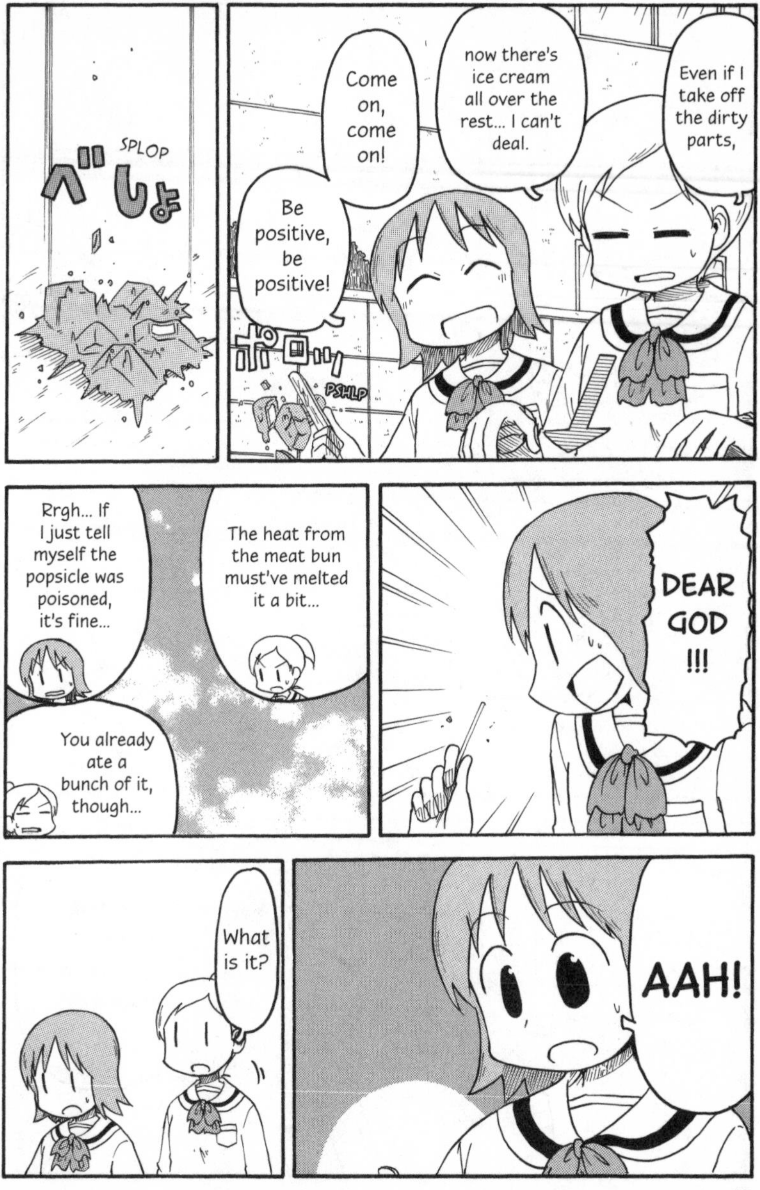

Even if I take off the dirty parts,
now there's ice cream all over the rest... I can't deal.
Come on, come on!
Be positive, be positive!
ポロッ
PSHLP
べしょ
SPLOP
DEAR GOD !!!
The heat from the meat bun must've melted it a bit...
Rrgh... If I just tell myself the popsicle was poisoned, it's fine...
You already ate a bunch of it, though...
AAH!
What is it?

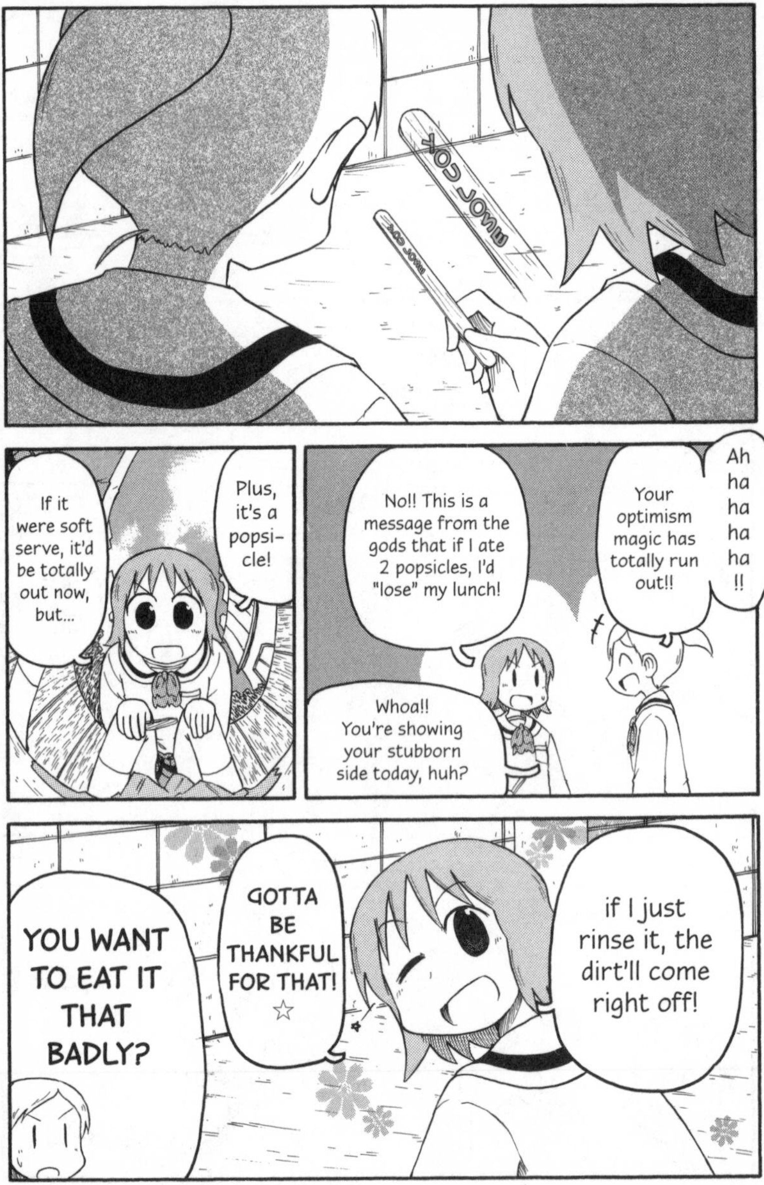

Ah ha ha ha ha !!
Your optimism magic has totally run out!!
No!! This is a message from the gods that if I ate 2 popsicles, I'd "lose" my lunch!
Whoa!! You're showing your stubborn side today, huh?
Plus, it's a popsi-cle!
If it were soft serve, it'd be totally out now, but...
if I just rinse it, the dirt'll come right off!
GOTTA BE THANKFUL FOR THAT! ☆
YOU WANT TO EAT IT THAT BADLY?

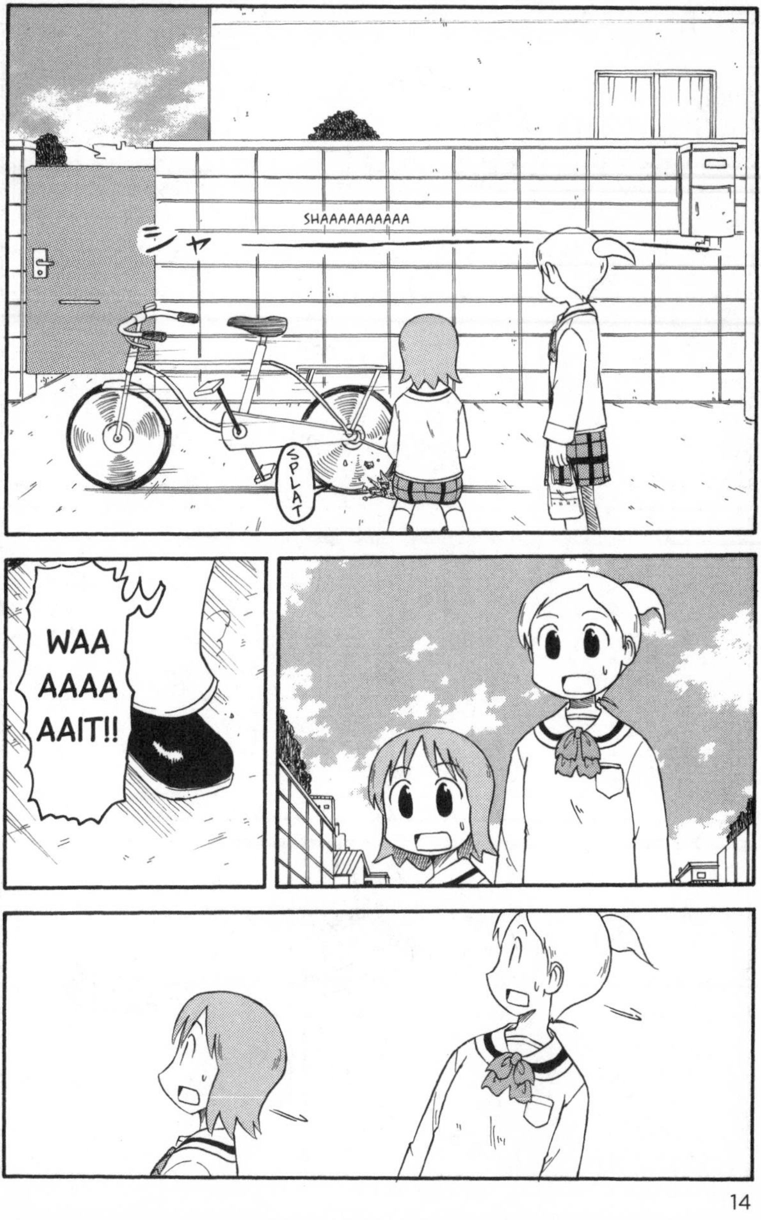
SHAAAAAAAAAA
シャ
SPLAT
WAA AAAA AAIT!!

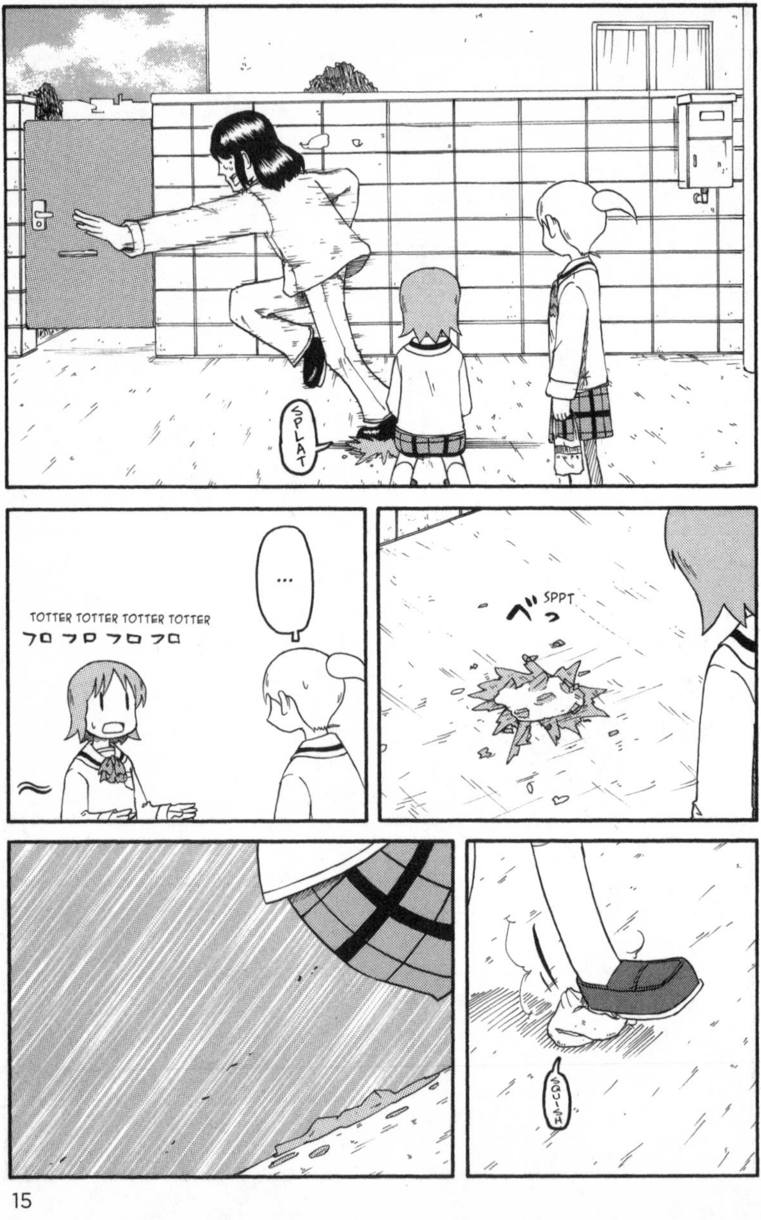
SPLAT
べっ
SPPT
...
TOTTER TOTTER TOTTER TOTTER
フロ フロ フロ フロ
SQUISH

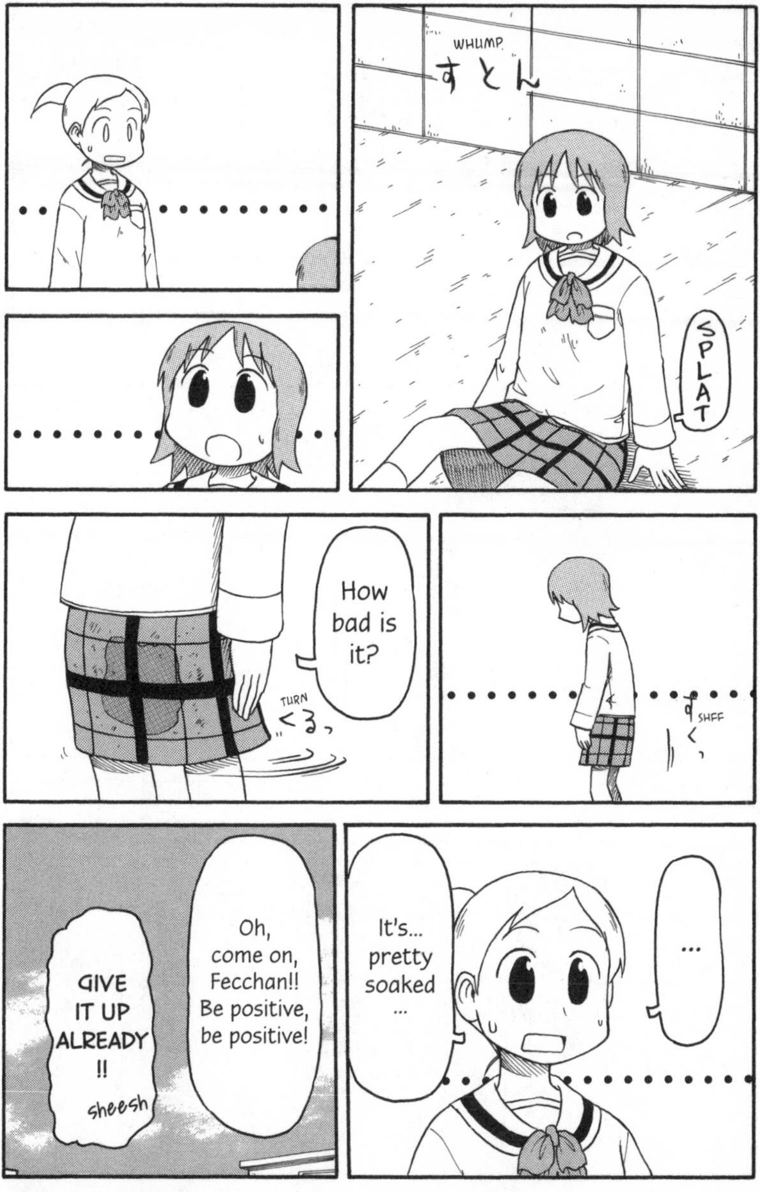
WHUMP
すとん
SPLAT
すく
SHFF
How bad is it?
TURN
くるっ
...
It's... pretty soaked ...
Oh, come on, Fecchan!! Be positive, be positive!
GIVE IT UP ALREADY !!
sheesh

chapter 90: end

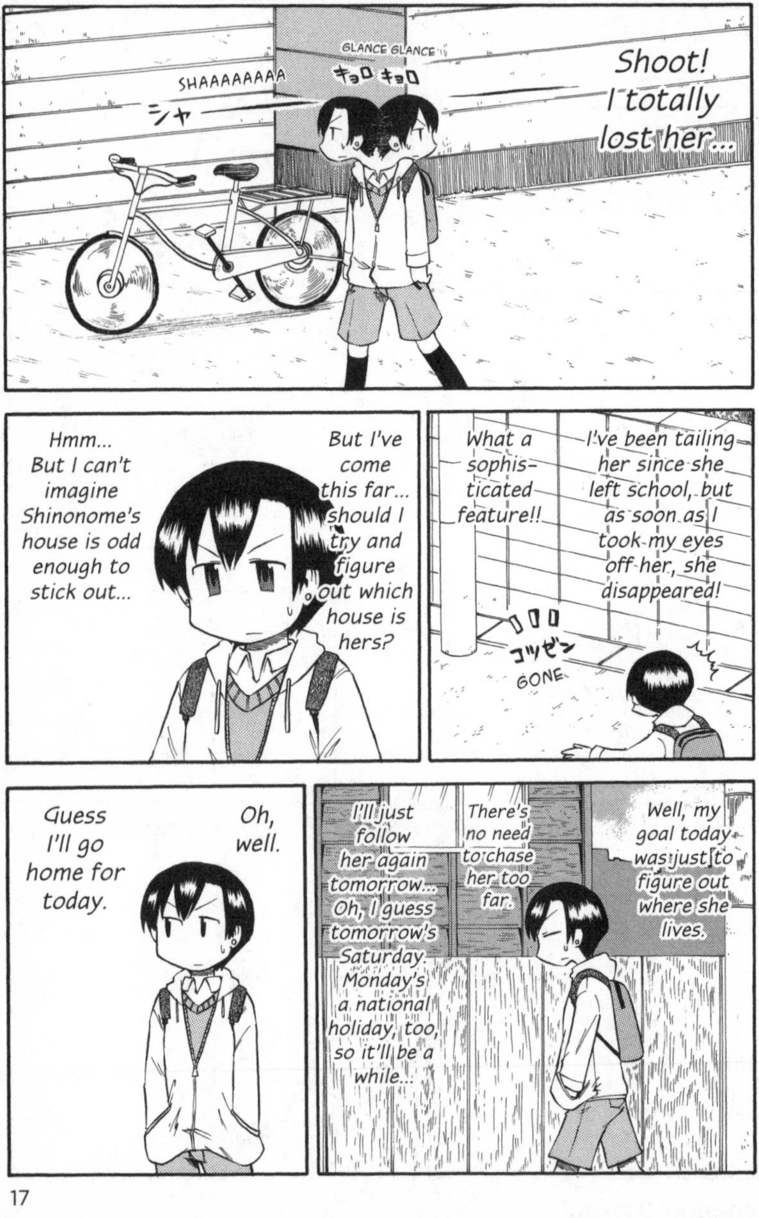
GLANCE GLANCE
キョロ キョロ
SHAAAAAAAA
シャ
Shoot! I totally lost her...
I've been tailing her since she left school, but as soon as I took my eyes off her, she disappeared!
What a sophis-ticated feature!!
コツゼン
GONE
But I've come this far... should I try and figure out which house is hers?
Hmm... But I can't imagine Shinonome's house is odd enough to stick out...
Well, my goal today was just to figure out where she lives.
There's no need to chase her too far.
I'll just follow her again tomorrow... Oh, I guess tomorrow's Saturday. Monday's a national holiday, too, so it'll be a while...
Oh, well.
Guess I'll go home for today.

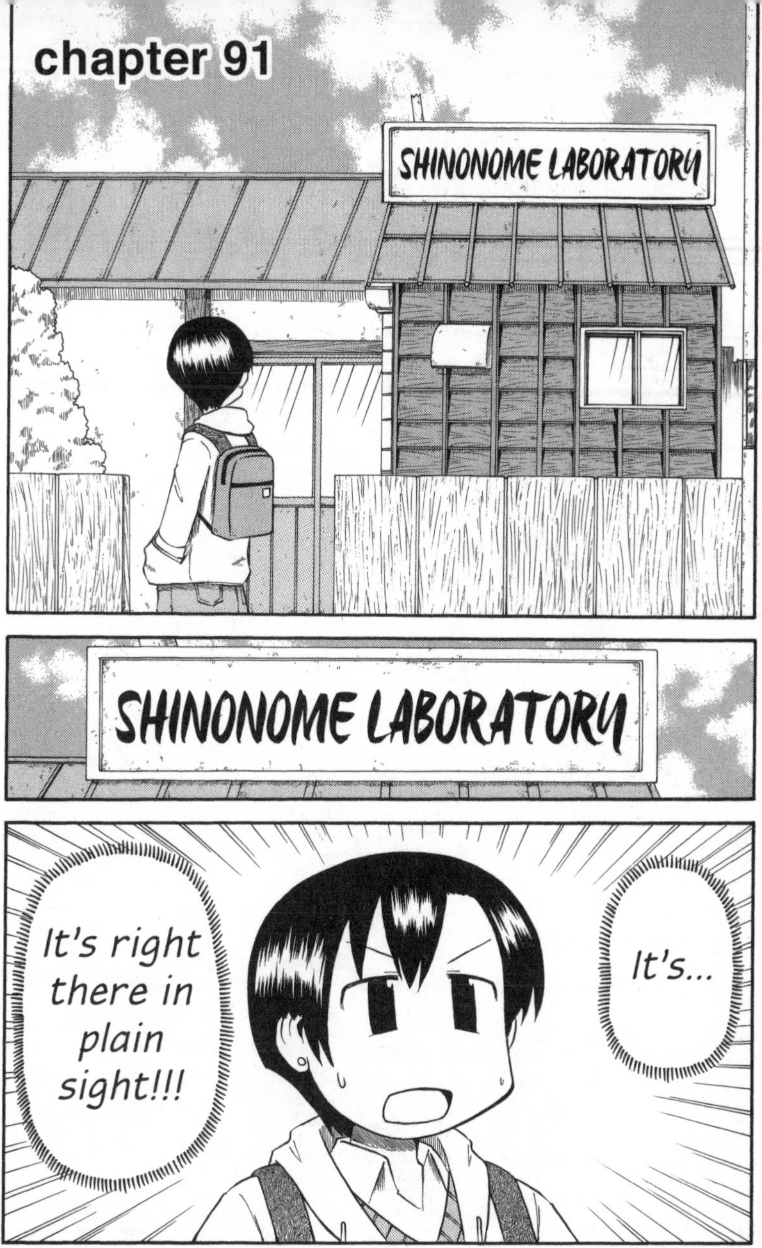
chapter 91
SHINONOME LABORATORY
SHINONOME LABORATORY
It's...
It's right there in plain sight!!!

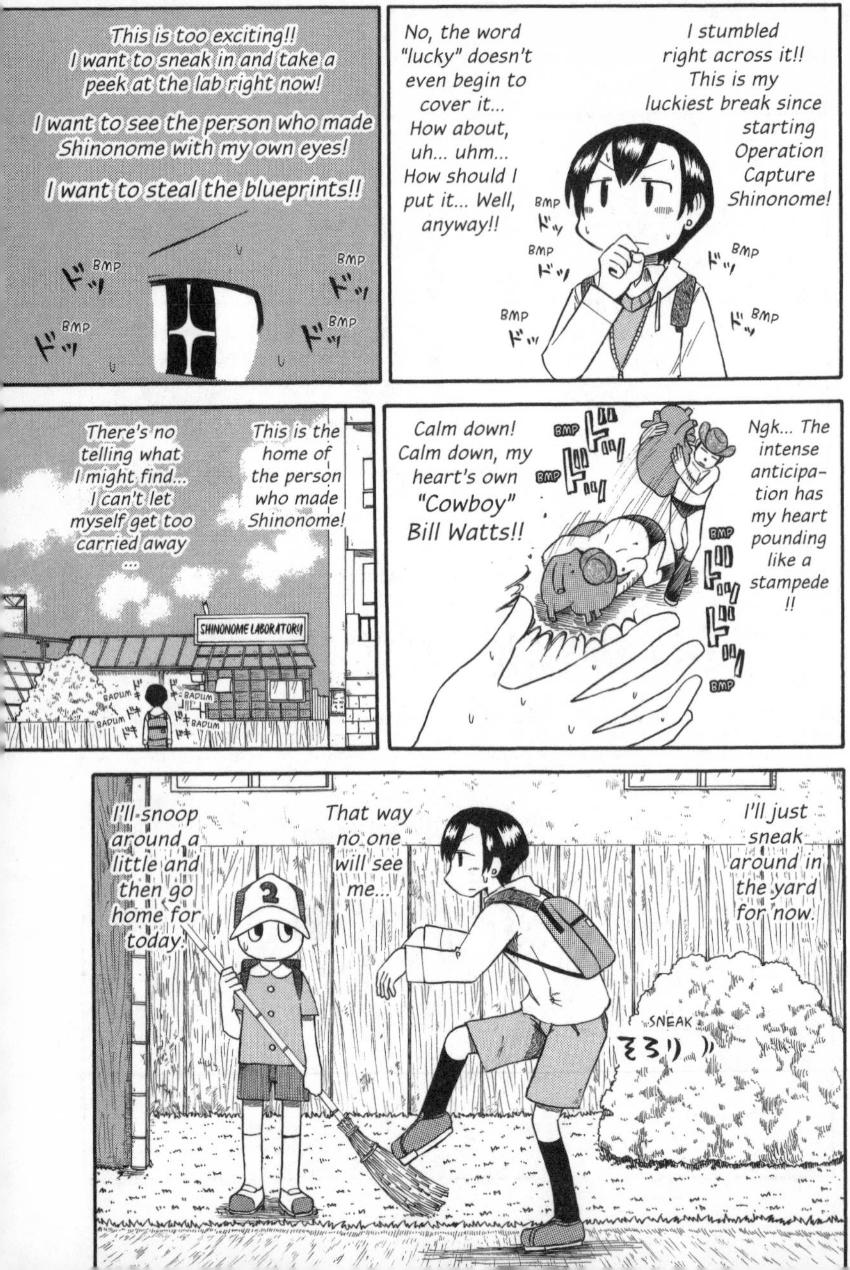
I stumbled right across it!! This is my luckiest break since starting Operation Capture Shinonome!
No, the word "lucky" doesn't even begin to cover it... How about, uh... uhm... How should I put it... Well, anyway!!
BMP ドッ
BMP ドッ
BMP ドッ
BMP ドッ
This is too exciting!! I want to sneak in and take a peek at the lab right now!
I want to see the person who made Shinonome with my own eyes!
I want to steal the blueprints!!
BMP ドッ
BMP ドッ
BMP ドッ
BMP ドッ
Ngk... The intense anticipation has my heart pounding like a stampede!!
Calm down! Calm down, my heart's own "Cowboy" Bill Watts!!
BMP ドッ
BMP ドッ
BMP ドッ
BMP ドッ
This is the home of the person who made Shinonome!
There's no telling what I might find... I can't let myself get too carried away...
SHINONOME LABORATORY
BADUM ドキ
BADUM ドキ
BADUM ドキ
BADUM ドキ
I'll just sneak around in the yard for now.
That way no one will see me...
I'll snoop around a little and then go home for today.
SNEAK そろり

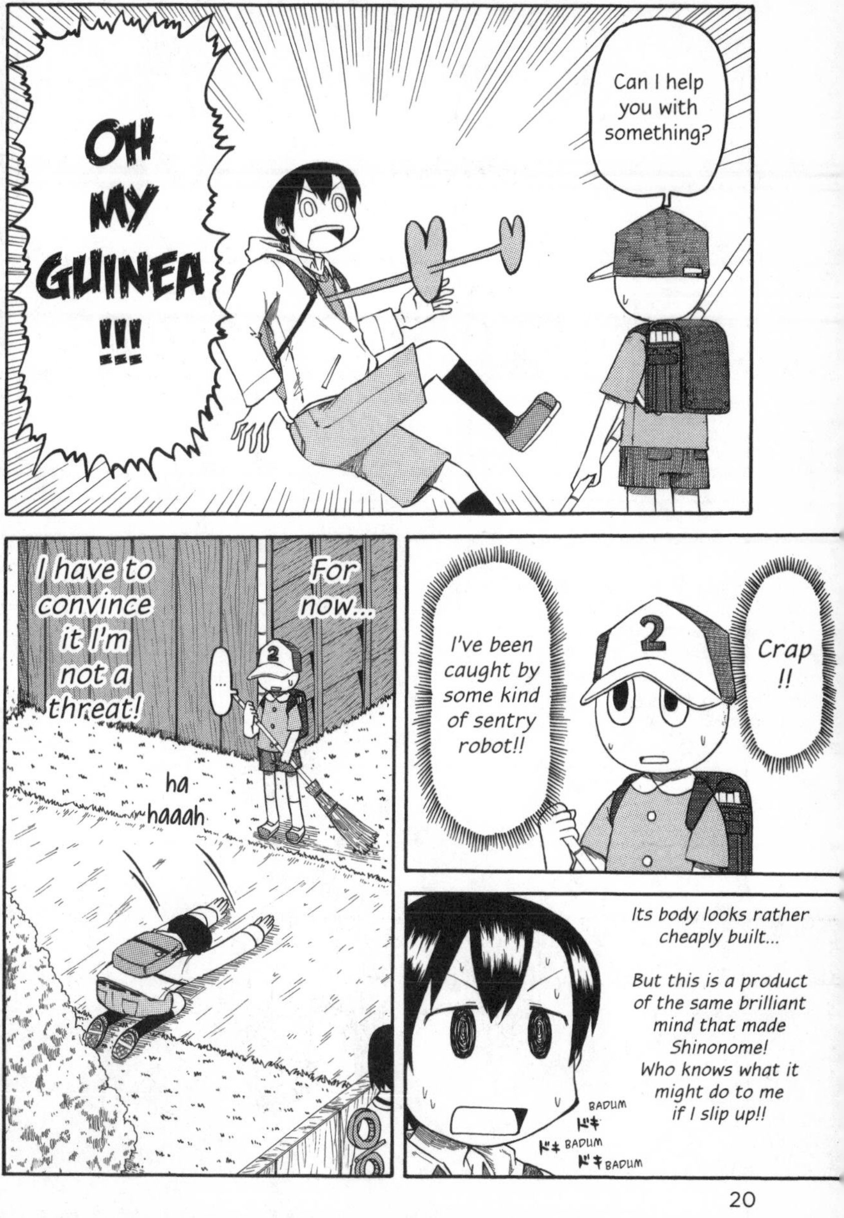
Can I help you with something?
OH MY GUINEA!!!
Crap!!
I've been caught by some kind of sentry robot!!
Its body looks rather cheaply built...
But this is a product of the same brilliant mind that made Shinonome! Who knows what it might do to me if I slip up!!
BADUM ドキ
ドキ BADUM
ドキ BADUM
For now...
I have to convince it I'm not a threat!
...
ha haaah

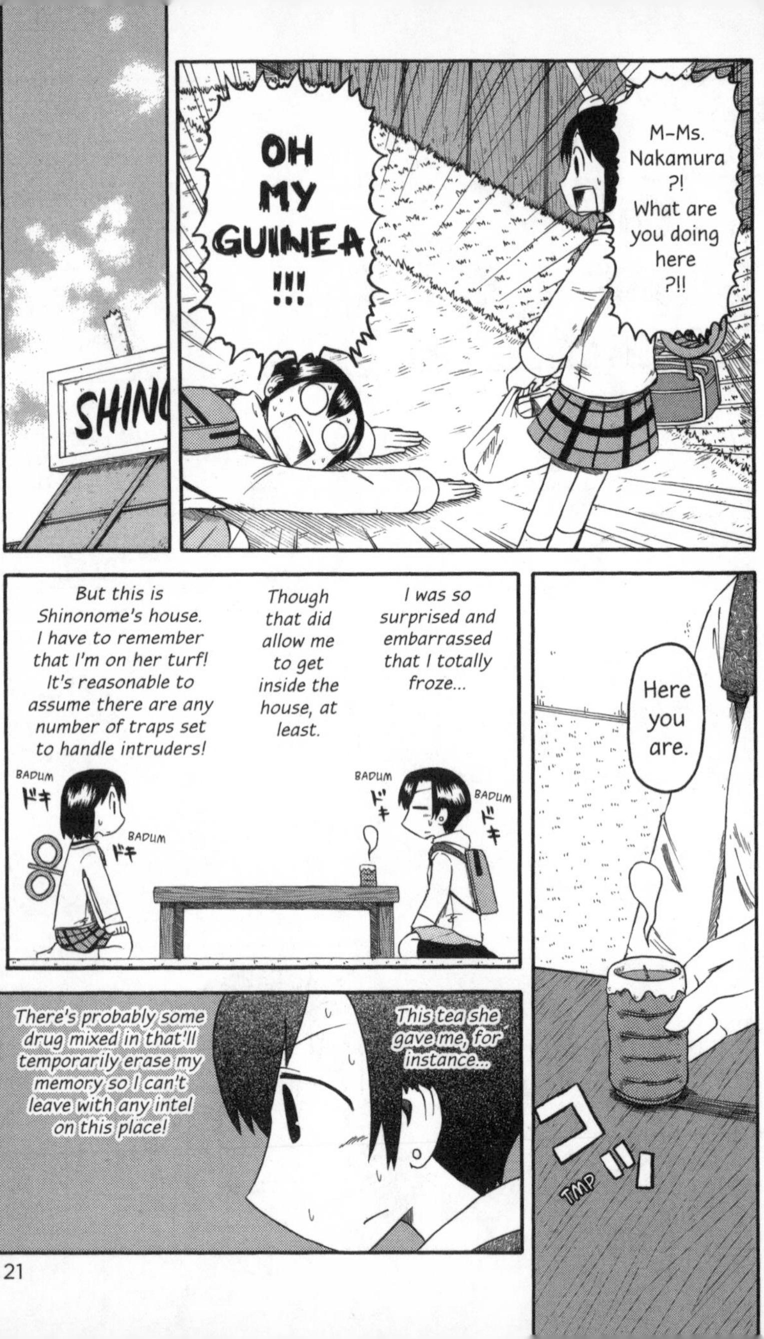

M–Ms. Nakamura ?! What are you doing here ?!!
OH MY GUINEA !!!
SHINO
Here you are.
コッ
TMP
I was so surprised and embarrassed that I totally froze...
BADUM
ドキ
BADUM
ドキ
Though that did allow me to get inside the house, at least.
But this is Shinonome's house. I have to remember that I'm on her turf! It's reasonable to assume there are any number of traps set to handle intruders!
BADUM
ドキ
BADUM
ドキ
This tea she gave me, for instance...
There's probably some drug mixed in that'll temporarily erase my memory so I can't leave with any intel on this place!

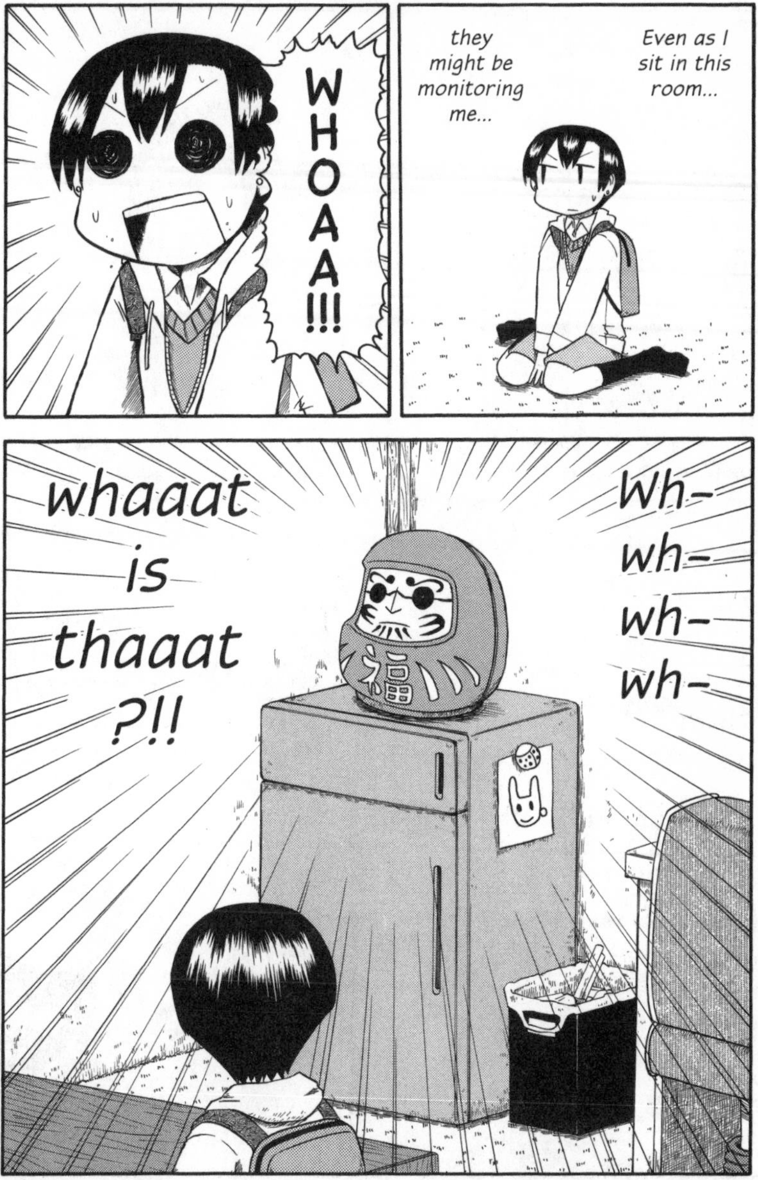
Even as I sit in this room...
they might be monitoring me...
WHOAA!!!
Wh-wh-wh-wh-
whaaat is thaaat?!!

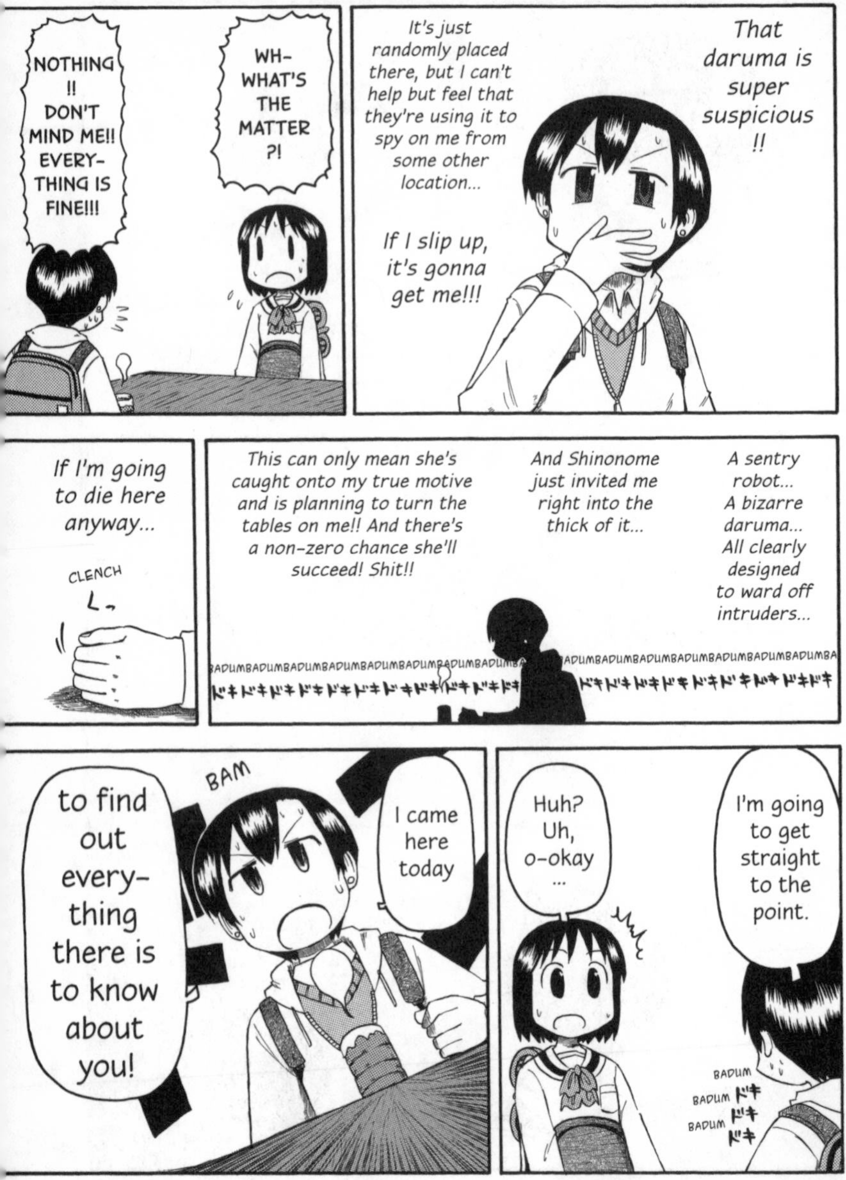

That daruma is super suspicious !!
It's just randomly placed there, but I can't help but feel that they're using it to spy on me from some other location...
If I slip up, it's gonna get me!!!
WH- WHAT'S THE MATTER ?!
NOTHING !! DON'T MIND ME!! EVERY-THING IS FINE!!!
A sentry robot... A bizarre daruma... All clearly designed to ward off intruders...
And Shinonome just invited me right into the thick of it...
This can only mean she's caught onto my true motive and is planning to turn the tables on me!! And there's a non-zero chance she'll succeed! Shit!!
BADUMBADUMBADUMBADUMBADUMBADUMBADUMBADUM
ドキドキドキドキドキドキドキドキ
If I'm going to die here anyway...
CLENCH
I'm going to get straight to the point.
Huh? Uh, o-okay ...
BADUM ドキ
BADUM ドキ
BADUM ドキ
I came here today
BAM
to find out every-thing there is to know about you!

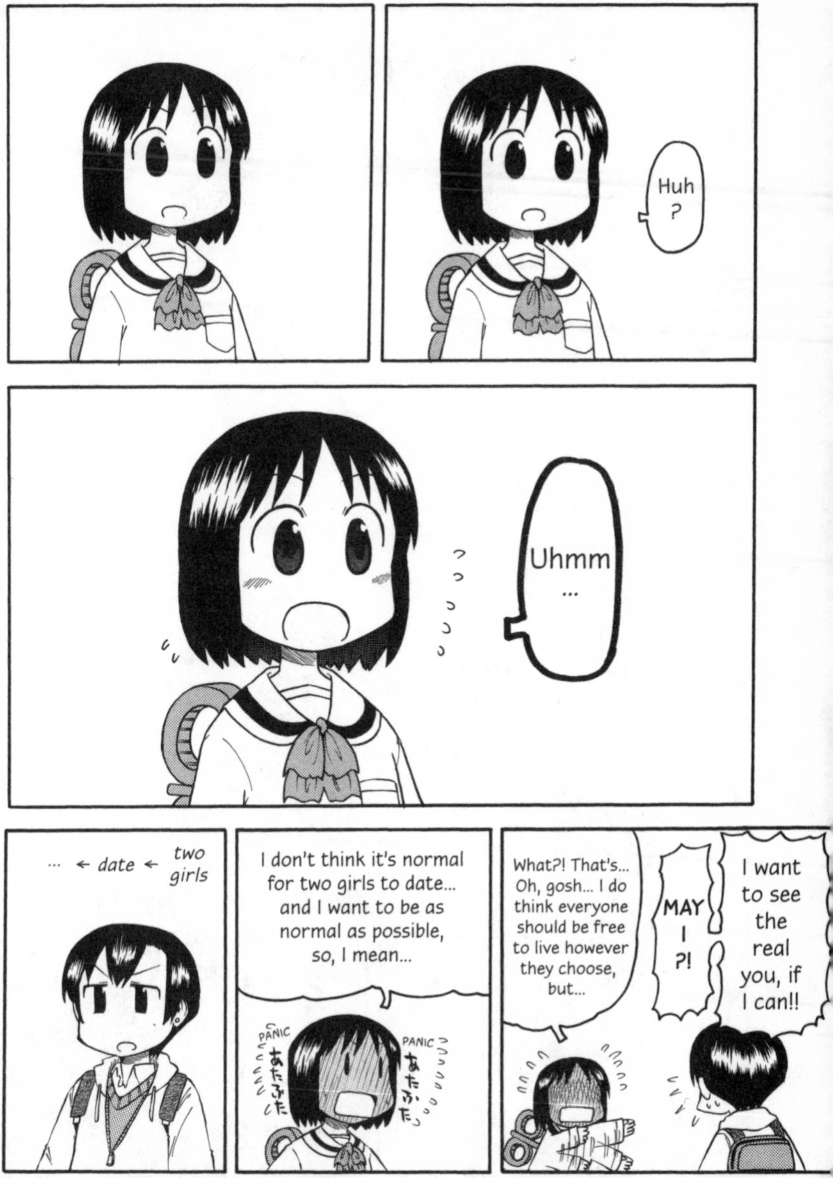
Huh?
Uhmm...
I want to see the real you, if I can!!
MAY I ?!
What?! That's... Oh, gosh... I do think everyone should be free to live however they choose, but...
PANIC あたふた
PANIC あたふた
I don't think it's normal for two girls to date... and I want to be as normal as possible, so, I mean...
two girls ← date ← ...

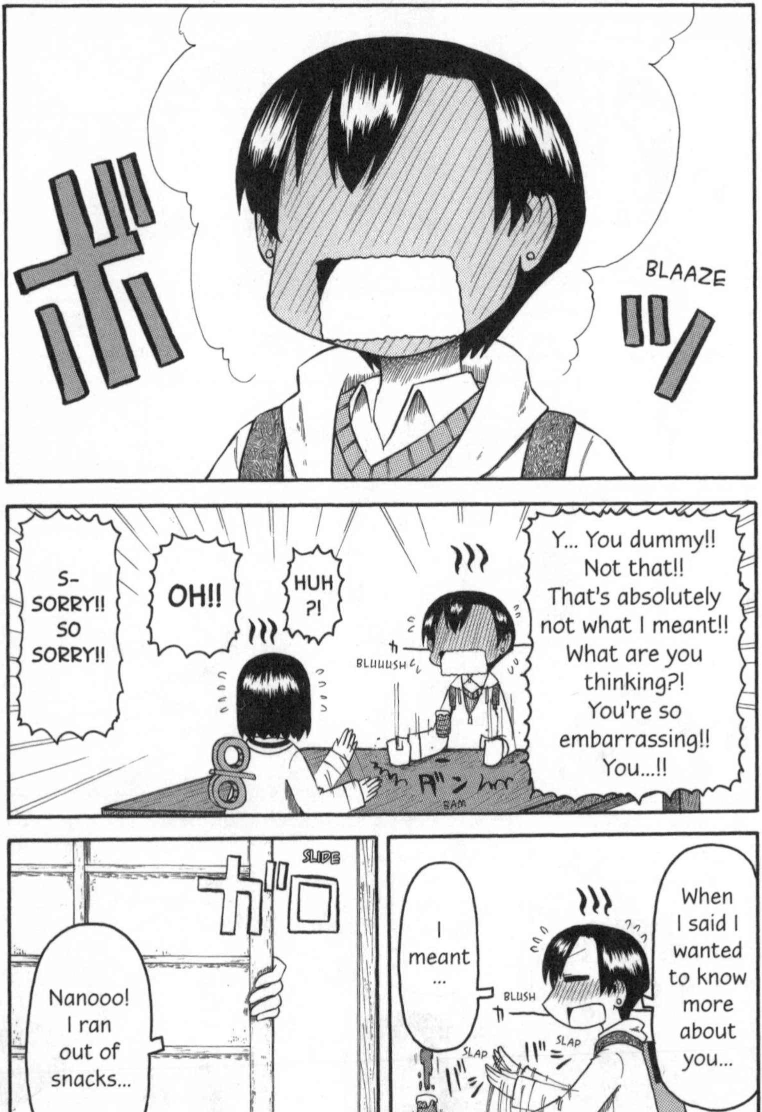
BLAAZE
Y... You dummy!! Not that!! That's absolutely not what I meant!! What are you thinking?! You're so embarrassing!! You...!!
BLUUUSH
HUH?!
OH!!
S-SORRY!! SO SORRY!!
SAM
When I said I wanted to know more about you...
BLUSH
SLAP
SLAP
I meant ...
SLIDE
Nanooo! I ran out of snacks...

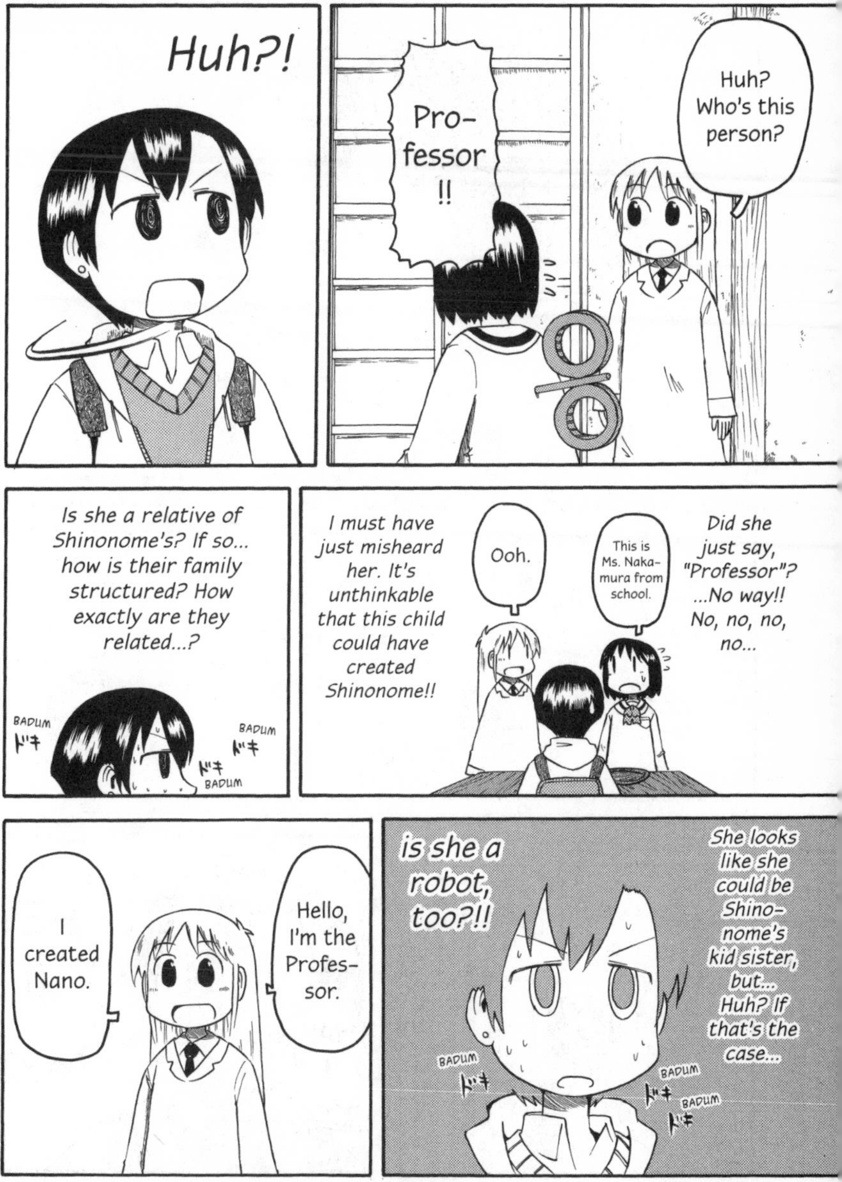
Huh? Who's this person?
Pro-fessor!!
Huh?!
Did she just say, "Professor"? ...No way!! No, no, no, no...
This is Ms. Nakamura from school.
Ooh.
I must have just misheard her. It's unthinkable that this child could have created Shinonome!!
Is she a relative of Shinonome's? If so... how is their family structured? How exactly are they related...?
BADUM
BADUM
BADUM
She looks like she could be Shino-nome's kid sister, but... Huh? If that's the case...
is she a robot, too?!!
BADUM
BADUM
BADUM
Hello, I'm the Profes-sor.
I created Nano.

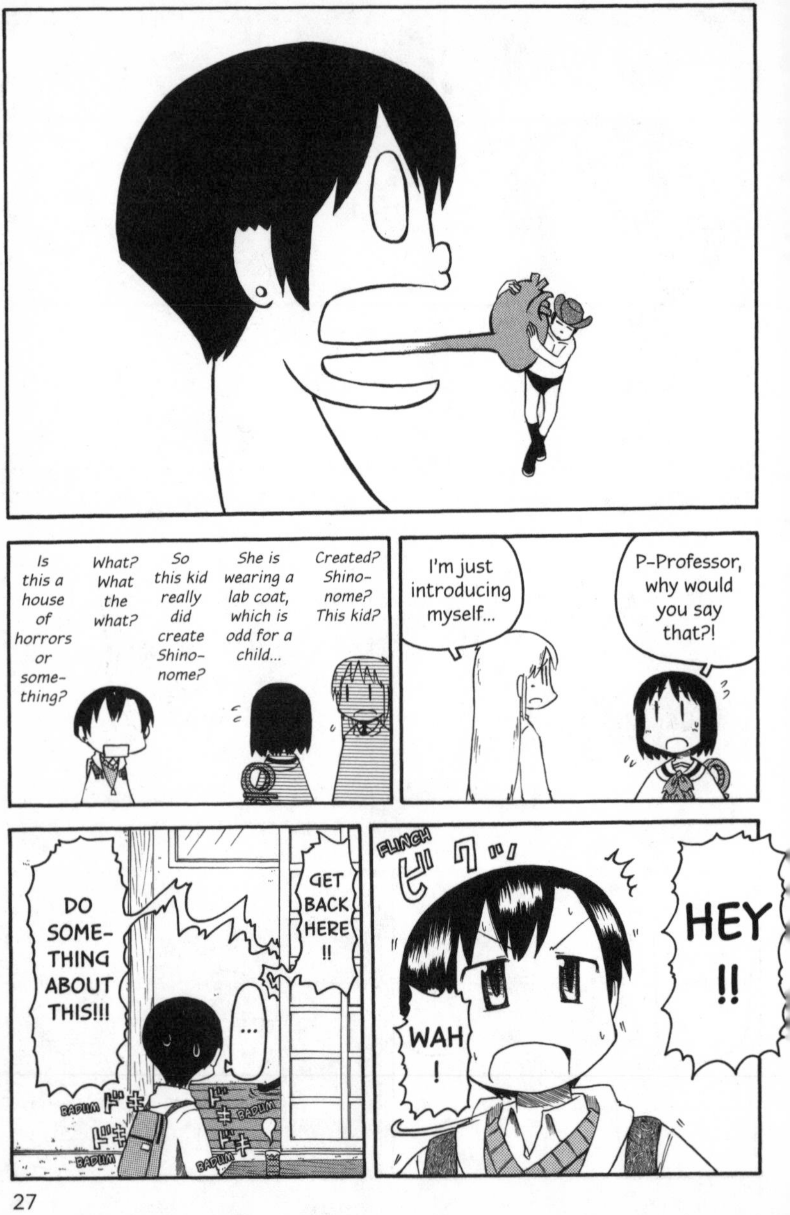

P-Professor, why would you say that?!
I'm just introducing myself...
Created? Shino-nome? This kid?
She is wearing a lab coat, which is odd for a child...
So this kid really did create Shino-nome?
What? What the what?
Is this a house of horrors or some-thing?
FLINCH
HEY !!
WAH !
GET BACK HERE !!
DO SOME-THING ABOUT THIS!!!
...
BADUM
BADUM
BADUM
BADUM

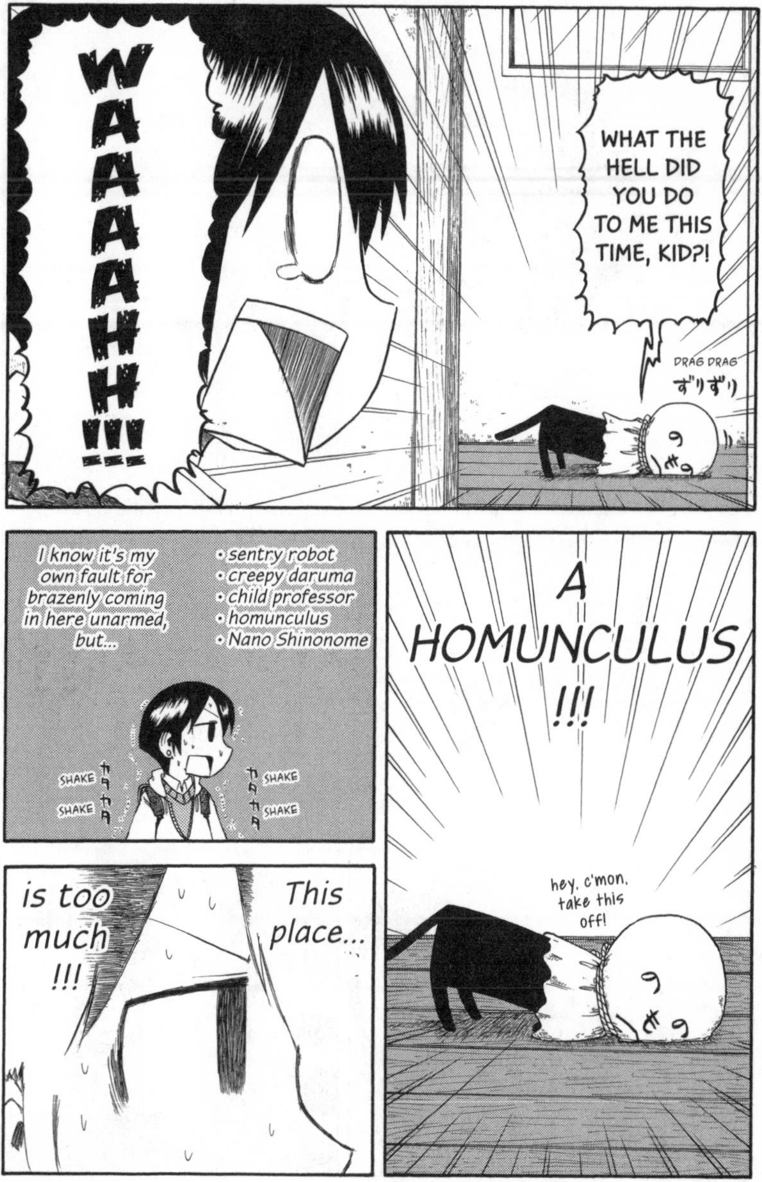
WHAT THE HELL DID YOU DO TO ME THIS TIME, KID?!
DRAG DRAG
ずりずり
WAAAAAHH!!!
A HOMUNCULUS!!!
hey, c'mon, take this off!
I know it's my own fault for brazenly coming in here unarmed, but...
• sentry robot
• creepy daruma
• child professor
• homunculus
• Nano Shinonome
SHAKE SHAKE
SHAKE SHAKE
This place...
is too much!!!

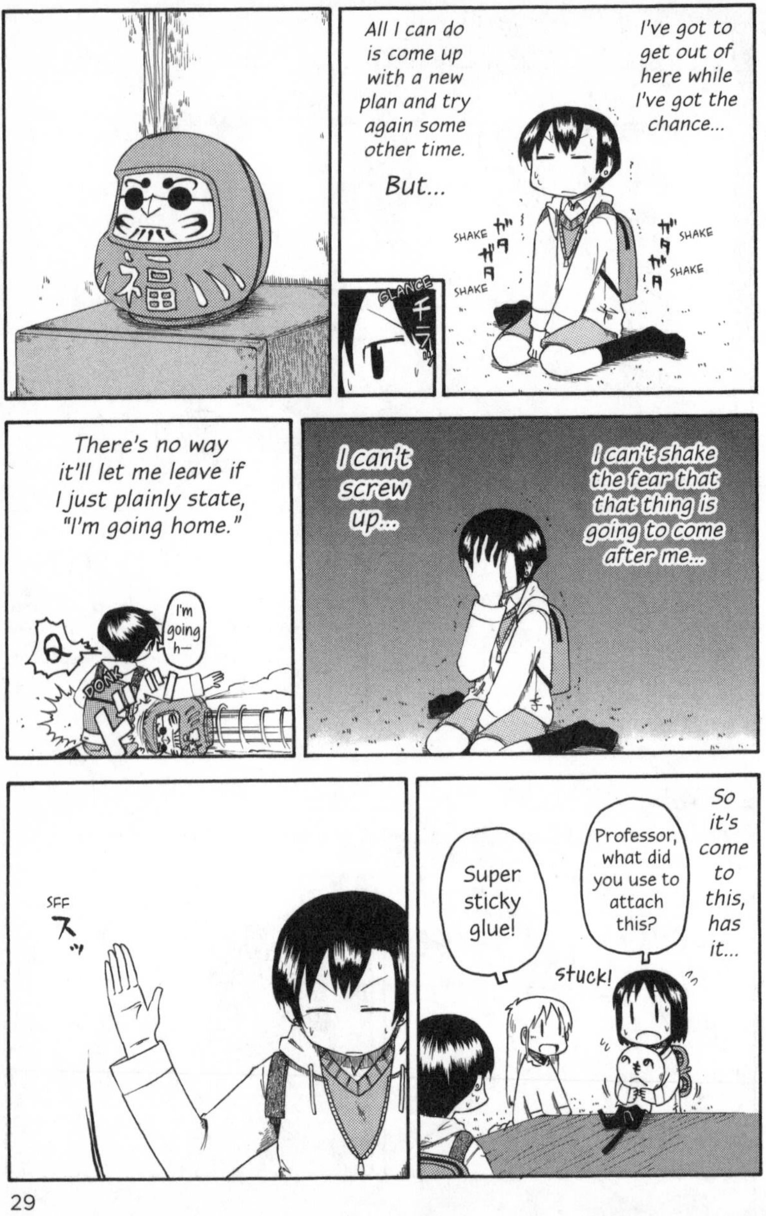
I've got to get out of here while I've got the chance...
All I can do is come up with a new plan and try again some other time.
But...
SHAKE
SHAKE
SHAKE
SHAKE
GLANCE
I can't shake the fear that that thing is going to come after me...
I can't screw up...
There's no way it'll let me leave if I just plainly state, "I'm going home."
I'm going h—
DONK
So it's come to this, has it...
Professor, what did you use to attach this?
Super sticky glue!
stuck!
SFF

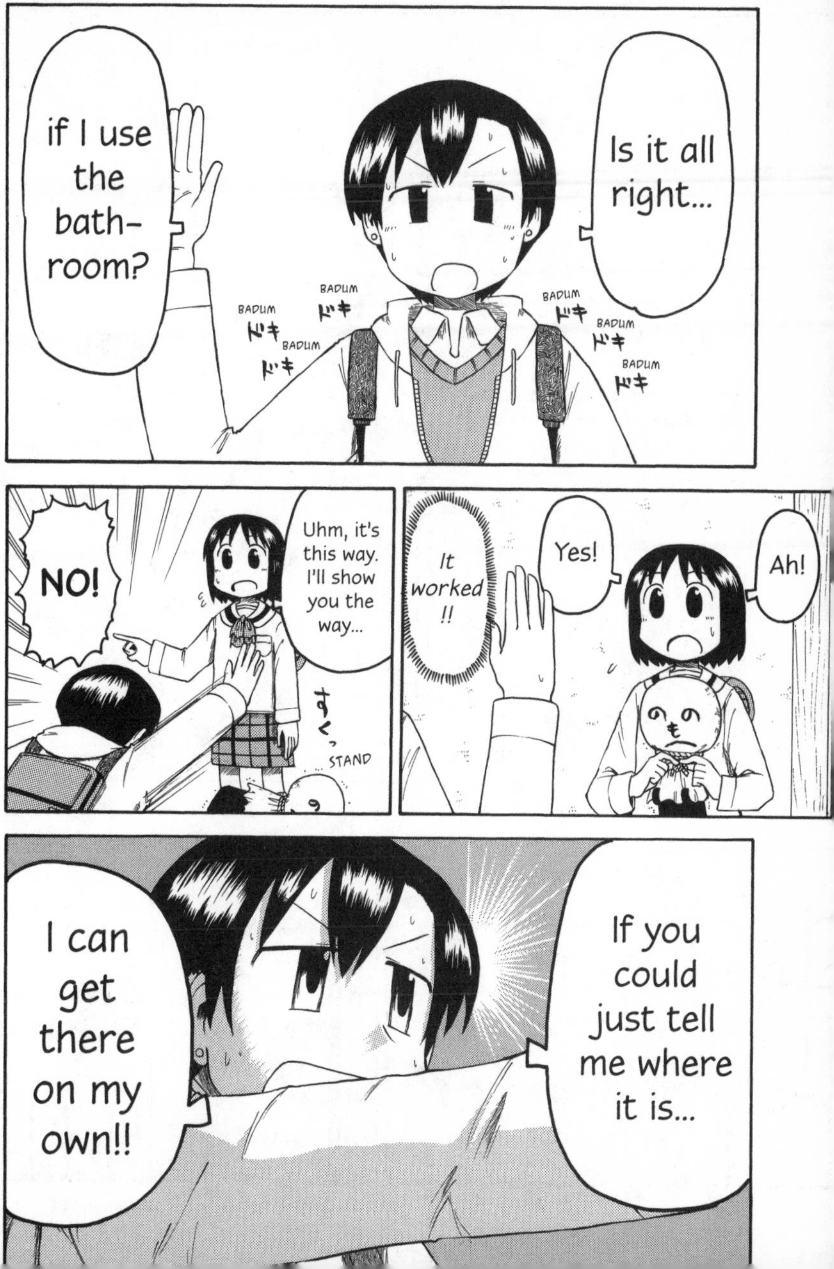
Is it all right...
if I use the bath-room?
BADUM ドキ
BADUM ドキ
BADUM ドキ
BADUM ドキ
BADUM ドキ
Ah!
Yes!
It worked!!
Uhm, it's this way. I'll show you the way...
NO!
すくっ STAND
If you could just tell me where it is...
I can get there on my own!!

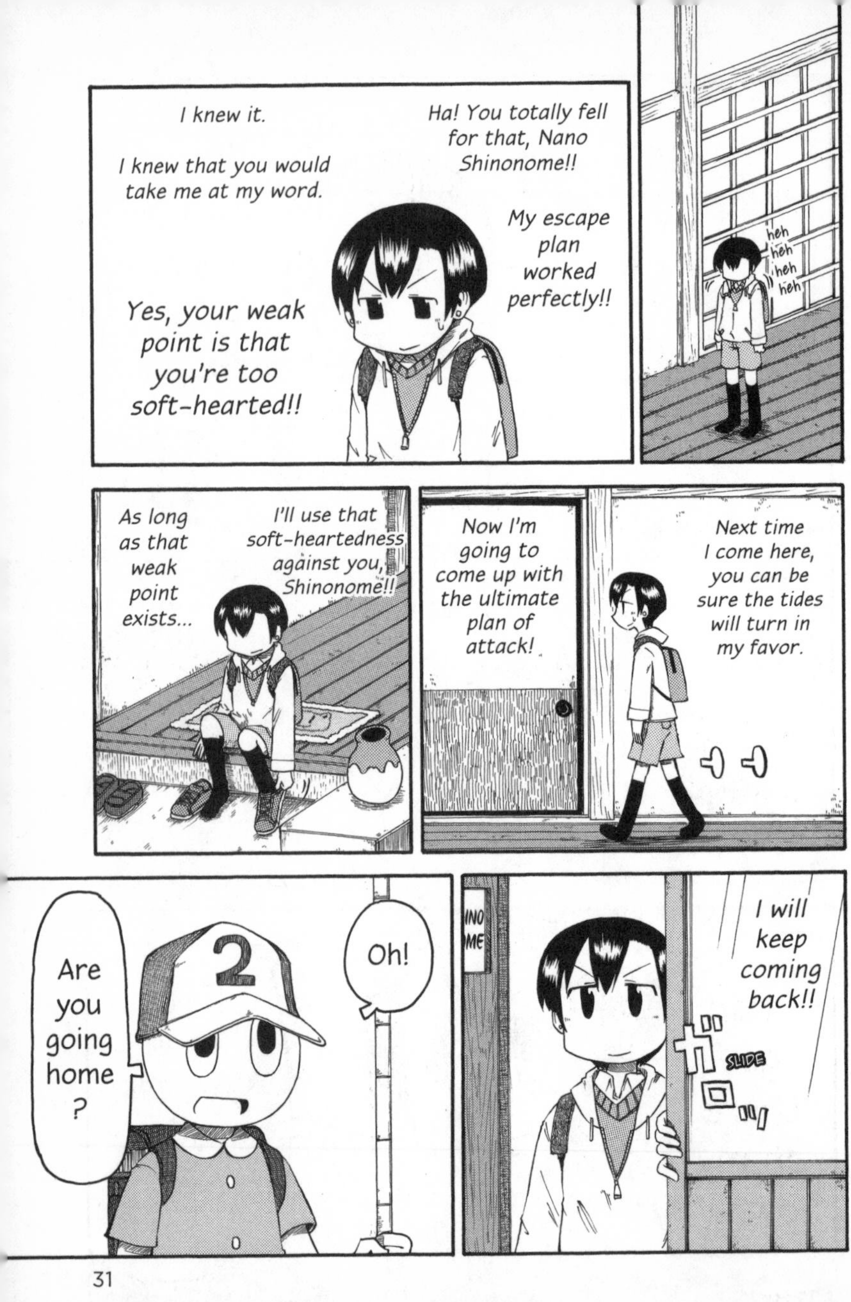
heh
heh
heh
heh
Ha! You totally fell for that, Nano Shinonome!!
My escape plan worked perfectly!!
I knew it.
I knew that you would take me at my word.
Yes, your weak point is that you're too soft-hearted!!
Next time I come here, you can be sure the tides will turn in my favor.
Now I'm going to come up with the ultimate plan of attack!
I'll use that soft-heartedness against you, Shinonome!!
As long as that weak point exists...
I will keep coming back!!
ガロ
SLIDE
INO
ME
Oh!
Are you going home?

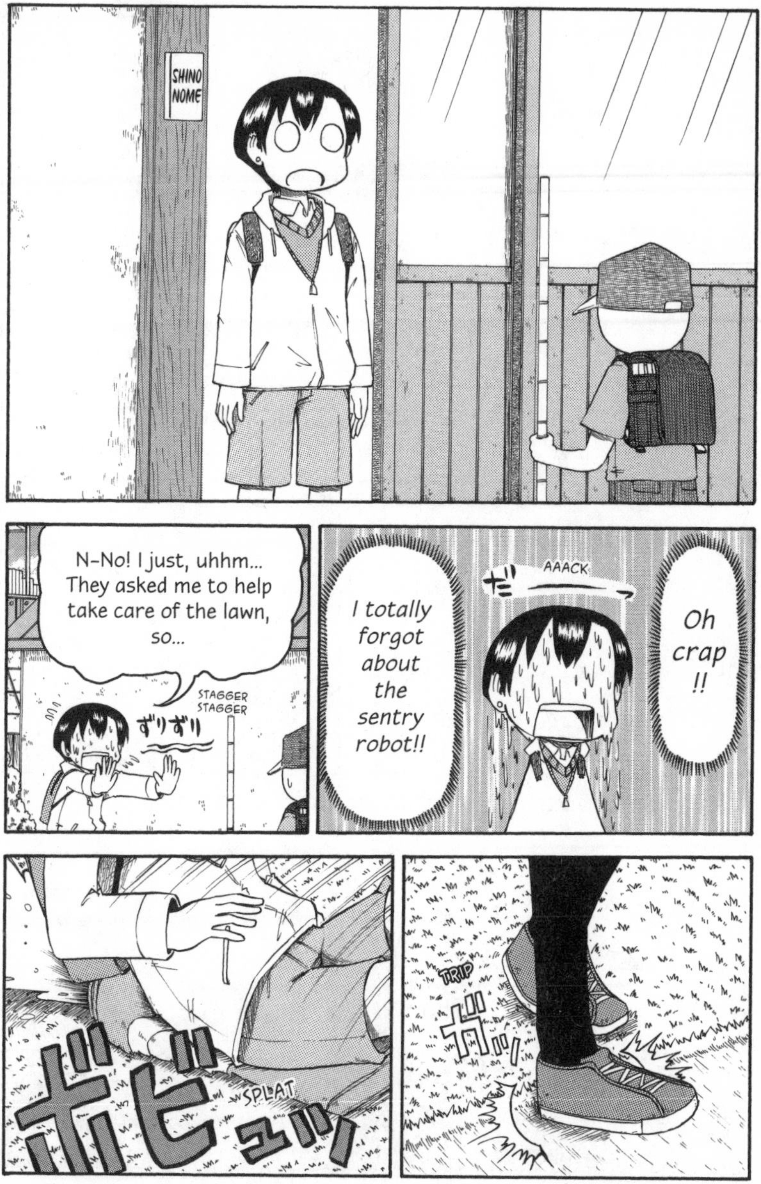
SHINO NOME
Oh crap !!
AAACK
I totally forgot about the sentry robot!!
N-No! I just, uhhm... They asked me to help take care of the lawn, so...
STAGGER STAGGER
ずりずり
TRIP
ガッ
SPLAT
ボビュッ

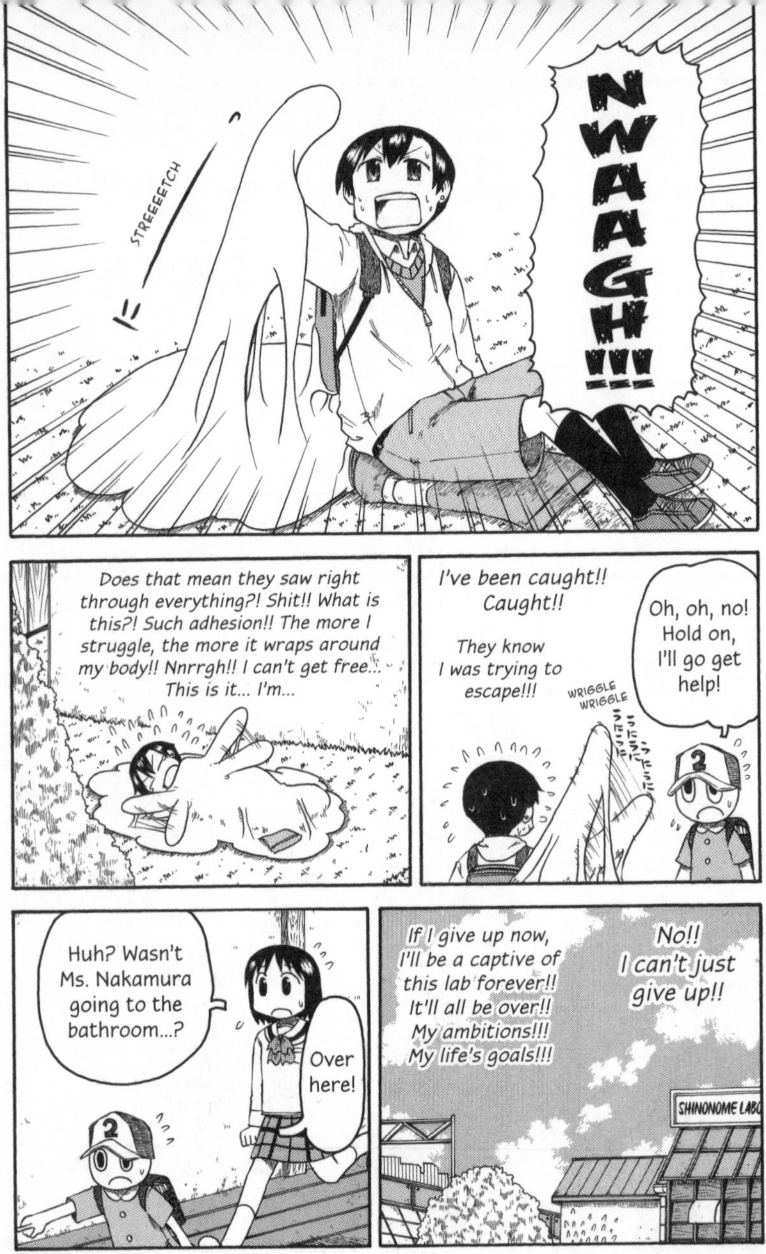
NWAAGH!!!
STREEEETCH
Oh, oh, no! Hold on, I'll go get help!
I've been caught!! Caught!!
They know I was trying to escape!!!
WRIGGLE WRIGGLE
Does that mean they saw right through everything?! Shit!! What is this?! Such adhesion!! The more I struggle, the more it wraps around my body!! Nnrrgh!! I can't get free... This is it... I'm...
No!! I can't just give up!!
If I give up now, I'll be a captive of this lab forever!! It'll all be over!! My ambitions!!! My life's goals!!!
SHINONOME LABO
Over here!
Huh? Wasn't Ms. Nakamura going to the bathroom...?

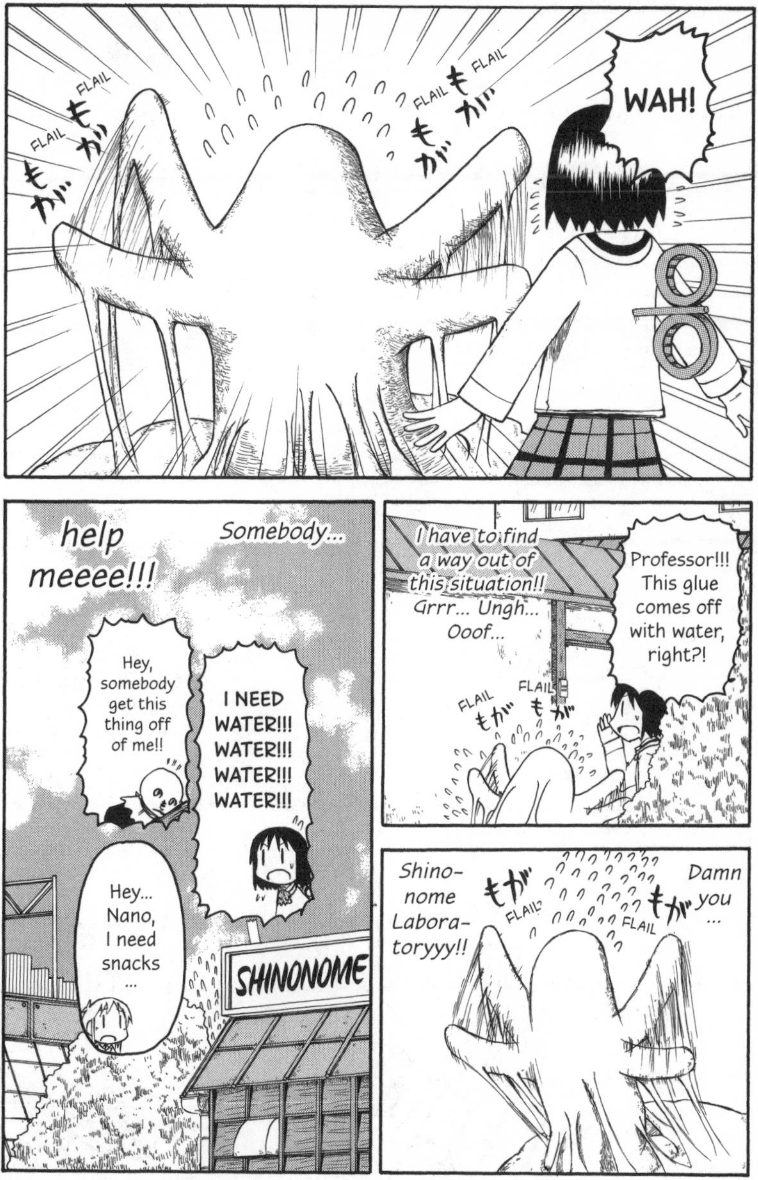
WAH!
FLAIL もが
FLAIL もが
FLAIL もが
FLAIL もが
Professor!!! This glue comes off with water, right?!
I have to find a way out of this situation!! Grrr... Ungh... Ooof...
FLAIL もが
FLAIL もが
Damn you ...
FLAIL もが
FLAIL もが
Shinonome Laboratoryyy!!
Somebody...
help meeeee!!!
I NEED WATER!!! WATER!!! WATER!!! WATER!!!
Hey, somebody get this thing off of me!!
SHINONOME
Hey... Nano, I need snacks ...

chapter 91: end

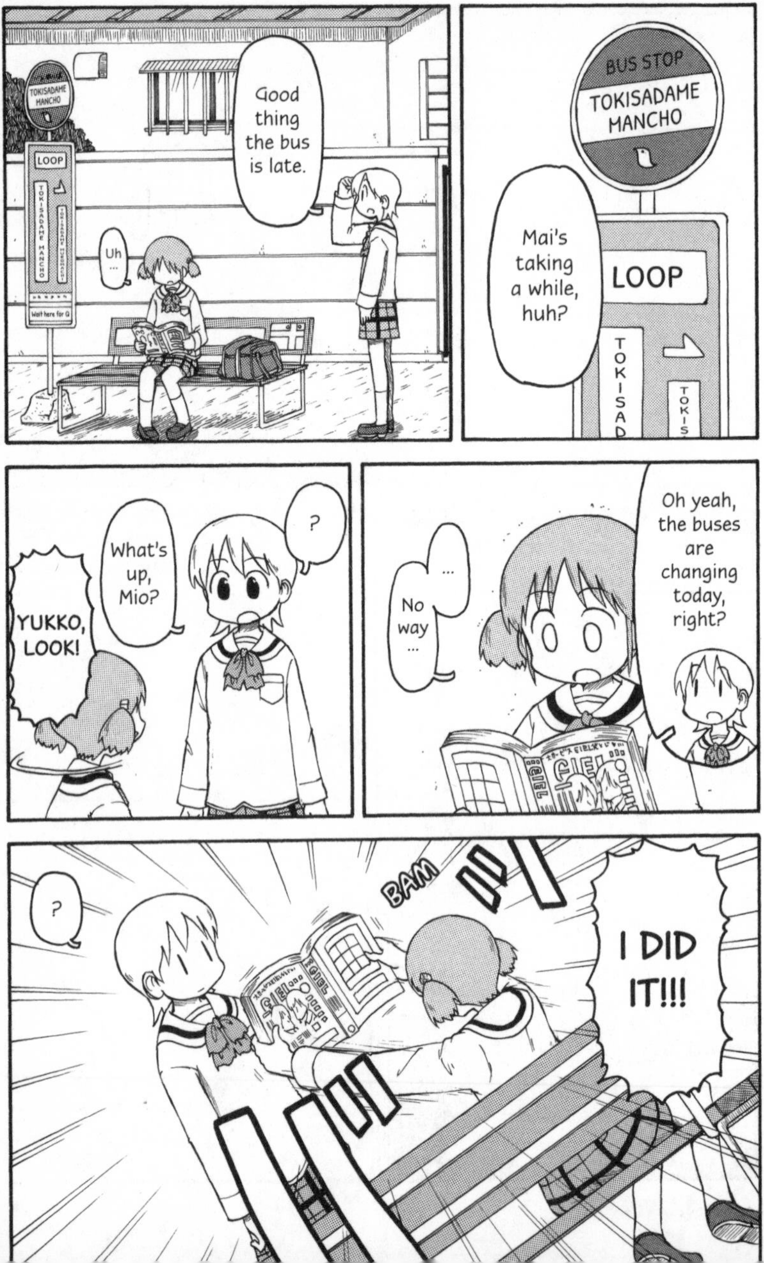

BUS STOP
TOKISADAME MANCHO
LOOP
Mai's taking a while, huh?
Good thing the bus is late.
TOKISADAME MANCHO
LOOP
Uh ...
Oh yeah, the buses are changing today, right?
... No way ...
GIEL
?
What's up, Mio?
YUKKO, LOOK!
I DID IT!!!
BAM
?

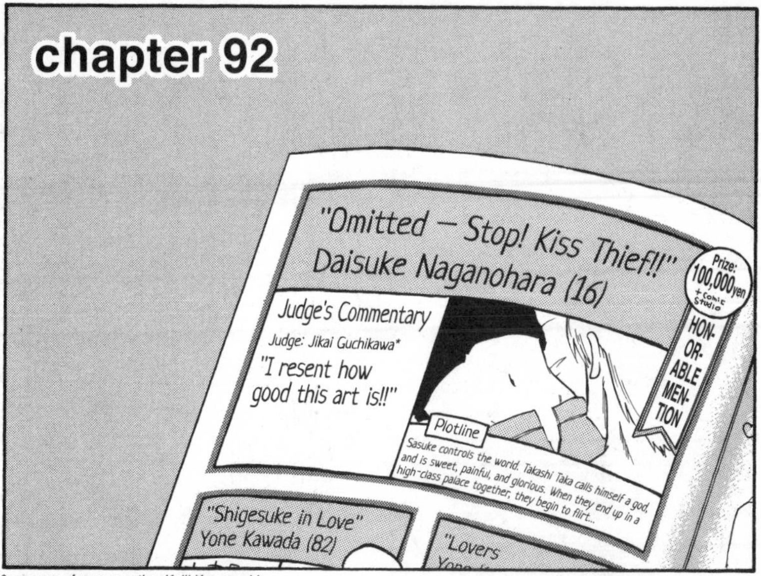
chapter 92
"Omitted — Stop! Kiss Thief!!"
Daisuke Naganohara (16)
Prize: 100,000yen +comic studio
HONORABLE MENTION
Judge's Commentary
Judge: Jikai Guchikawa*
"I resent how good this art is!!"
Plotline
Sasuke controls the world. Takashi Taka calls himself a god, and is sweet, painful, and glorious. When they end up in a high-class palace together, they begin to flirt...
"Shigesuke in Love"
Yone Kawada (82)
"Lovers

*anagram of manga author Kaiji Kawaguchi

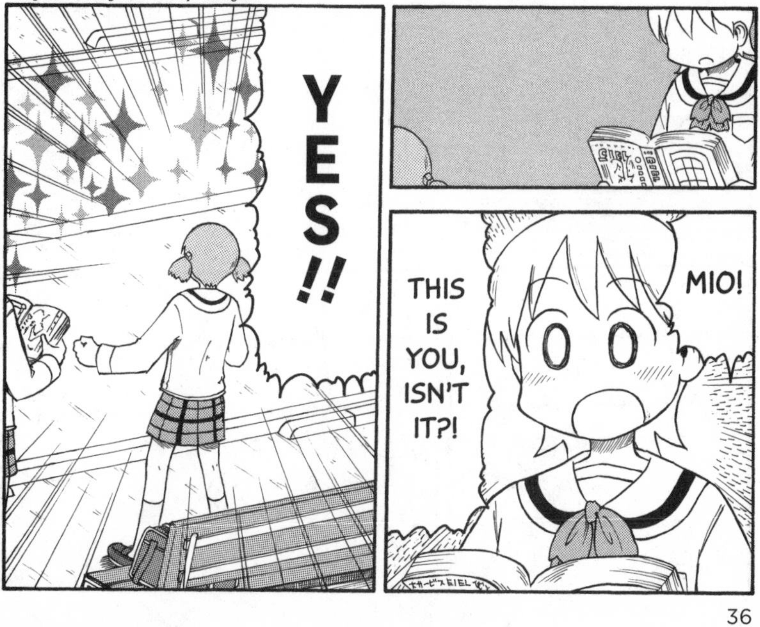
MIO!
THIS IS YOU, ISN'T IT?!
YES!!

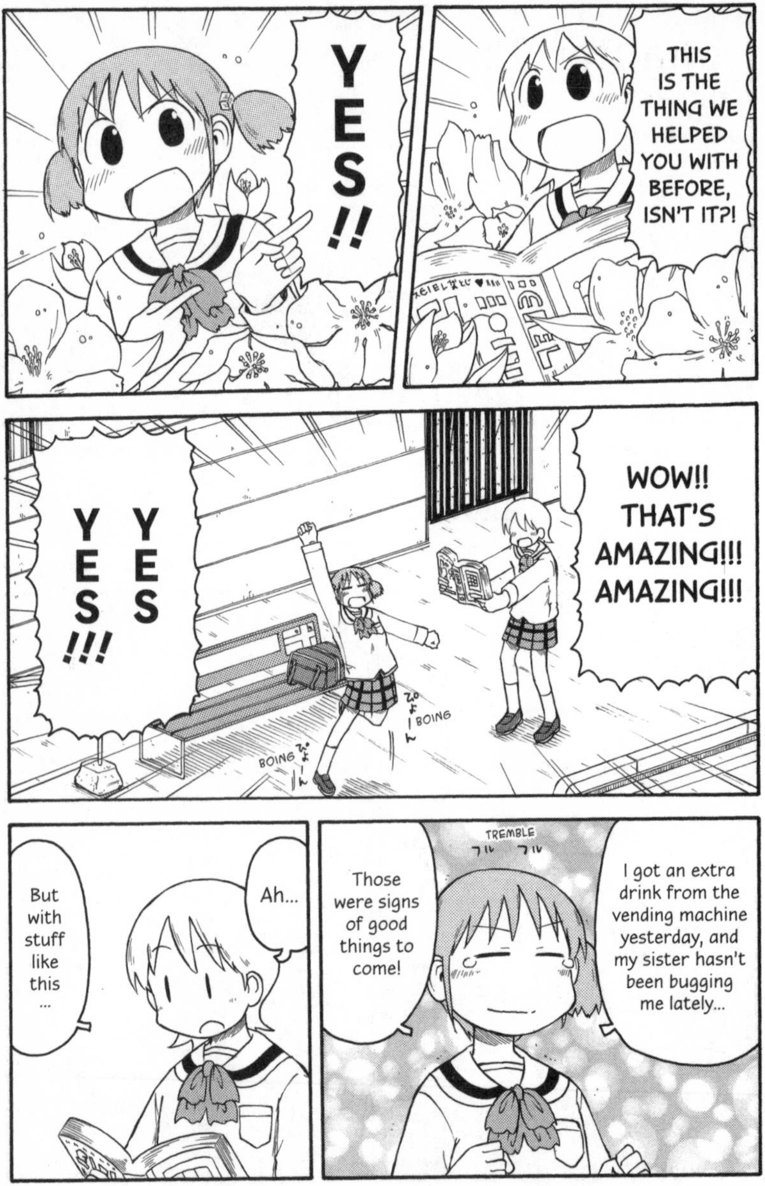
THIS IS THE THING WE HELPED YOU WITH BEFORE, ISN'T IT?!
YES!!
WOW!! THAT'S AMAZING!!! AMAZING!!!
YES YES YES!!!
BOING
BOING
TREMBLE
I got an extra drink from the vending machine yesterday, and my sister hasn't been bugging me lately...
Those were signs of good things to come!
Ah...
But with stuff like this ...

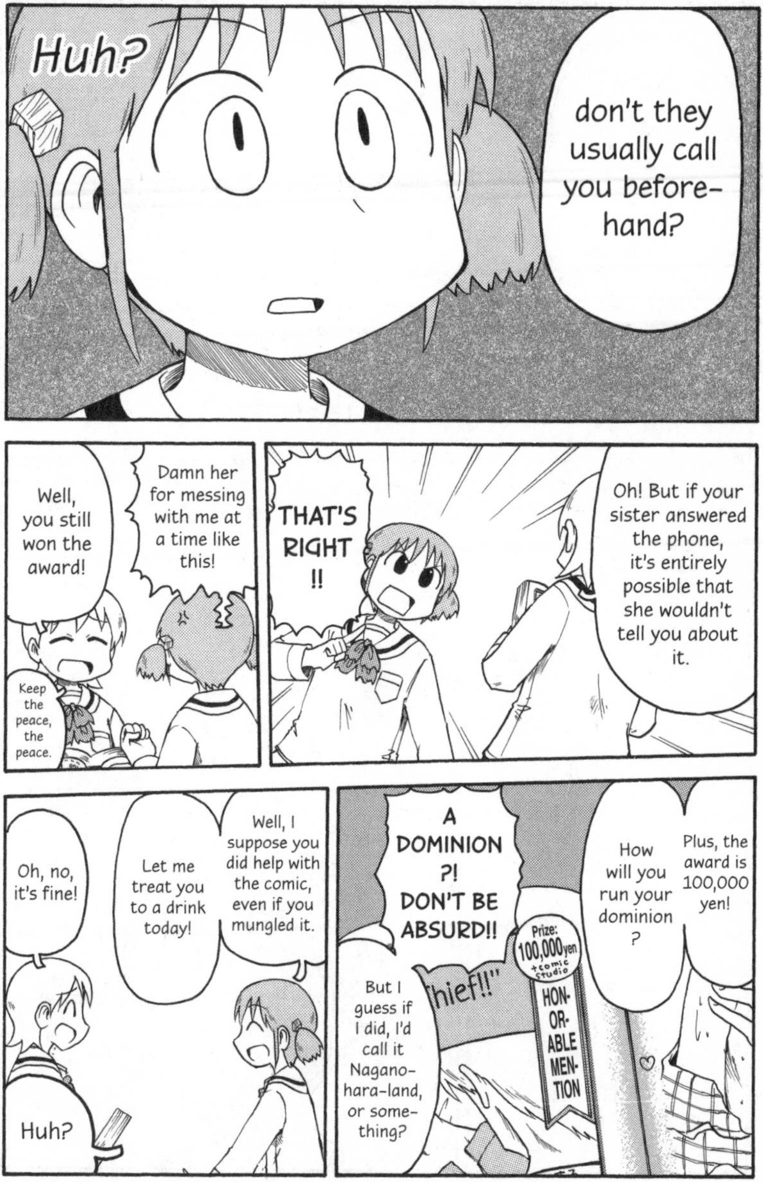
don't they usually call you before-hand?
Huh?
Oh! But if your sister answered the phone, it's entirely possible that she wouldn't tell you about it.
THAT'S RIGHT !!
Damn her for messing with me at a time like this!
Well, you still won the award!
Keep the peace, the peace.
Plus, the award is 100,000 yen!
How will you run your dominion ?
A DOMINION ?! DON'T BE ABSURD!!
Prize: 100,000yen +comic studio
HON-OR-ABLE MEN-TION
"Thief!!"
But I guess if I did, I'd call it Nagano-hara-land, or some-thing?
Well, I suppose you did help with the comic, even if you mungled it.
Let me treat you to a drink today!
Oh, no, it's fine!
Huh?

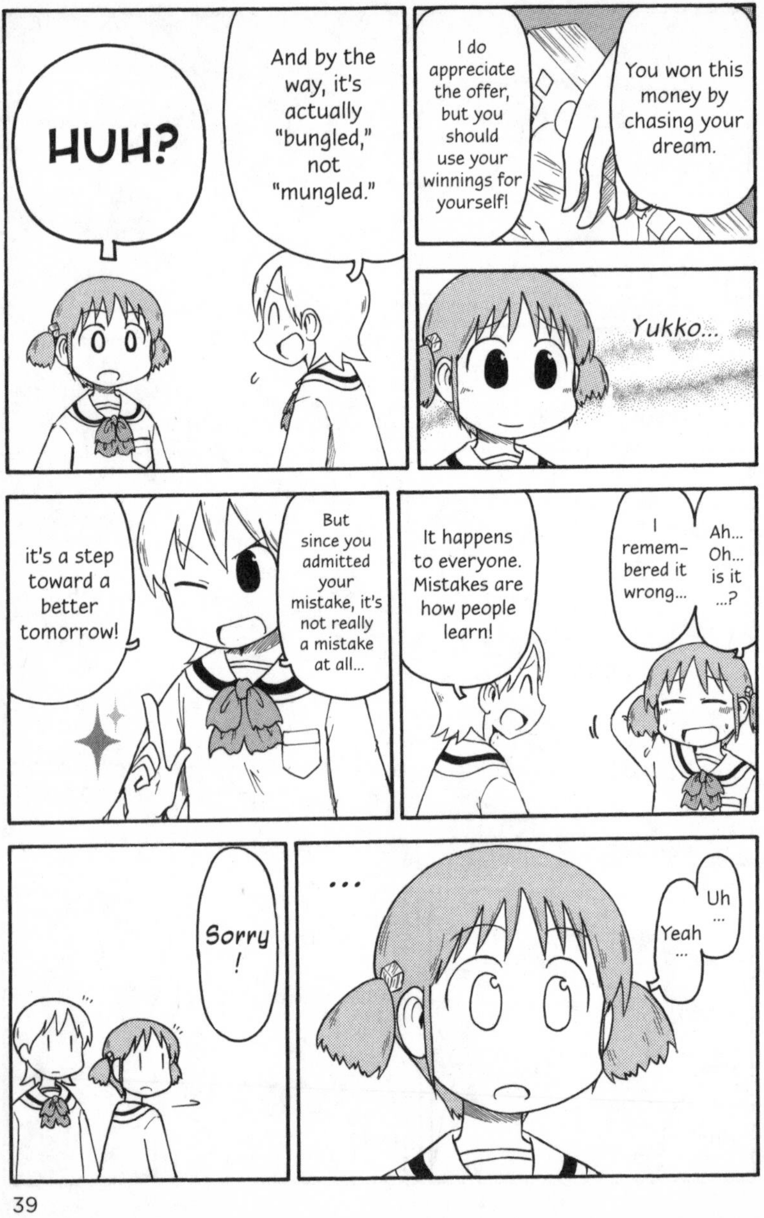
You won this money by chasing your dream.
I do appreciate the offer, but you should use your winnings for yourself!
Yukko...
And by the way, it's actually "bungled," not "mungled."
HUH?
Ah... Oh... is it ...?
I remembered it wrong...
It happens to everyone. Mistakes are how people learn!
But since you admitted your mistake, it's not really a mistake at all...
it's a step toward a better tomorrow!
Uh... Yeah...
...
Sorry!

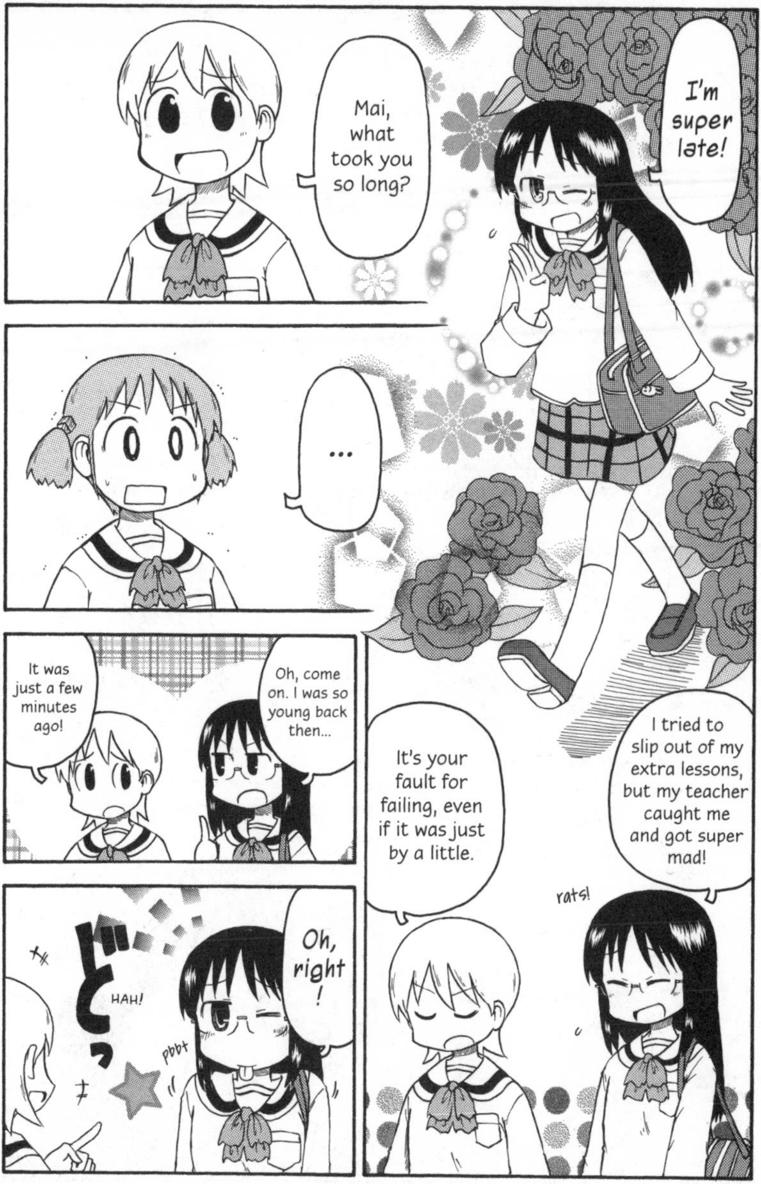
I'm super late!
Mai, what took you so long?
...
I tried to slip out of my extra lessons, but my teacher caught me and got super mad!
It's your fault for failing, even if it was just by a little.
rats!
Oh, come on. I was so young back then...
It was just a few minutes ago!
Oh, right!
どっ
HAH!
pbbt

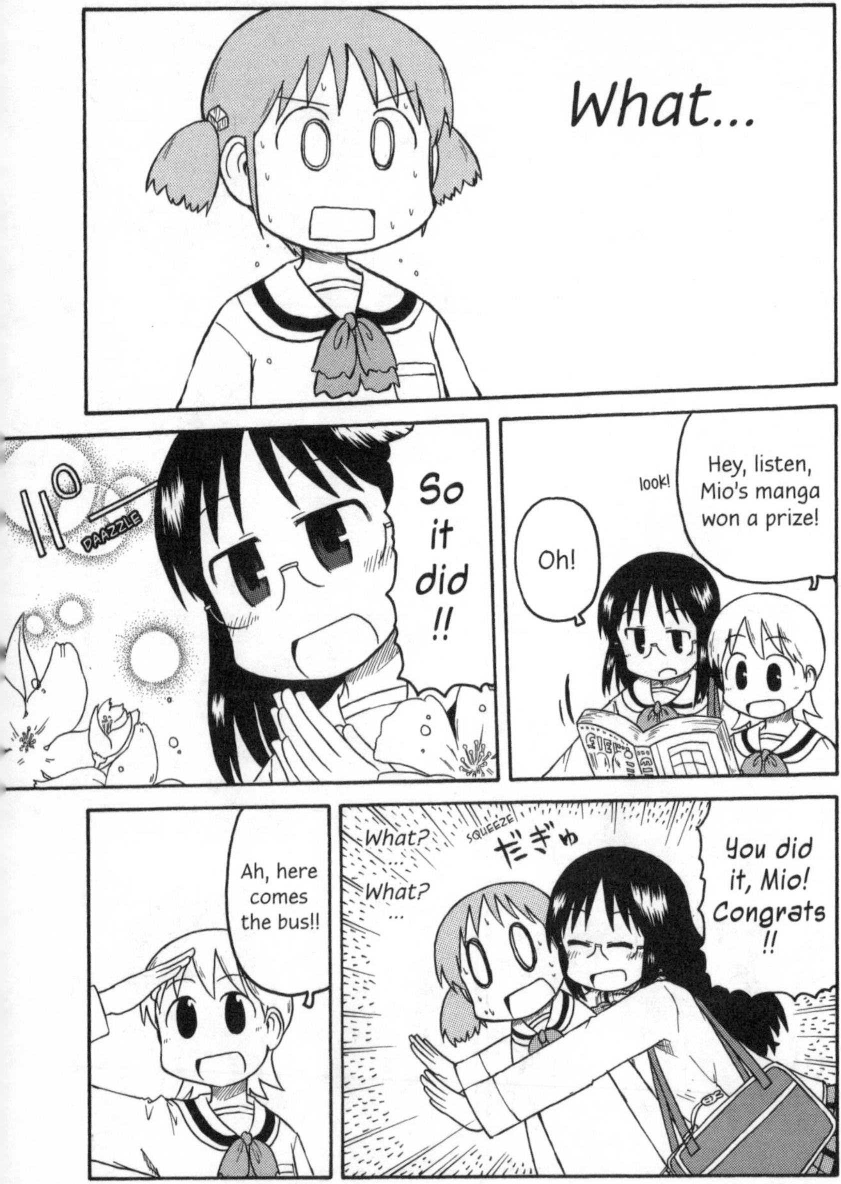
What...
Hey, listen, Mio's manga won a prize!
look!
Oh!
So it did !!
DAAZZLE
You did it, Mio! Congrats !!
だぎゅ
SQUEEZE
What? ... What? ...
Ah, here comes the bus!!

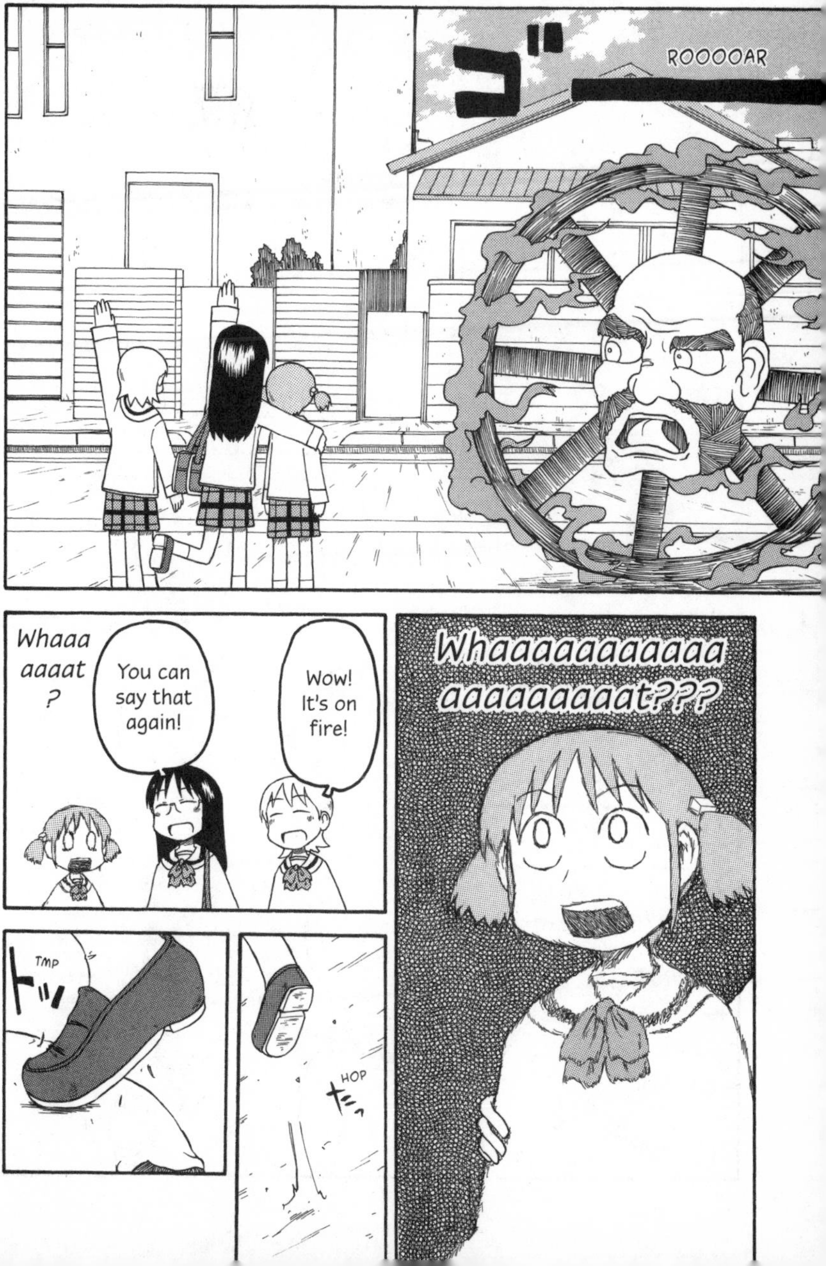
ゴー
ROOOOAR
Whaaaaaaaaaaa aaaaaaaaat???
Wow! It's on fire!
You can say that again!
Whaaa aaaat ?
HOP
トッ
TMP

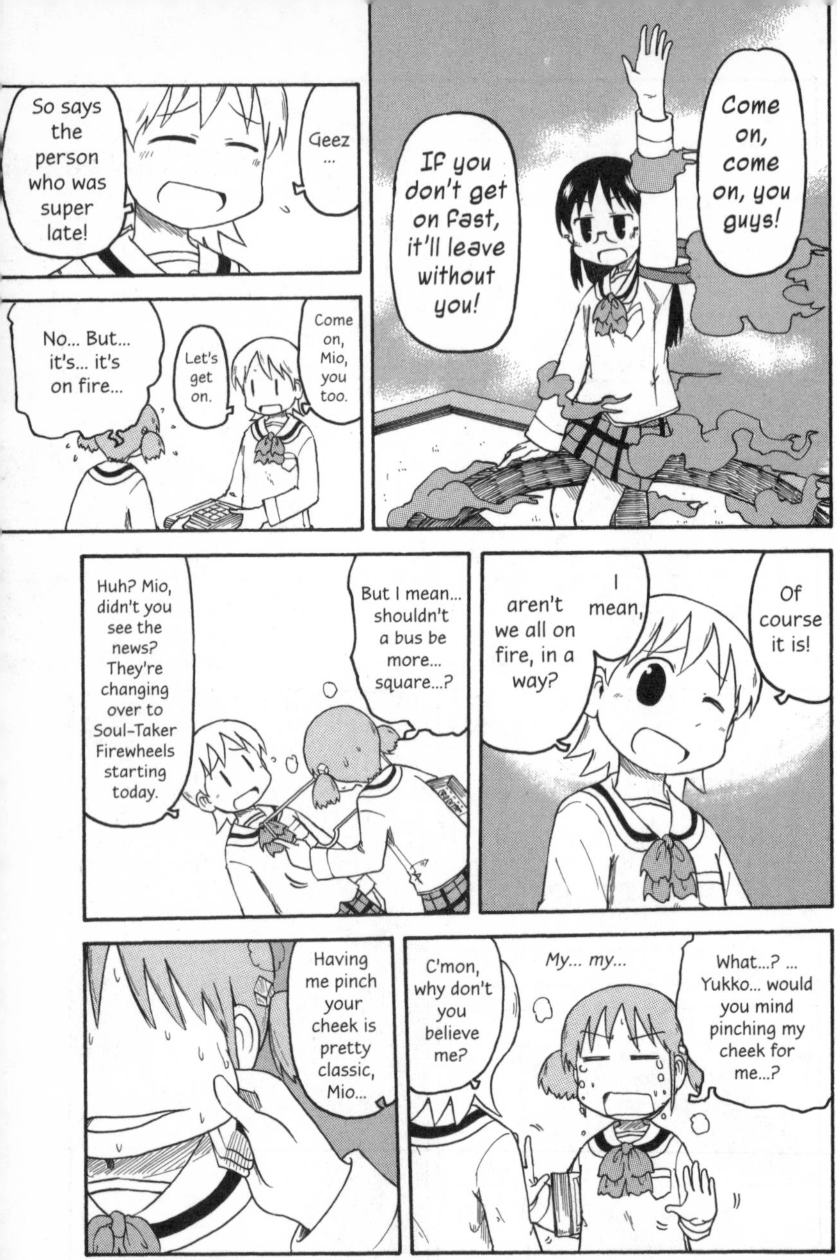
Come on, come on, you guys!
If you don't get on fast, it'll leave without you!
Geez ...
So says the person who was super late!
Come on, Mio, you too.
Let's get on.
No... But... it's... it's on fire...
Of course it is!
I mean,
aren't we all on fire, in a way?
But I mean... shouldn't a bus be more... square...?
Huh? Mio, didn't you see the news? They're changing over to Soul-Taker Firewheels starting today.
What...? ... Yukko... would you mind pinching my cheek for me...?
My... my...
C'mon, why don't you believe me?
Having me pinch your cheek is pretty classic, Mio...

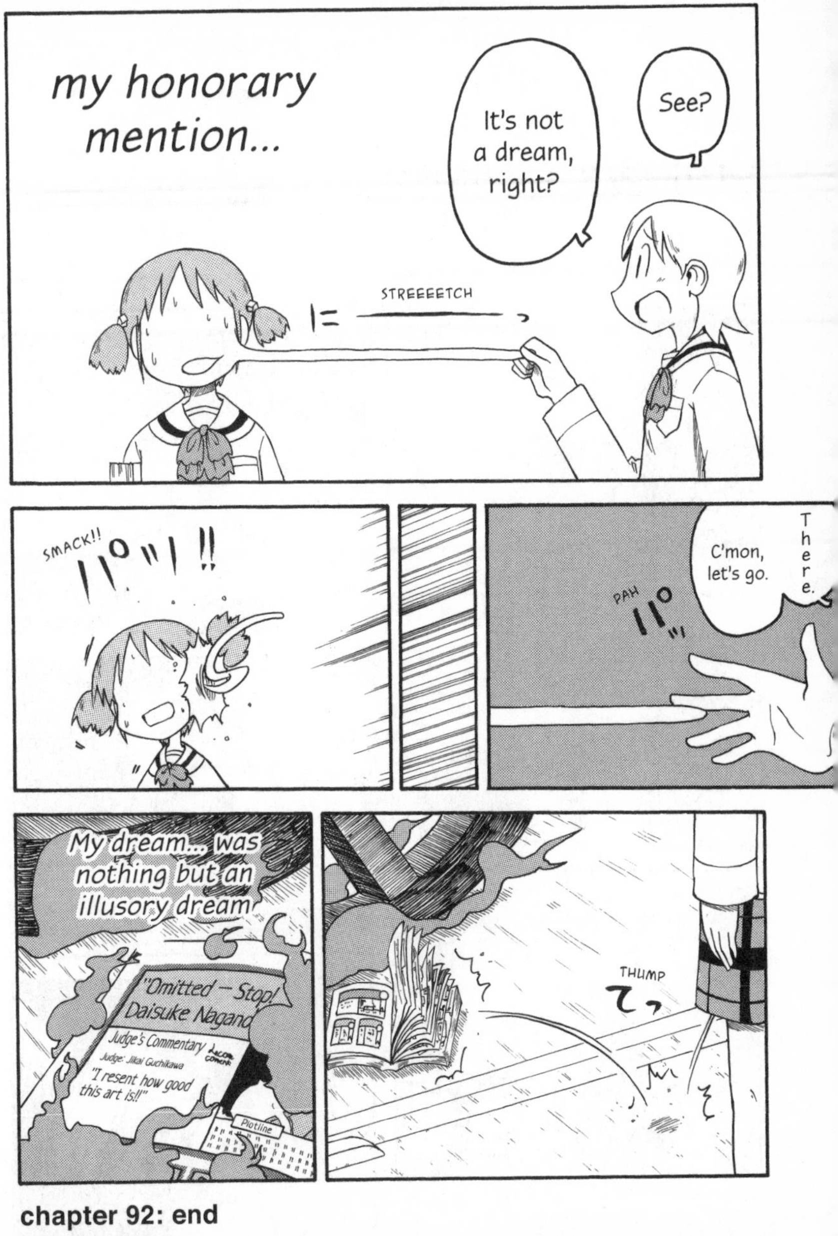
See?
It's not a dream, right?
my honorary mention...
STREEEETCH
There.
C'mon, let's go.
PAH
SMACK!!
THUMP
My dream... was nothing but an illusory dream
"Omitted — Stop!
Daisuke Nagan
Judge's Commentary
Judge: Jikai Guchikawa
"I resent how good this art is!!"
Plotline

chapter 92: end

ordinary shorts 8

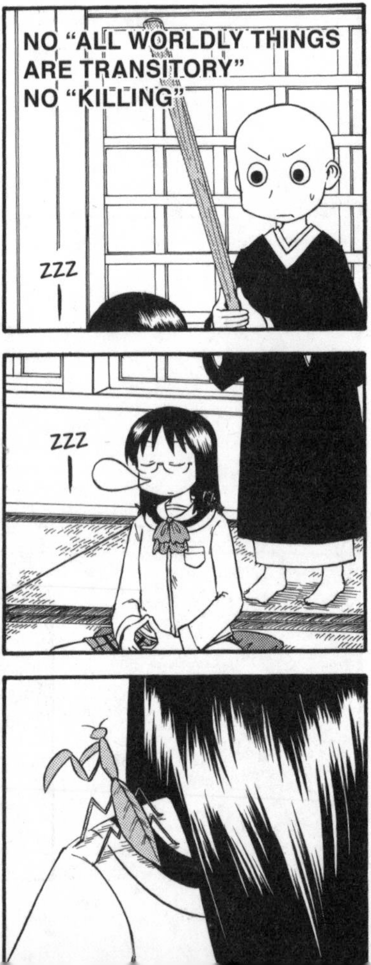
NO “ALL WORLDLY THINGS ARE TRANSITORY” NO “KILLING”
ZZZ
ZZZ

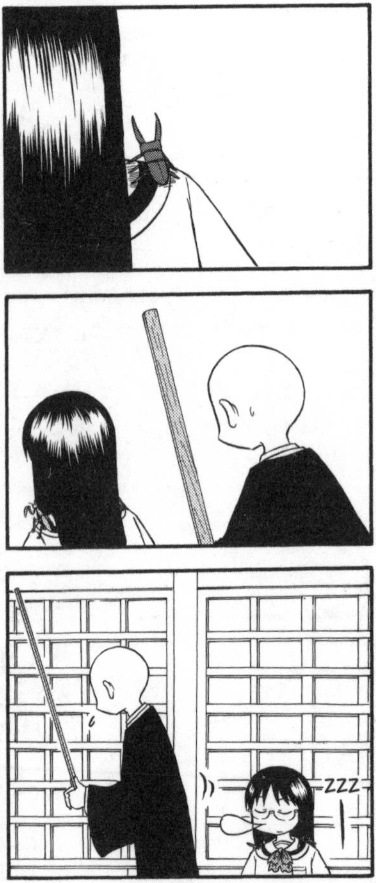
ZZZ

izumi

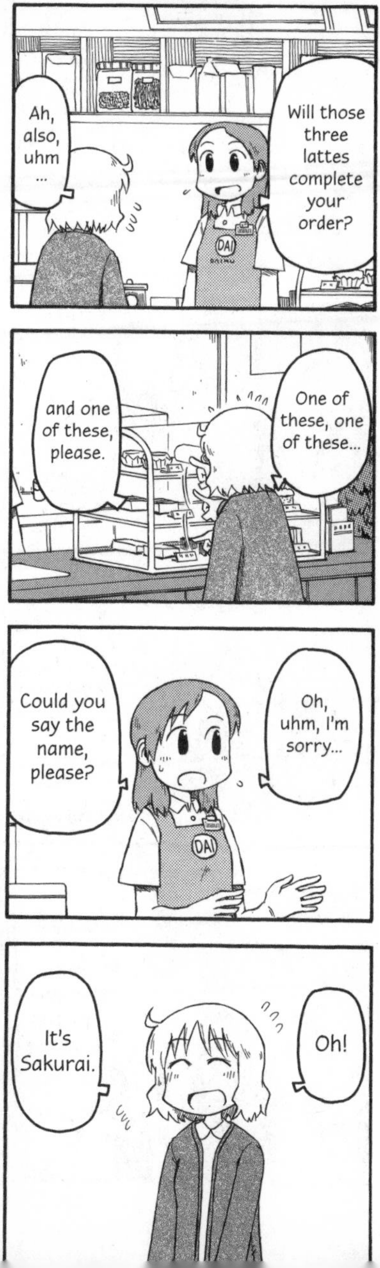

Will those three lattes complete your order?
Ah, also, uhm ...
One of these, one of these...
and one of these, please.
Oh, uhm, I'm sorry...
Could you say the name, please?
Oh!
It's Sakurai.

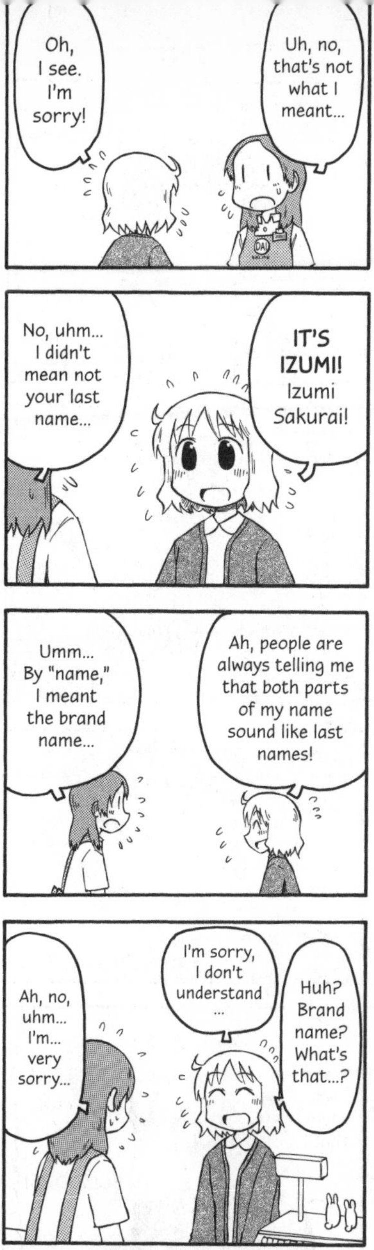

Uh, no, that's not what I meant...
Oh, I see. I'm sorry!
IT'S IZUMI! Izumi Sakurai!
No, uhm... I didn't mean not your last name...
Ah, people are always telling me that both parts of my name sound like last names!
Umm... By "name," I meant the brand name...
Huh? Brand name? What's that...?
I'm sorry, I don't understand ...
Ah, no, uhm... I'm... very sorry...

1-B

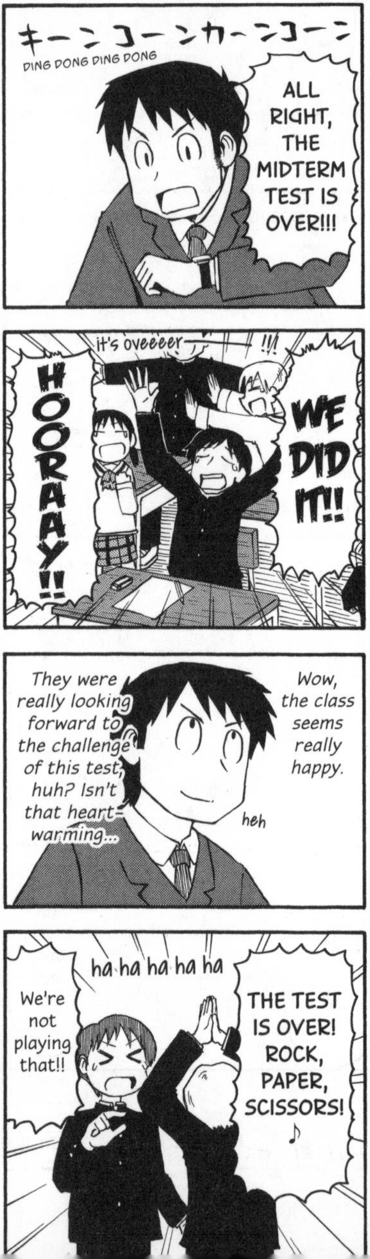
キーンコーンカーンコーン
DING DONG DING DONG
ALL RIGHT, THE MIDTERM TEST IS OVER!!!
it's oveeeer !!!
WE DID IT!!
HOORAAY!!
Wow, the class seems really happy.
heh
They were really looking forward to the challenge of this test, huh? Isn't that heart-warming...
THE TEST IS OVER! ROCK, PAPER, SCISSORS! ♪
ha ha ha ha ha
We're not playing that!!

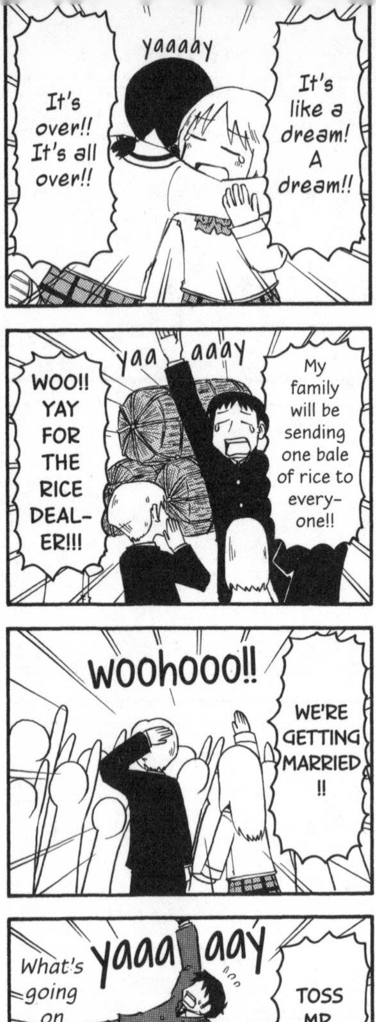
It's like a dream! A dream!!
yaaaay
It's over!! It's all over!!
My family will be sending one bale of rice to everyone!!
yaa aaay
WOO!! YAY FOR THE RICE DEALER!!!
woohooo!!
WE'RE GETTING MARRIED !!
TOSS MR. TAKASAKI IN THE AIR!!
yaaa aay
What's going on here?!!

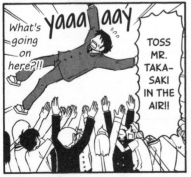

river fishing

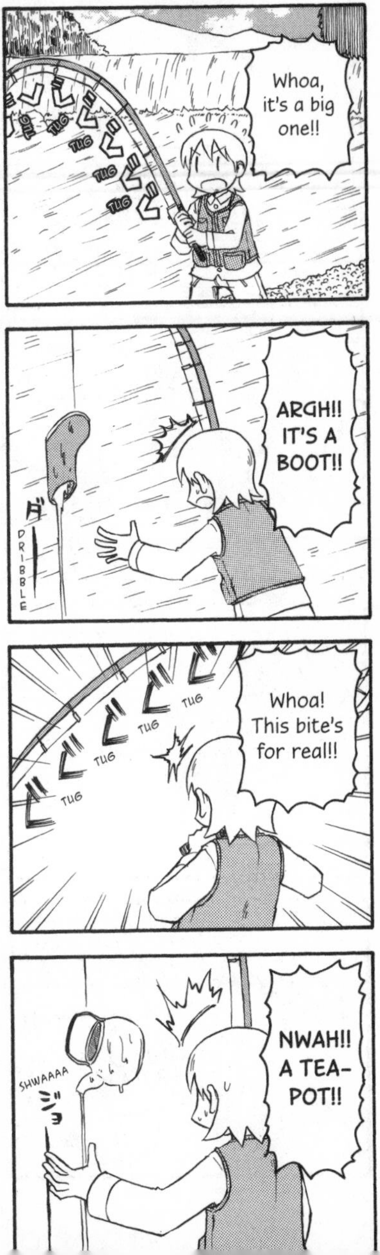
Whoa, it's a big one!!
TUG
TUG
TUG
TUG
ARGH!! IT'S A BOOT!!
DRIBBLE
Whoa! This bite's for real!!
TUG
TUG
TUG
TUG
NWAH!! A TEA-POT!!
SHWAAAA

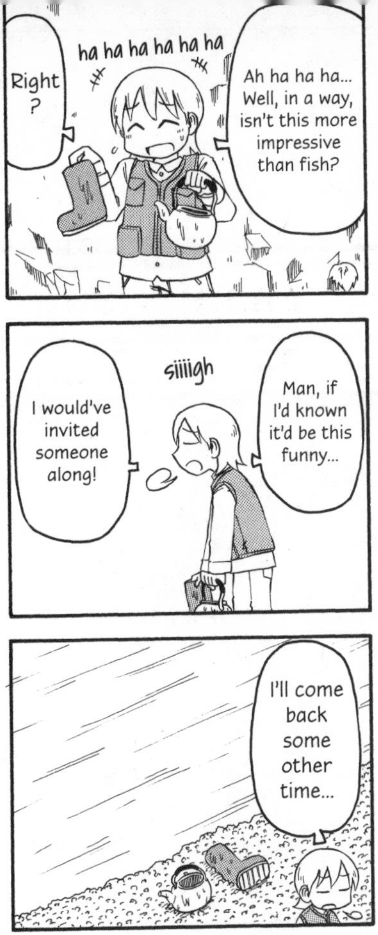
Ah ha ha ha... Well, in a way, isn't this more impressive than fish?
ha ha ha ha ha ha ha
Right?
Man, if I'd known it'd be this funny...
siiiigh
I would've invited someone along!
I'll come back some other time...
WHOOSH

ordinary shorts 8: end

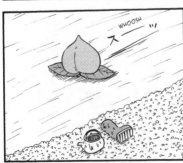

chapter 93

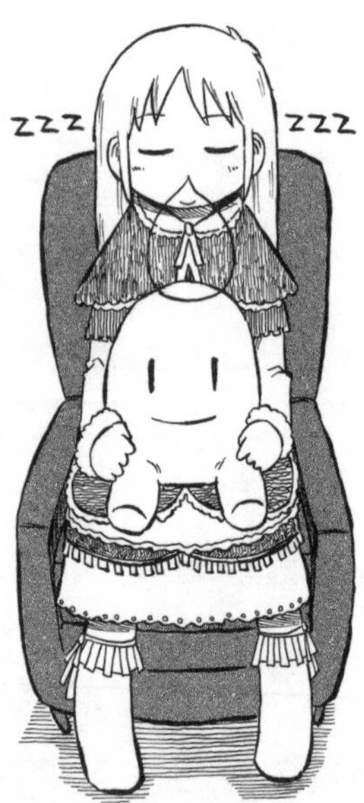
ZZZ
ZZZ

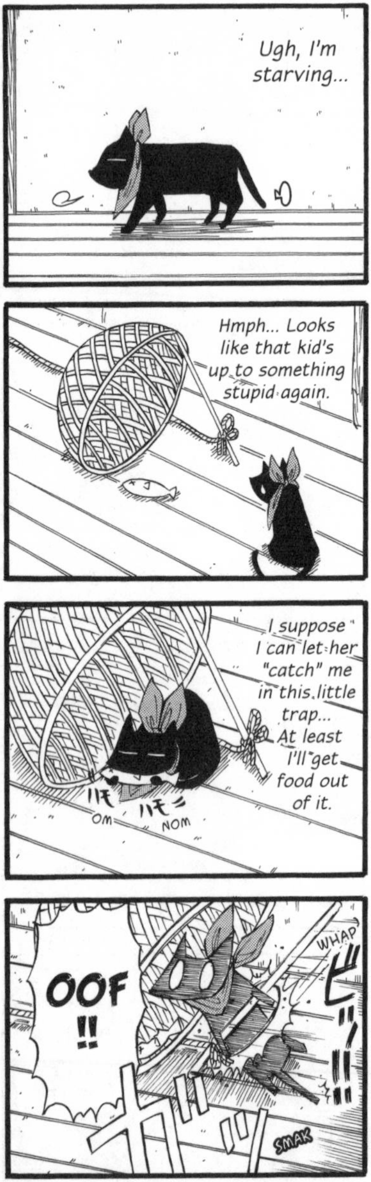
Ugh, I'm starving...
Hmph... Looks like that kid's up to something stupid again.
I suppose I can let her "catch" me in this little trap... At least I'll get food out of it.
OM
NOM
WHAP
OOF !!
SMAK

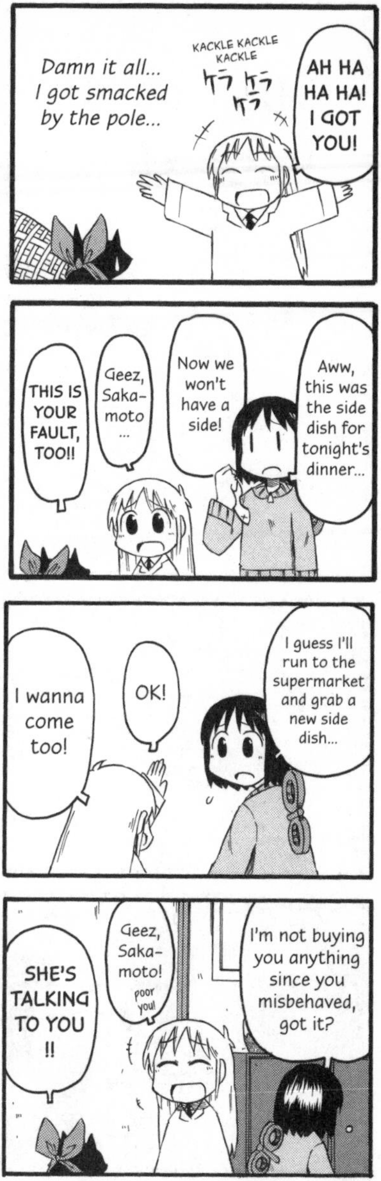
AH HA HA HA! I GOT YOU!
KACKLE KACKLE KACKLE
ケラ ケラ ケラ
Damn it all... I got smacked by the pole...
Aww, this was the side dish for tonight's dinner...
Now we won't have a side!
Geez, Saka-moto ...
THIS IS YOUR FAULT, TOO!!
I guess I'll run to the supermarket and grab a new side dish...
OK!
I wanna come too!
I'm not buying you anything since you misbehaved, got it?
Geez, Saka-moto!
poor you!
SHE'S TALKING TO YOU !!

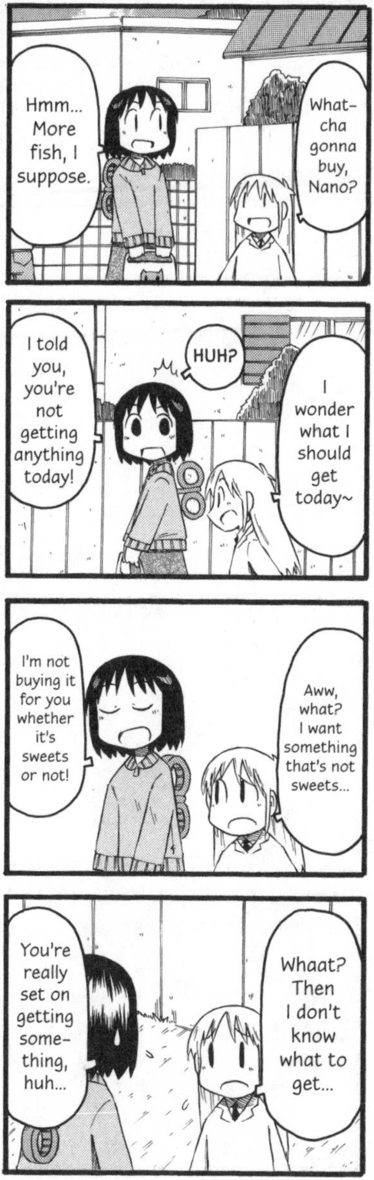
What-cha gonna buy, Nano?
Hmm... More fish, I suppose.
I wonder what I should get today~
HUH?
I told you, you're not getting anything today!
Aww, what? I want something that's not sweets...
I'm not buying it for you whether it's sweets or not!
Whaat? Then I don't know what to get...
You're really set on getting some-thing, huh...

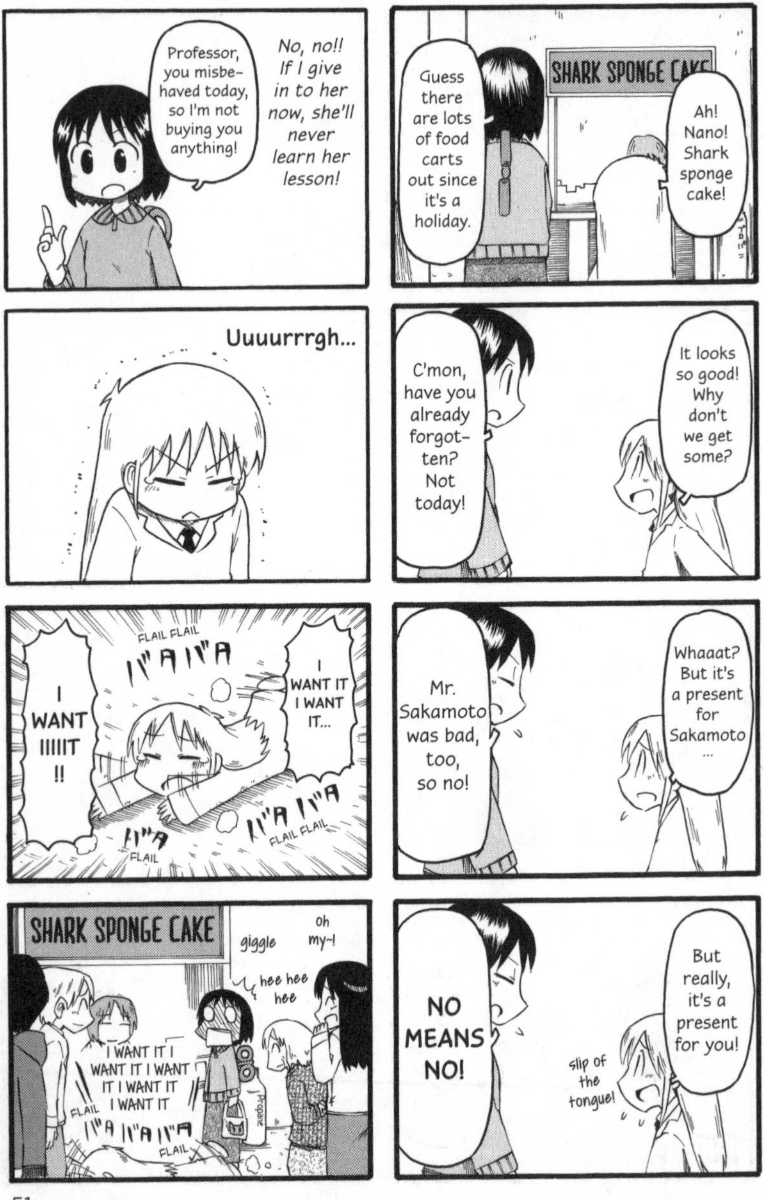
SHARK SPONGE CAKE
Ah! Nano! Shark sponge cake!
Guess there are lots of food carts out since it's a holiday.
It looks so good! Why don't we get some?
C'mon, have you already forgotten? Not today!
Whaaat? But it's a present for Sakamoto ...
Mr. Sakamoto was bad, too, so no!
But really, it's a present for you!
slip of the tongue!
NO MEANS NO!
No, no!! If I give in to her now, she'll never learn her lesson!
Professor, you misbehaved today, so I'm not buying you anything!
Uuuurrrgh...
FLAIL FLAIL
バタバタ
I WANT IT I WANT IT...
I WANT IIIIIT !!
バタバタ
FLAIL FLAIL
バタ
FLAIL
SHARK SPONGE CAKE
oh my~!
giggle
hee hee hee
I WANT IT I WANT IT I WANT IT I WANT IT I WANT IT
FLAIL
バタバタバタ
FLAIL
Propane

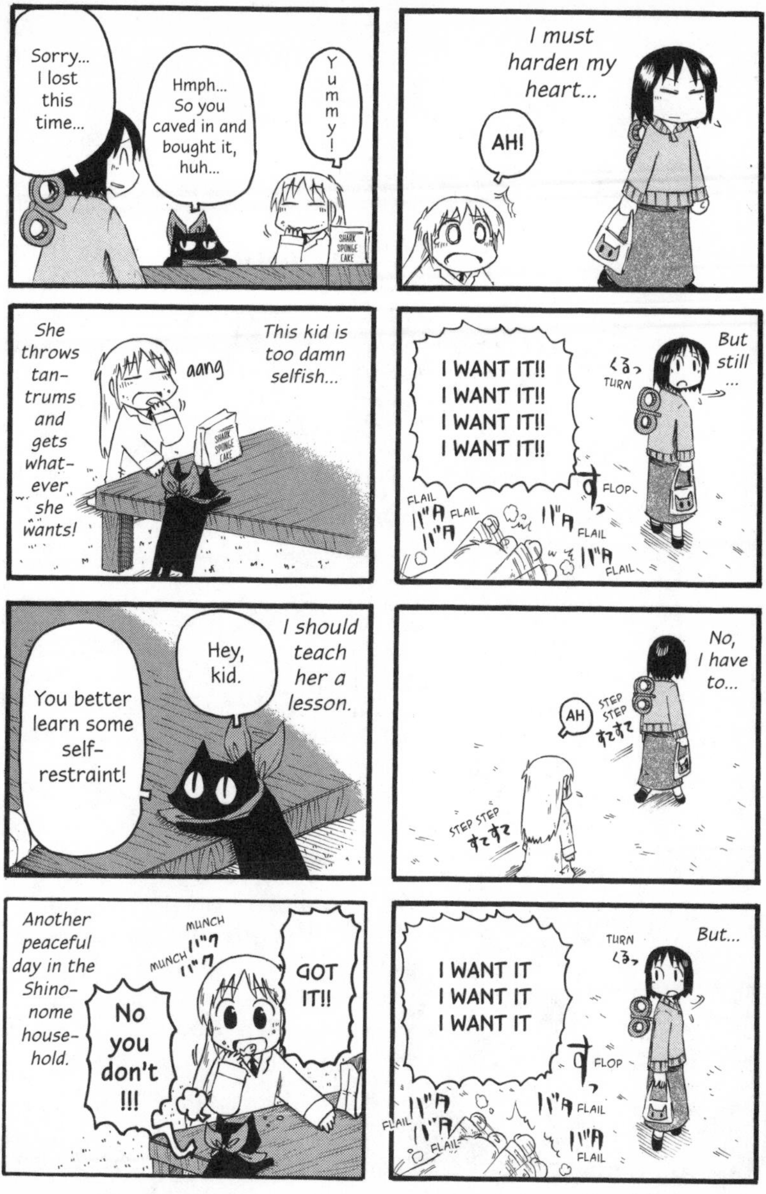
I must harden my heart...
AH!
But still...
TURN くるっ
I WANT IT!! I WANT IT!! I WANT IT!! I WANT IT!!
FLOP すっ
FLAIL バタ FLAIL バタ FLAIL バタ FLAIL バタ
No, I have to...
STEP STEP すてすて
AH
STEP STEP すてすて
But...
TURN くるっ
I WANT IT I WANT IT I WANT IT
FLOP すっ
FLAIL バタ FLAIL バタ FLAIL バタ FLAIL バタ
Sorry... I lost this time...
Hmph... So you caved in and bought it, huh...
Yummy!
SHARK SPONGE CAKE
This kid is too damn selfish...
She throws tan-trums and gets what-ever she wants!
aang
SHARK SPONGE CAKE
I should teach her a lesson.
Hey, kid.
You better learn some self-restraint!
GOT IT!!
MUNCH バク MUNCH バク
No you don't!!!
Another peaceful day in the Shino-nome house-hold.

chapter 93: end

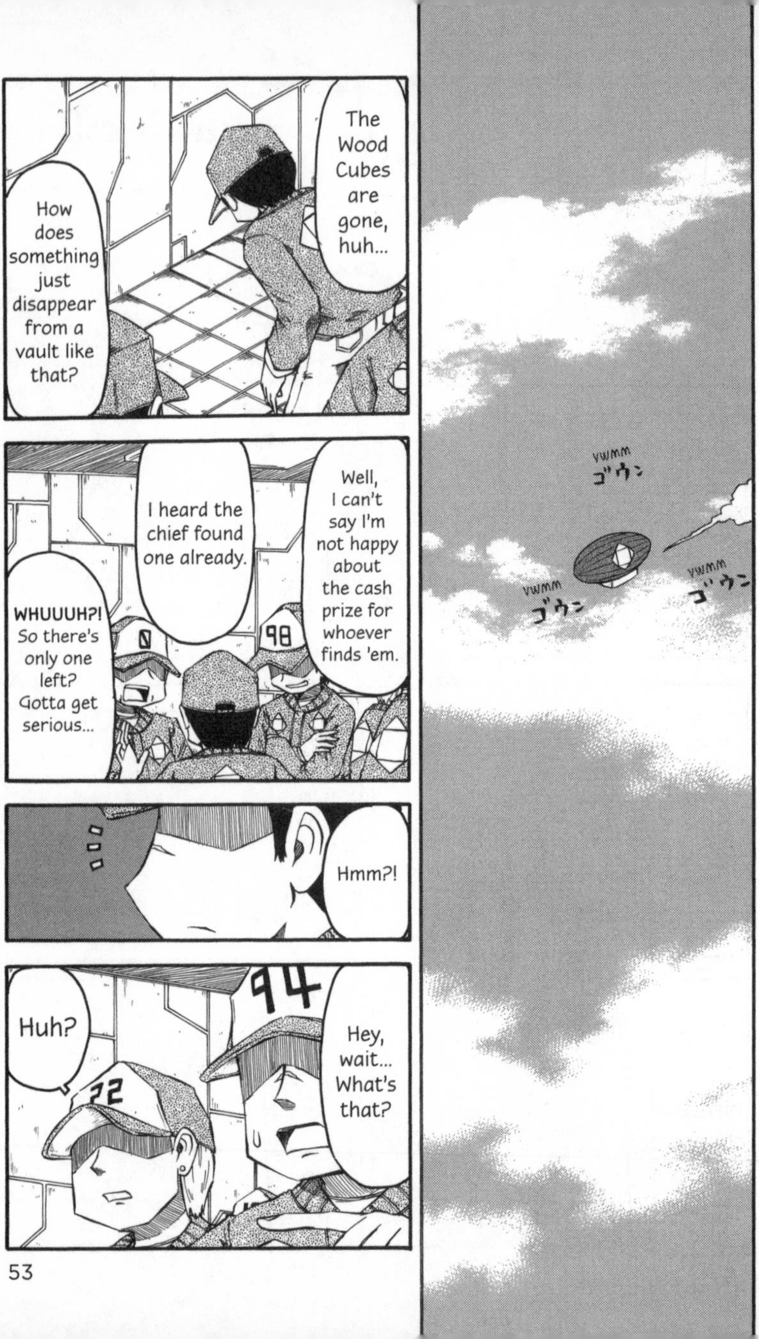
VWMM
ゴウン
VWMM
ゴウン
VWMM
ゴウン
The Wood Cubes are gone, huh...
How does something just disappear from a vault like that?
Well, I can't say I'm not happy about the cash prize for whoever finds 'em.
I heard the chief found one already.
WHUUUH?! So there's only one left? Gotta get serious...
Hmm?!
Hey, wait... What's that?
Huh?

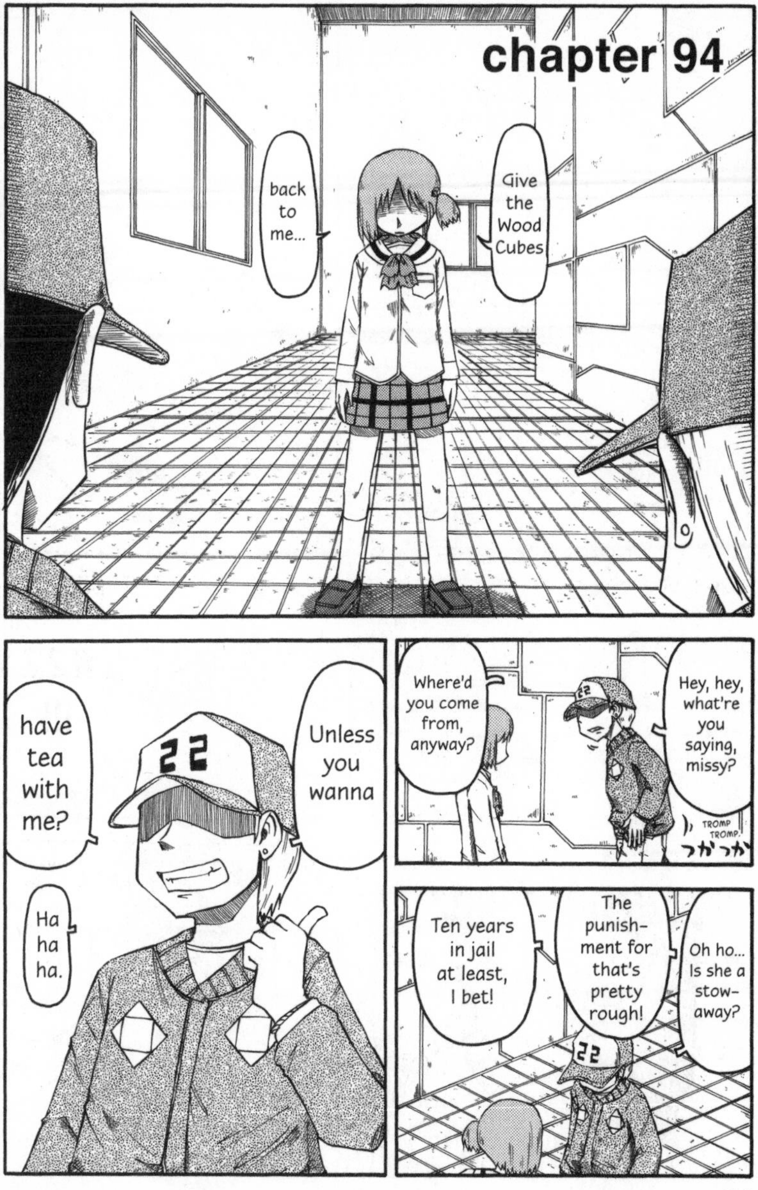
chapter 94
Give the Wood Cubes
back to me...
Hey, hey, what're you saying, missy?
Where'd you come from, anyway?
TROMP TROMP.
つかつか
Oh ho... Is she a stow-away?
The punish-ment for that's pretty rough!
Ten years in jail at least, I bet!
Unless you wanna
have tea with me?
Ha ha ha.

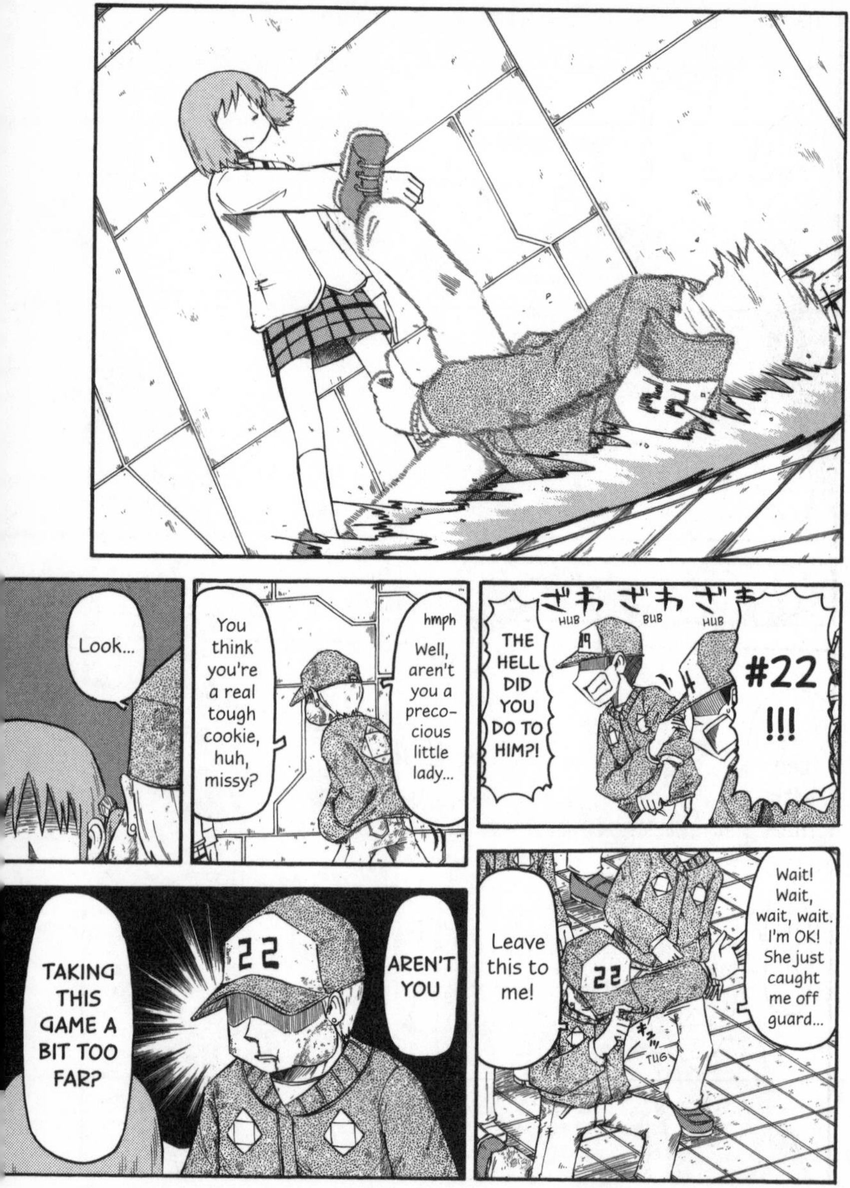
HUB
BUB
HUB
#22 !!!
THE HELL DID YOU DO TO HIM?!
hmph
Well, aren't you a preco-cious little lady...
You think you're a real tough cookie, huh, missy?
Look...
Wait! Wait, wait, wait. I'm OK! She just caught me off guard...
Leave this to me!
TUG
AREN'T YOU
TAKING THIS GAME A BIT TOO FAR?

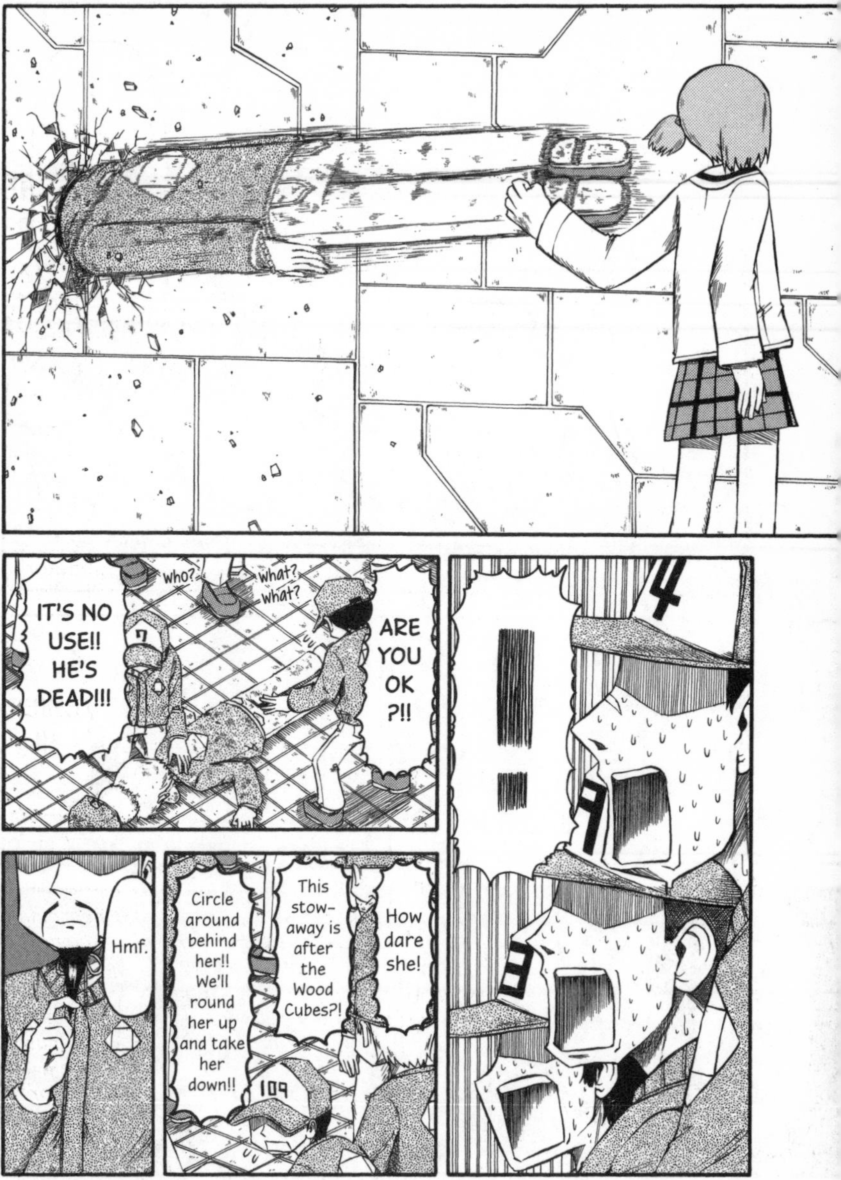
!!
ARE YOU OK ?!!
what? what?
who?
IT'S NO USE!! HE'S DEAD!!!
How dare she!
This stow-away is after the Wood Cubes?!
Circle around behind her!! We'll round her up and take her down!!
Hmf.

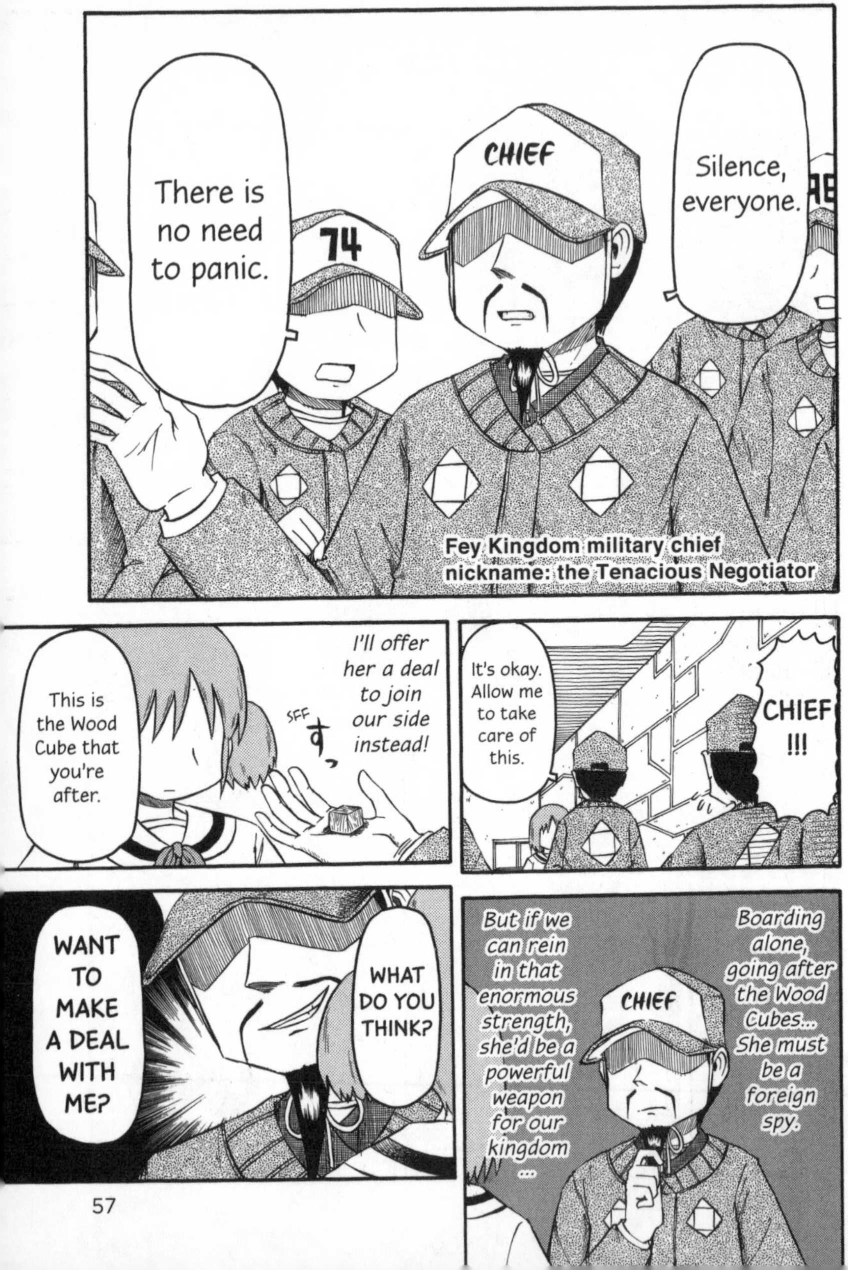
CHIEF
Silence, everyone.
74
There is no need to panic.
Fey Kingdom military chief
nickname: the Tenacious Negotiator
CHIEF !!!
It's okay. Allow me to take care of this.
I'll offer her a deal to join our side instead!
SFF
This is the Wood Cube that you're after.
Boarding alone, going after the Wood Cubes... She must be a foreign spy.
But if we can rein in that enormous strength, she'd be a powerful weapon for our kingdom ...
CHIEF
WHAT DO YOU THINK?
WANT TO MAKE A DEAL WITH ME?

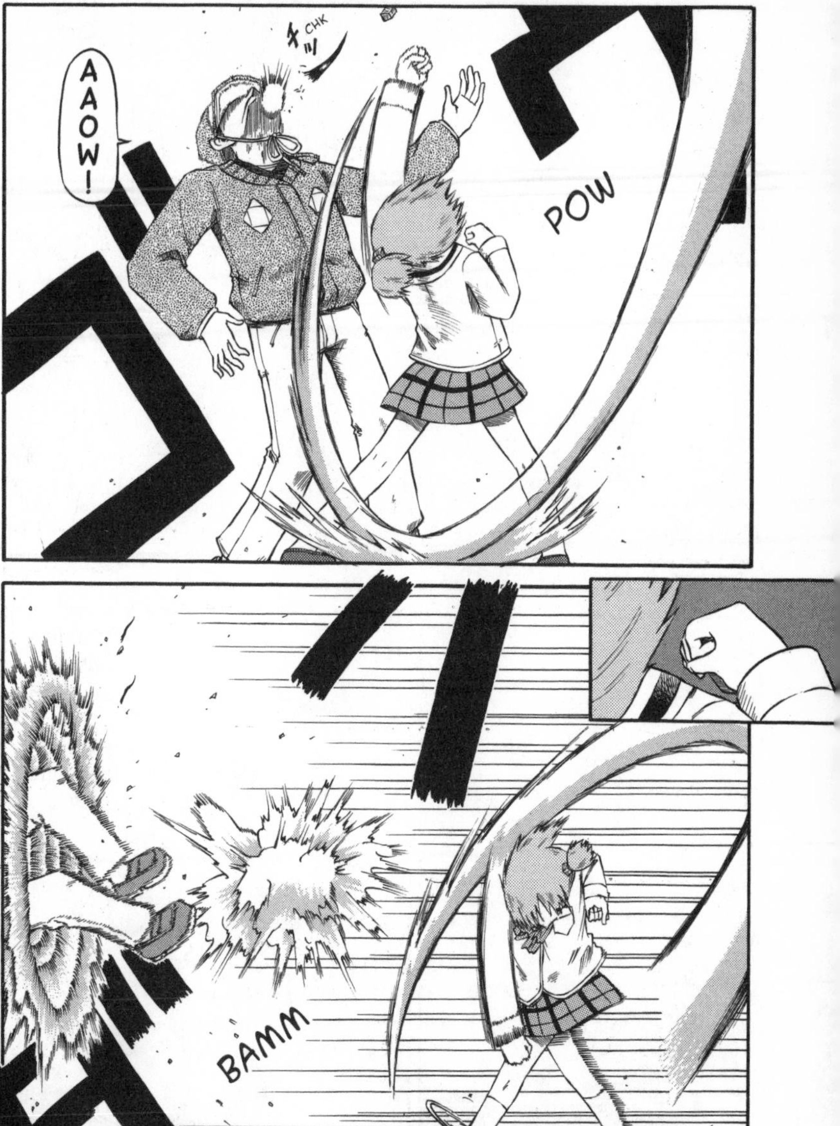
CHK
POW
AAOW!
BAMM

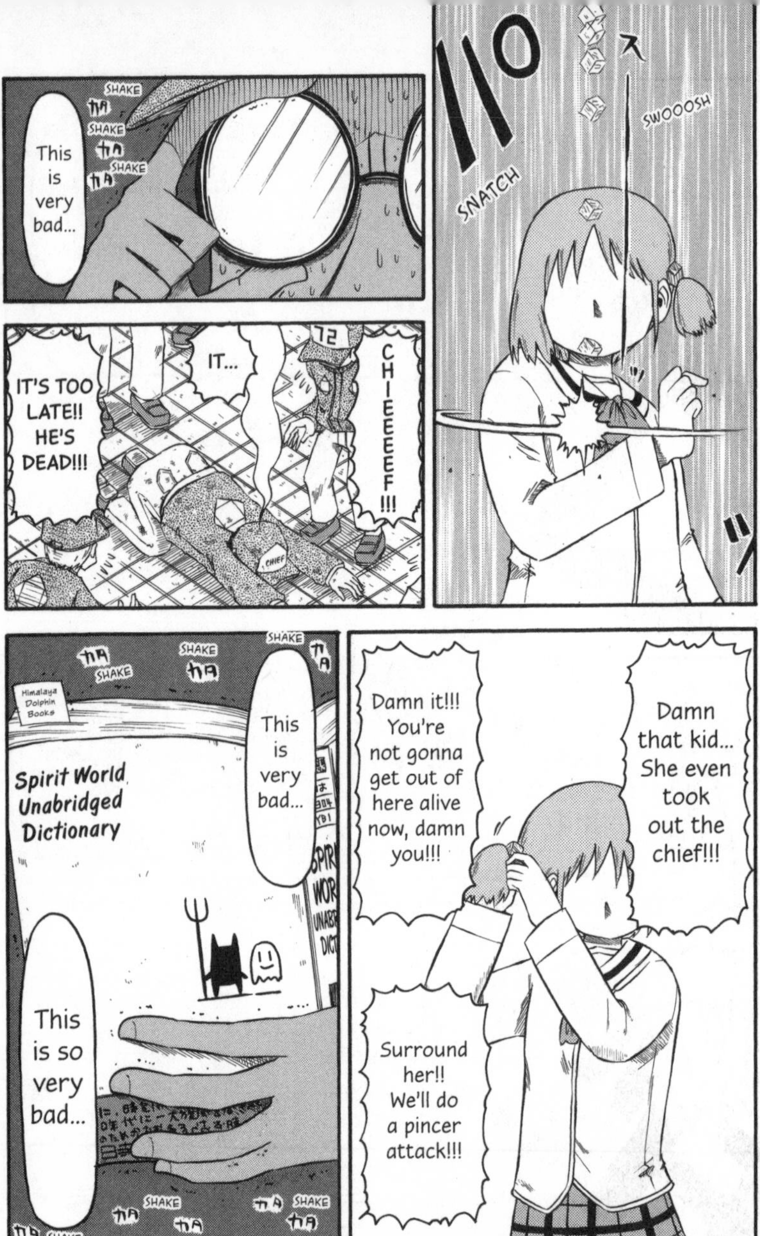
SWOOOSH
SNATCH
SHAKE
SHAKE
SHAKE
This is very bad...
72
CHIEEEEEF!!!
IT...
IT'S TOO LATE!! HE'S DEAD!!!
CHIEF
Damn that kid... She even took out the chief!!!
Damn it!!! You're not gonna get out of here alive now, damn you!!!
Surround her!! We'll do a pincer attack!!!
SHAKE
SHAKE
SHAKE
This is very bad...
Himalaya Dolphin Books
Spirit World Unabridged Dictionary
This is so very bad...
SHAKE
SHAKE
SHAKE

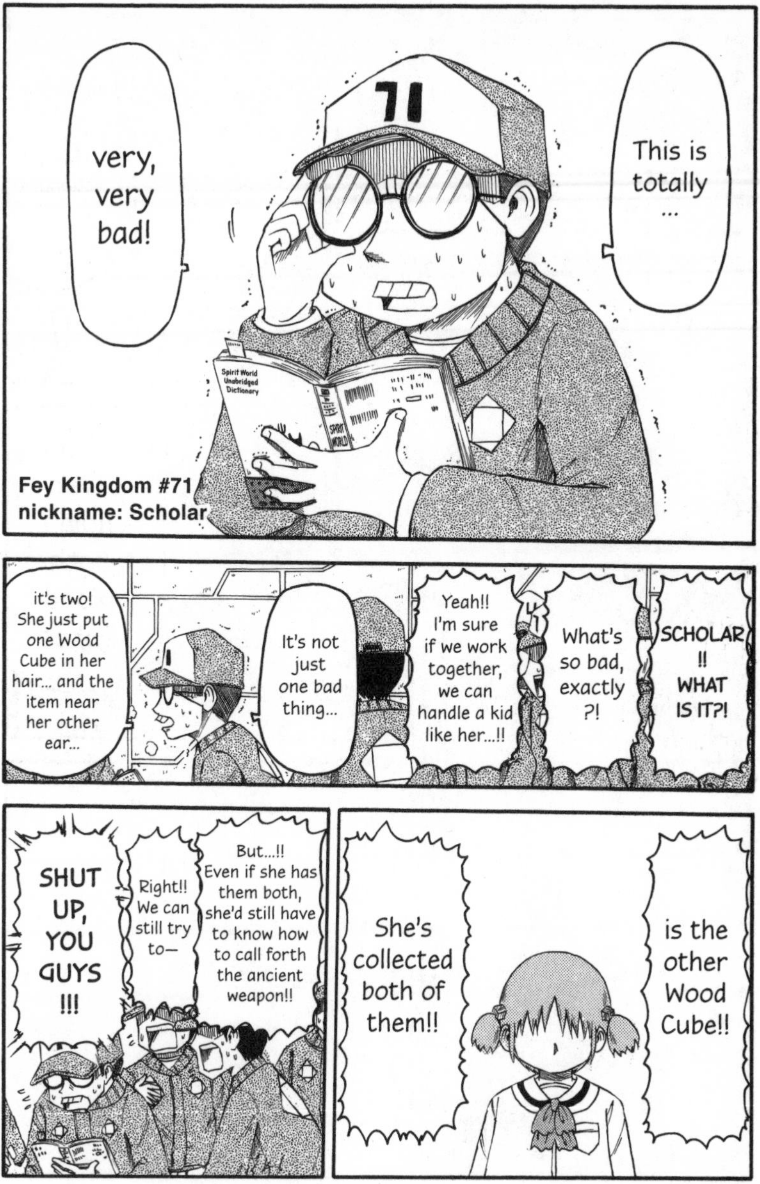
This is totally ...
very, very bad!
Spirit World Unabridged Dictionary
SPIRIT WORLD
Fey Kingdom #71
nickname: Scholar
SCHOLAR!! WHAT IS IT?!
What's so bad, exactly?!
Yeah!! I'm sure if we work together, we can handle a kid like her...!!
It's not just one bad thing...
it's two! She just put one Wood Cube in her hair... and the item near her other ear...
is the other Wood Cube!!
She's collected both of them!!
But...!! Even if she has them both, she'd still have to know how to call forth the ancient weapon!!
Right!! We can still try to—
SHUT UP, YOU GUYS!!!

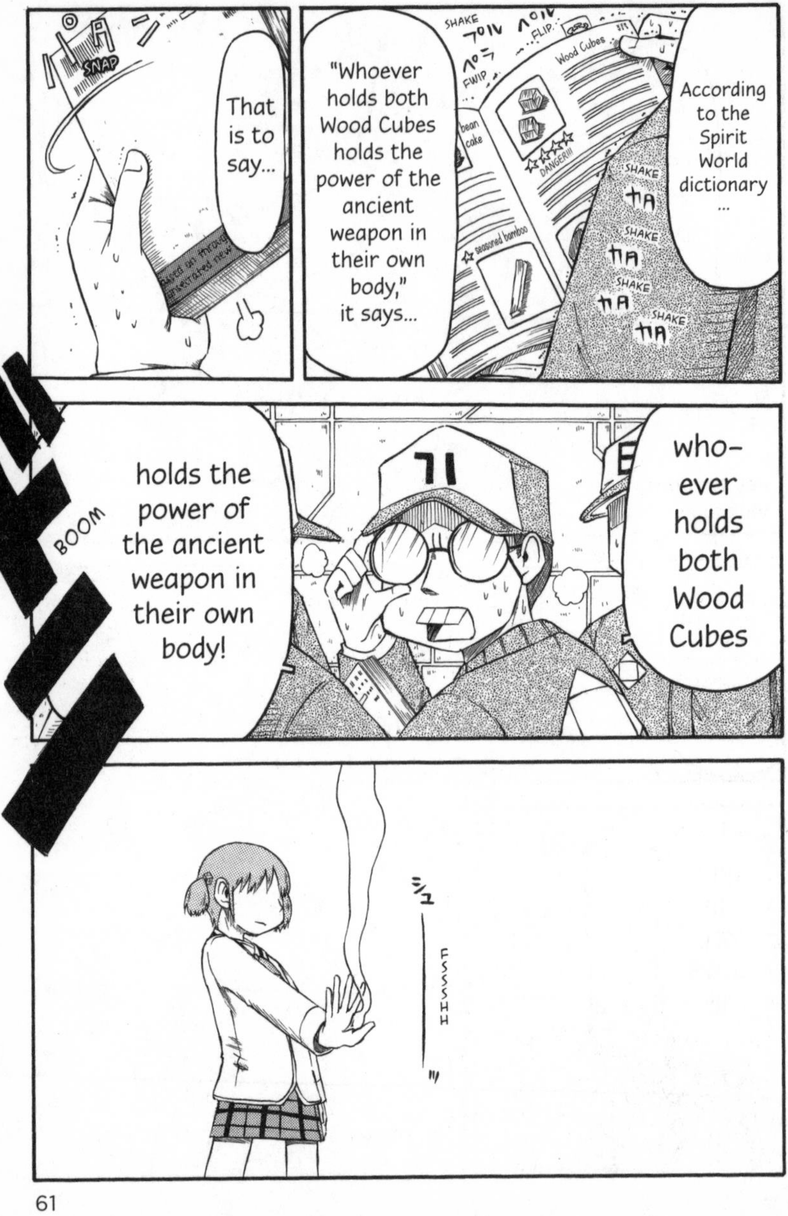
According to the Spirit World dictionary...
SHAKE
SHAKE
SHAKE
SHAKE
FLIP
FWIP
Wood Cubes
DANGER!!!
bean cake
seasoned bamboo
"Whoever holds both Wood Cubes holds the power of the ancient weapon in their own body," it says...
SNAP
That is to say...
who-ever holds both Wood Cubes
holds the power of the ancient weapon in their own body!
BOOM
FSSSHH

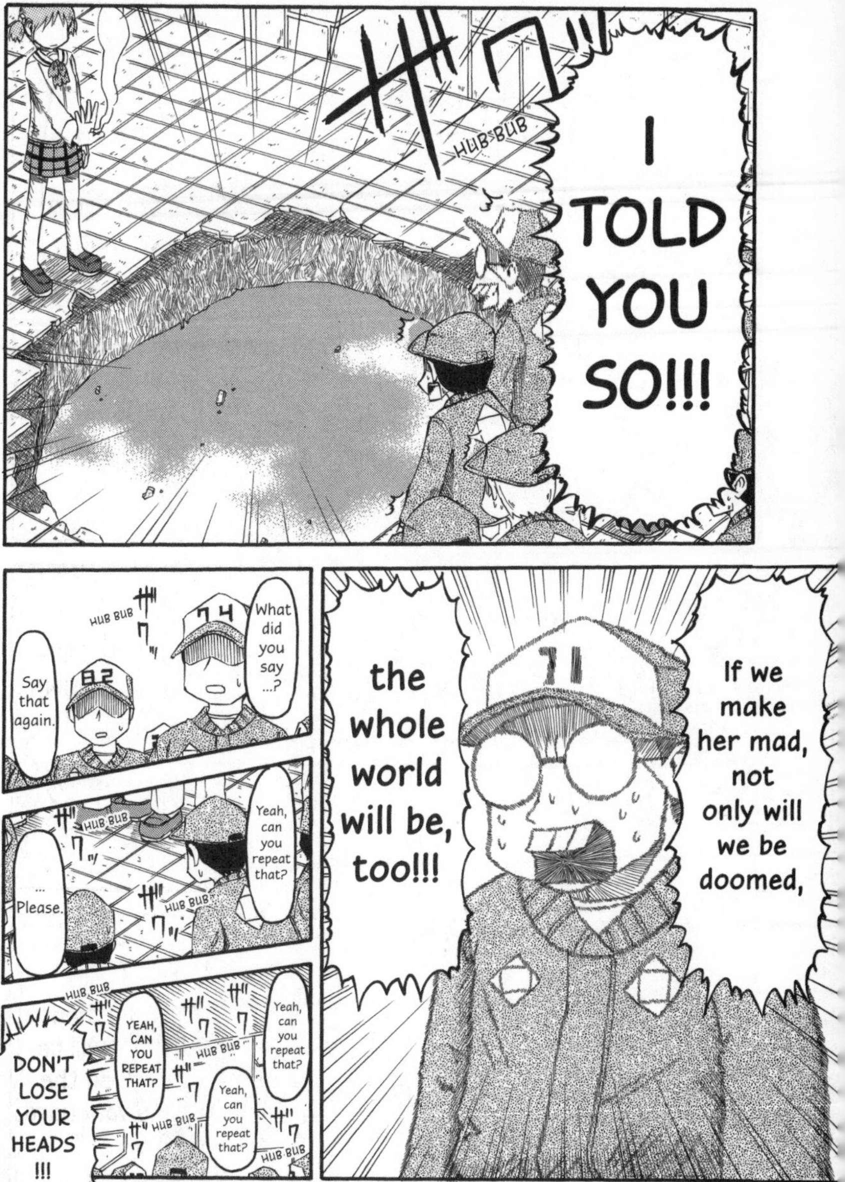
HUB BUB
I TOLD YOU SO!!!
If we make her mad, not only will we be doomed,
the whole world will be, too!!!
HUB BUB
What did you say ...?
Say that again.
HUB BUB
Yeah, can you repeat that?
HUB BUB
... Please.
HUB BUB
Yeah, can you repeat that?
HUB BUB
YEAH, CAN YOU REPEAT THAT?
Yeah, can you repeat that?
HUB BUB
HUB BUB
DON'T LOSE YOUR HEADS !!!

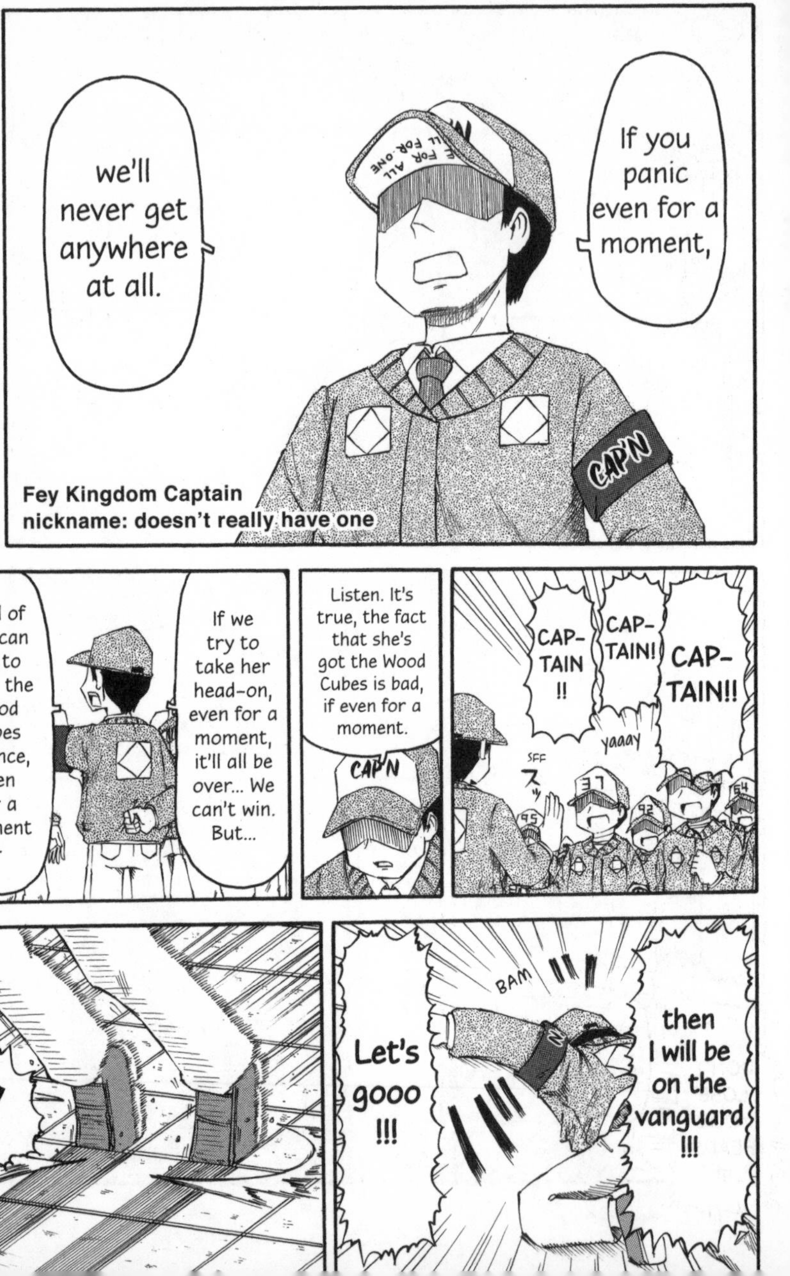
If you panic even for a moment,
we'll never get anywhere at all.
Fey Kingdom Captain
nickname: doesn't really have one
CAP'N
CAP-TAIN!!
CAP-TAIN!
CAP-TAIN !!
yaaay
SFF
Listen. It's true, the fact that she's got the Wood Cubes is bad, if even for a moment.
CAP'N
If we try to take her head-on, even for a moment, it'll all be over... We can't win. But...
if all of you can try to steal the Wood Cubes at once, even for a moment ...
then I will be on the vanguard !!!
BAM
Let's gooo !!!
!

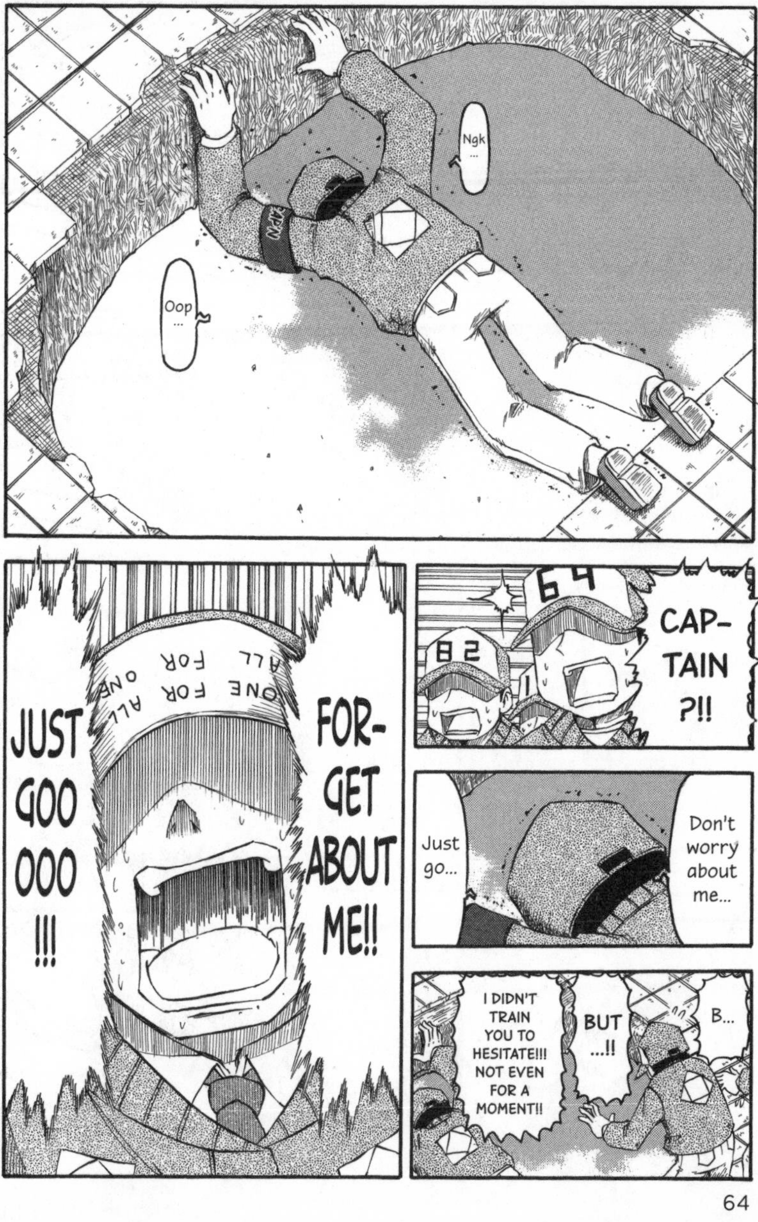
Ngk ...
Oop ...
CAP-TAIN ?!!
Don't worry about me...
Just go...
B...
BUT ...!!
I DIDN'T TRAIN YOU TO HESITATE!!! NOT EVEN FOR A MOMENT!!
FOR-GET ABOUT ME!!
JUST GOOOOO !!!

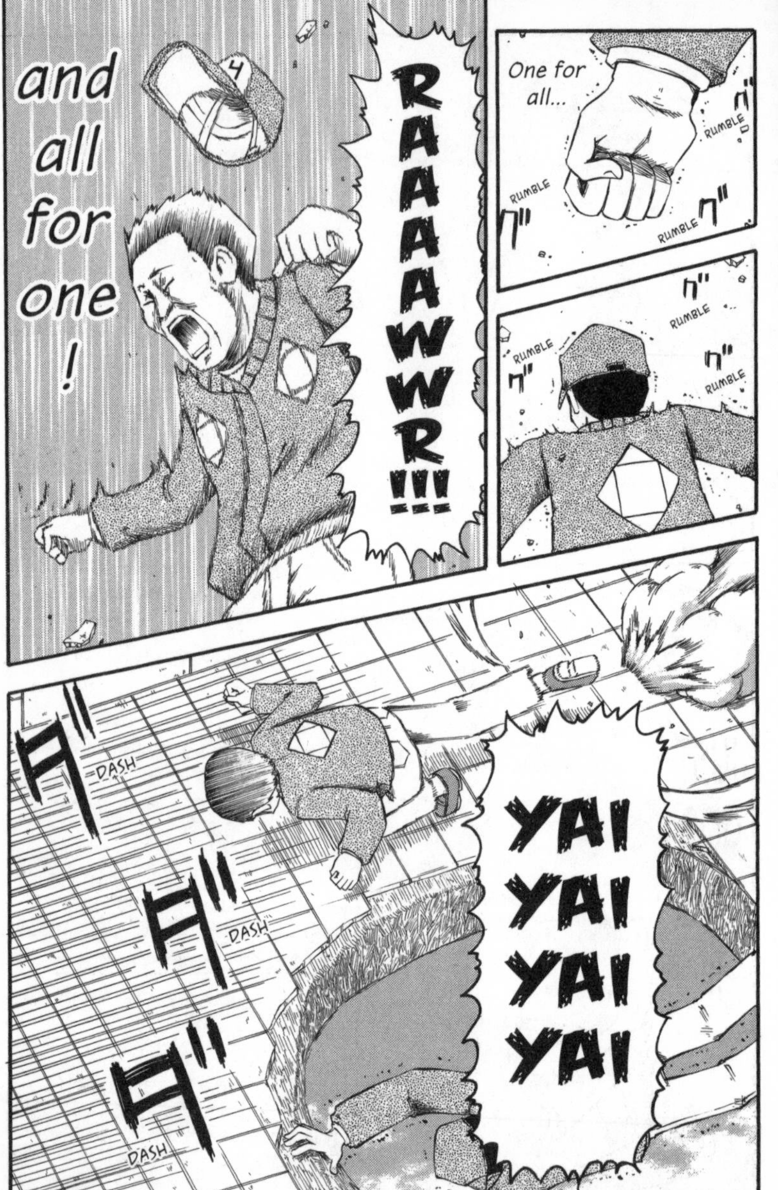

One for all...
RUMBLE
RUMBLE
RUMBLE
RUMBLE
RUMBLE
RUMBLE
RUMBLE
RAAAAWWR!!!
and all for one!
YAI YAI YAI YAI
DASH
DASH
DASH

ONE FOR ALL
ALL FOR ONE
CAP'N
ONE FOR ALL
ALL FOR ONE

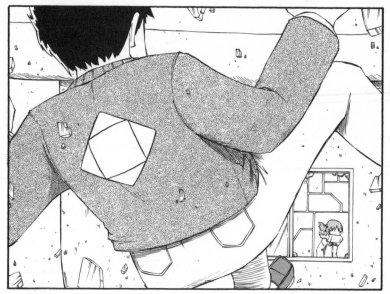

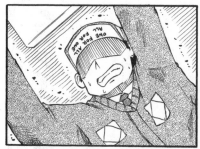

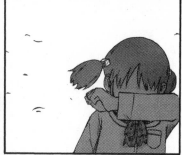

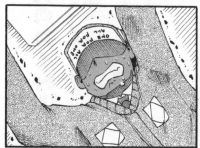

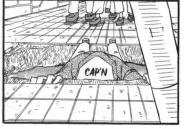

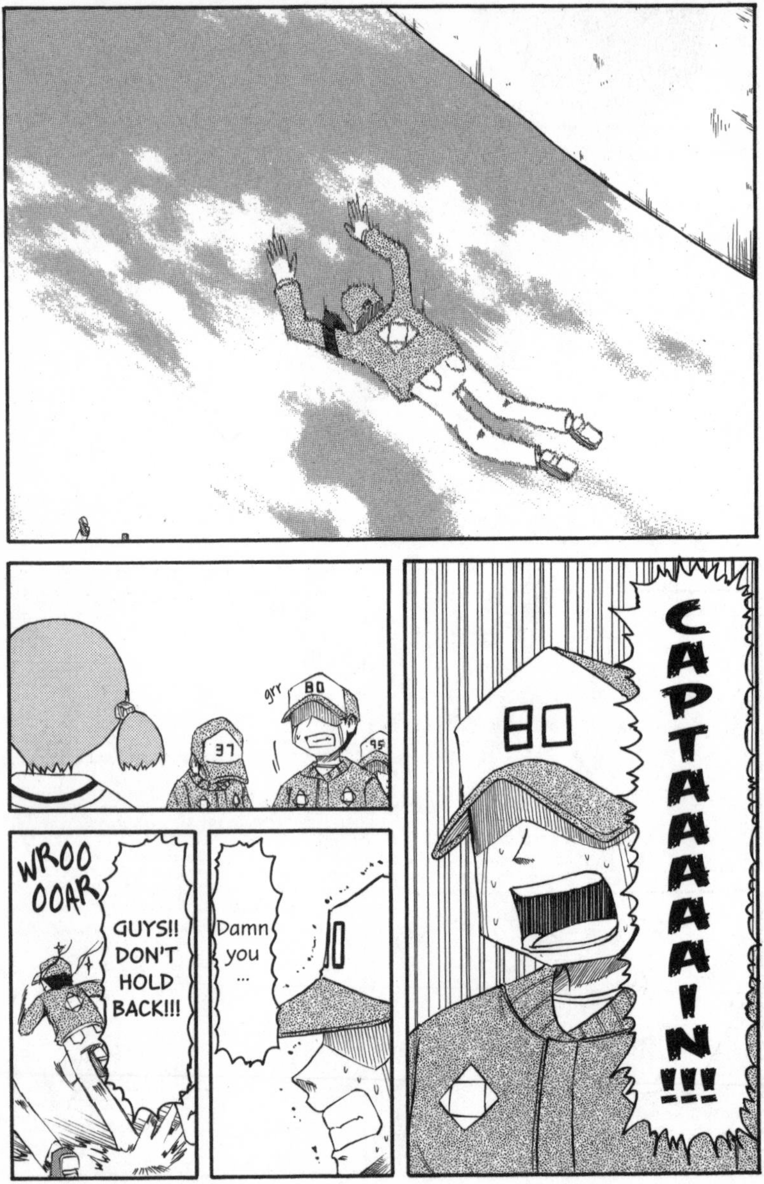
CAPTAAAAAAIN!!!
grr
Damn you ...
WROOOOAR
GUYS!! DON'T HOLD BACK!!!

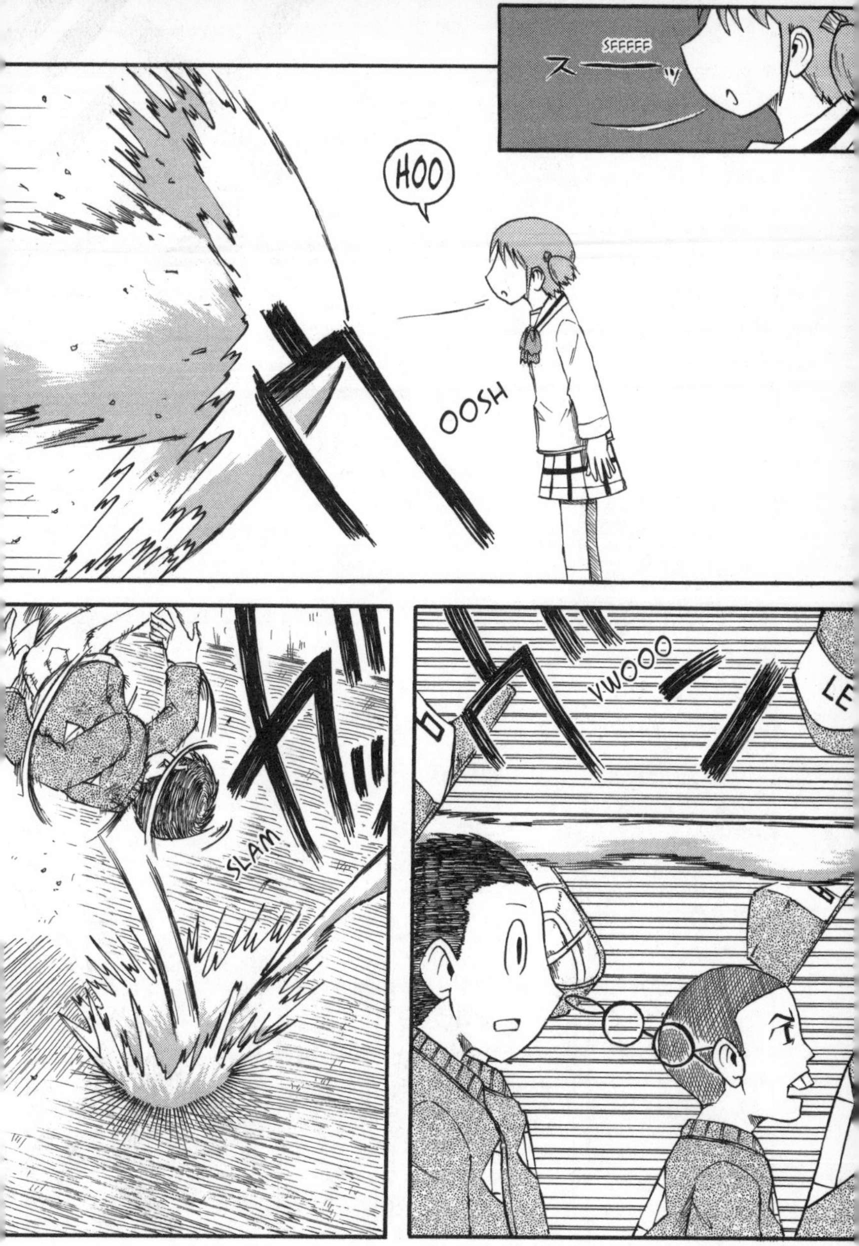
SFFFFF
HOO
OOSH
VWOOO
SLAM

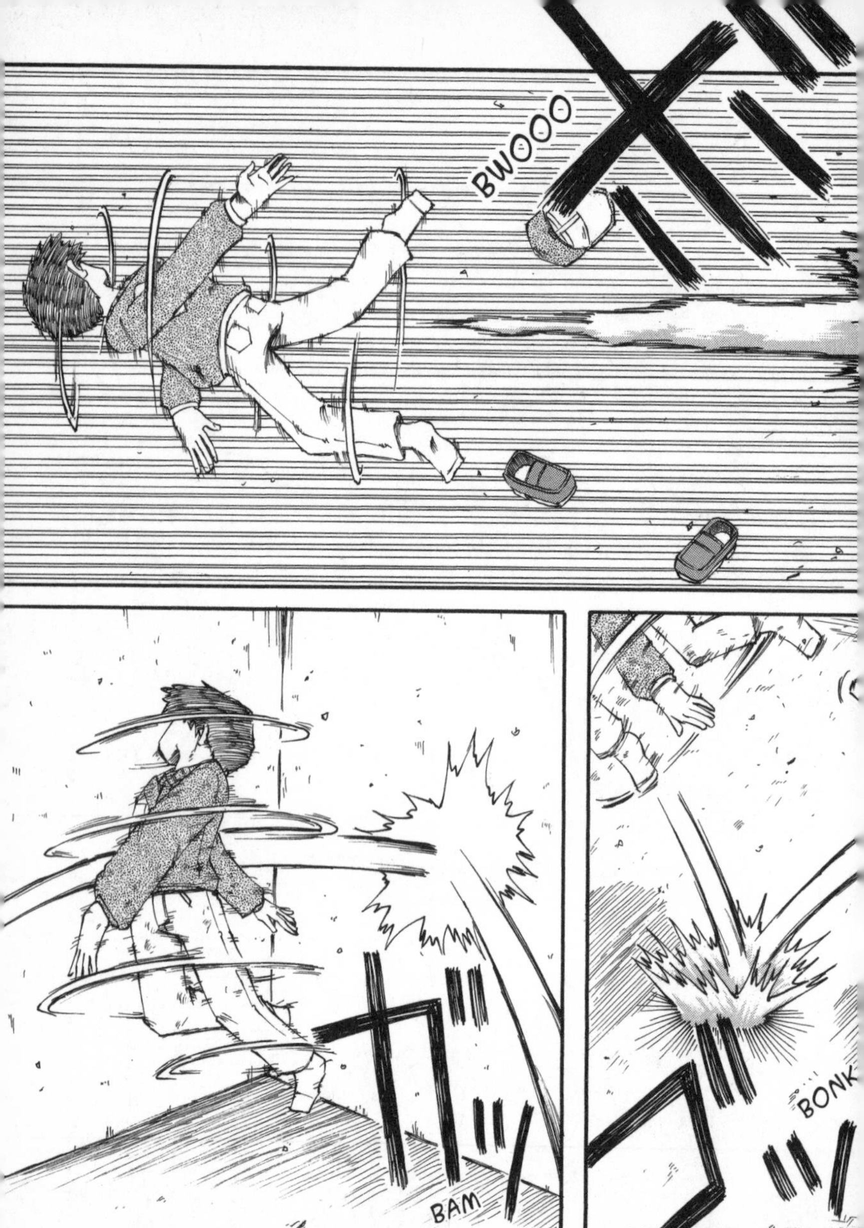
BWOOO
BONK
BAM

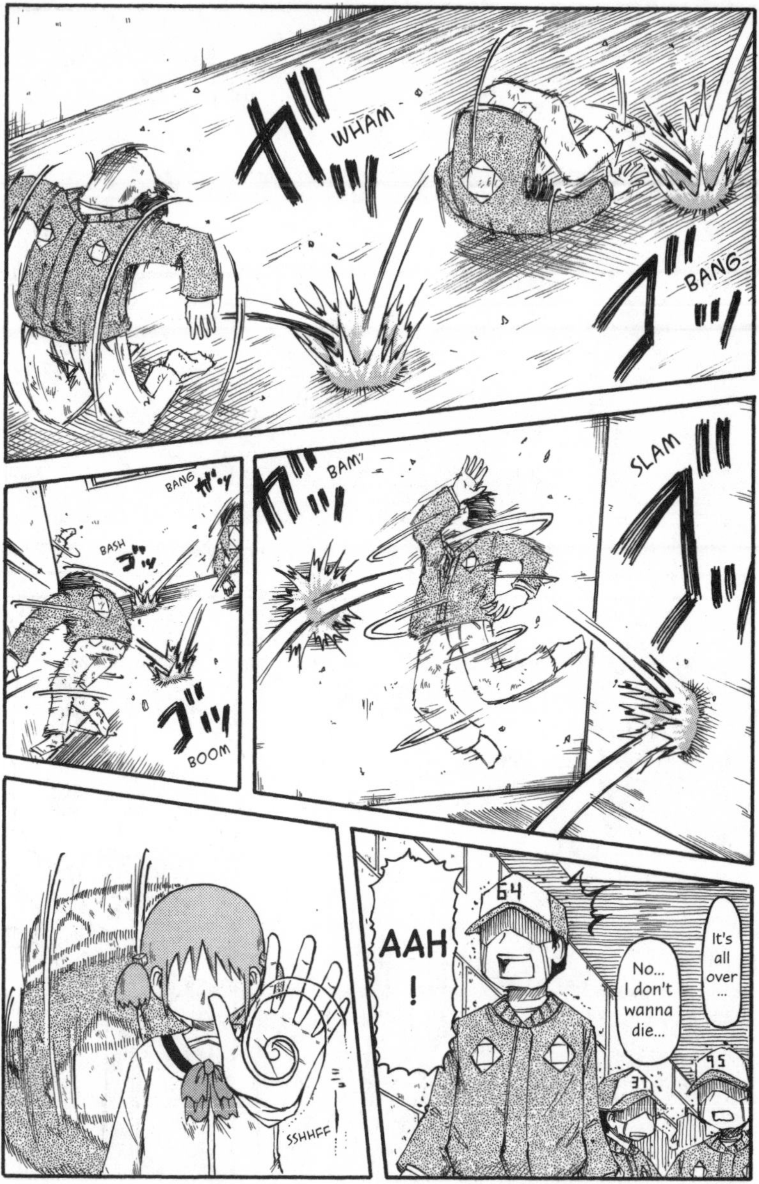
WHAM
BANG
SLAM
BAM
BANG
BASH
BOOM
AAH!
It's all over...
No... I don't wanna die...
SSHHFF

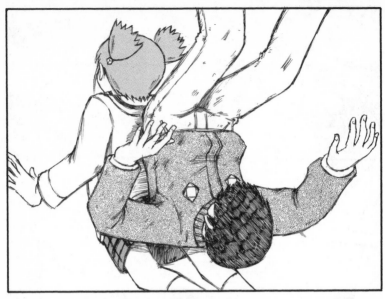

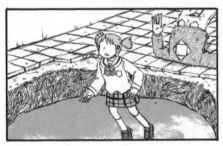

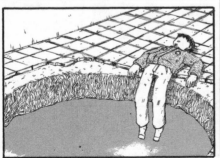

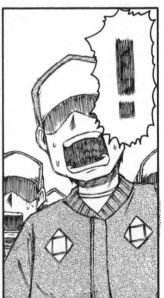

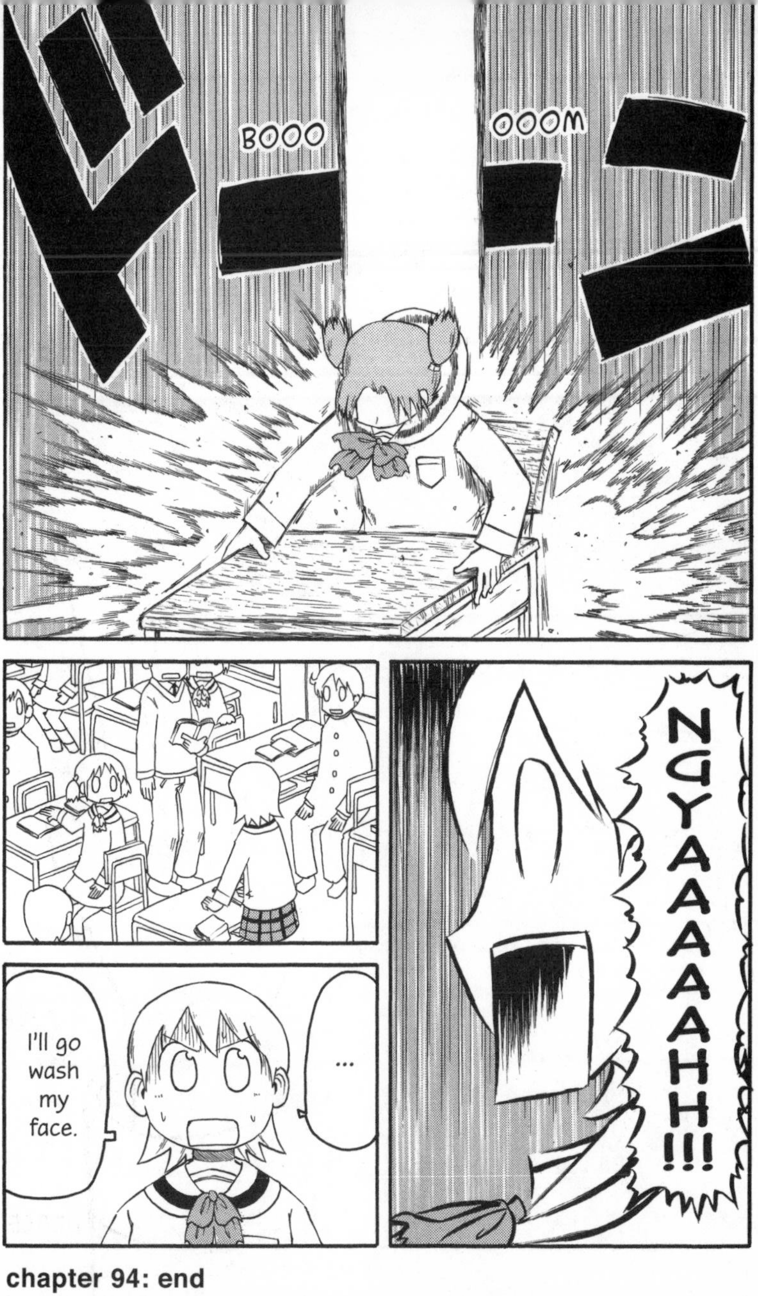
BOOO
OOOM
NGYAAAAAAHH!!!
...
I'll go wash my face.

chapter 94: end

chapter 95

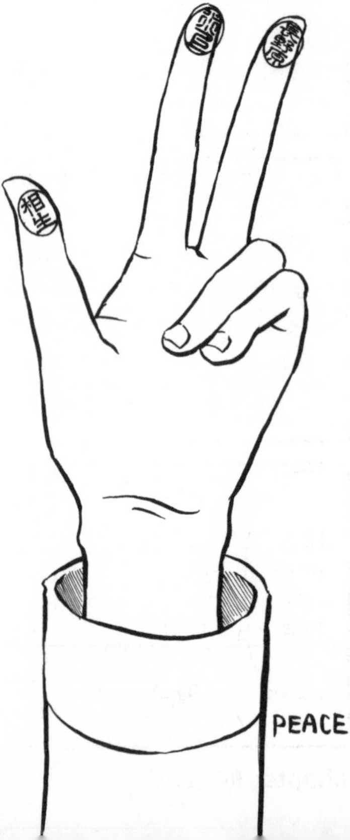
PEACE

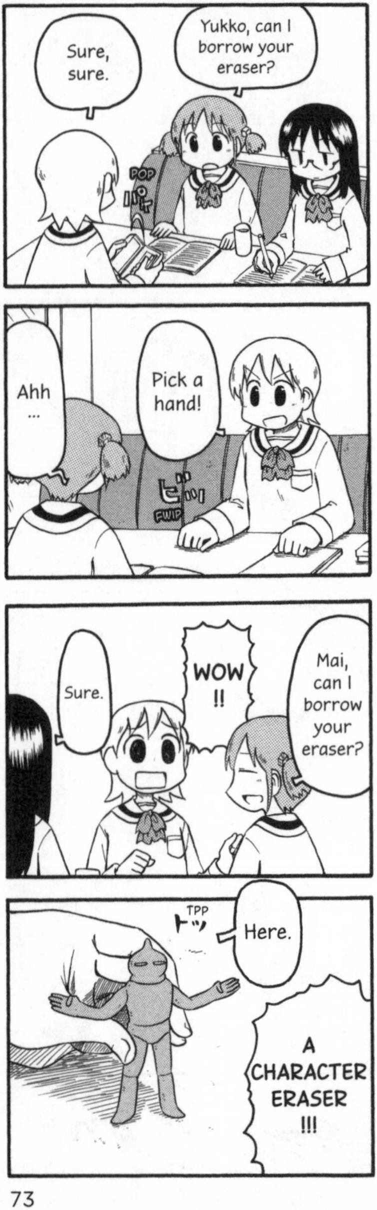
Yukko, can I borrow your eraser?
Sure, sure.
POP
Pick a hand!
Ahh ...
FWIP
Mai, can I borrow your eraser?
WOW !!
Sure.
Here.
TPP
A CHARACTER ERASER !!!

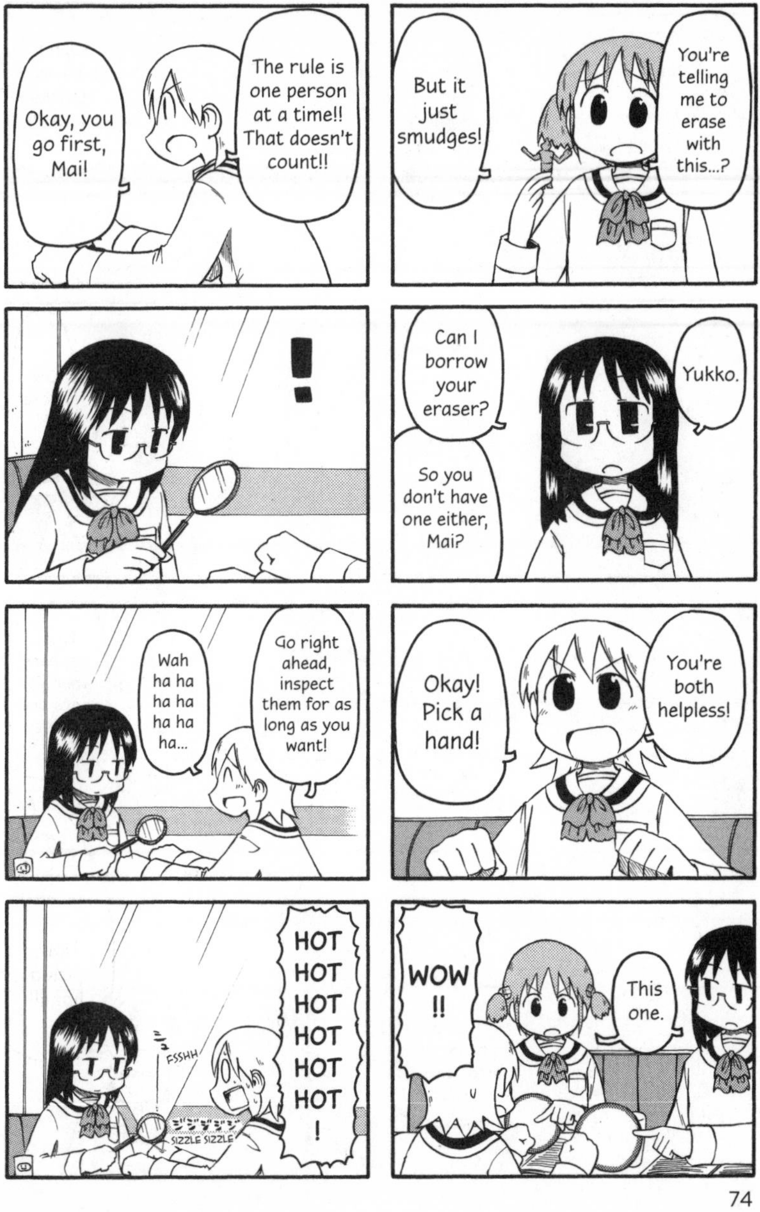
You're telling me to erase with this...?
But it just smudges!
Yukko.
Can I borrow your eraser?
So you don't have one either, Mai?
You're both helpless!
Okay! Pick a hand!
This one.
WOW !!
The rule is one person at a time!! That doesn't count!!
Okay, you go first, Mai!
!
Go right ahead, inspect them for as long as you want!
Wah ha ha ha ha ha ha ha...
HOT HOT HOT HOT HOT HOT !
FSSHH
ジジジジ
SIZZLE SIZZLE

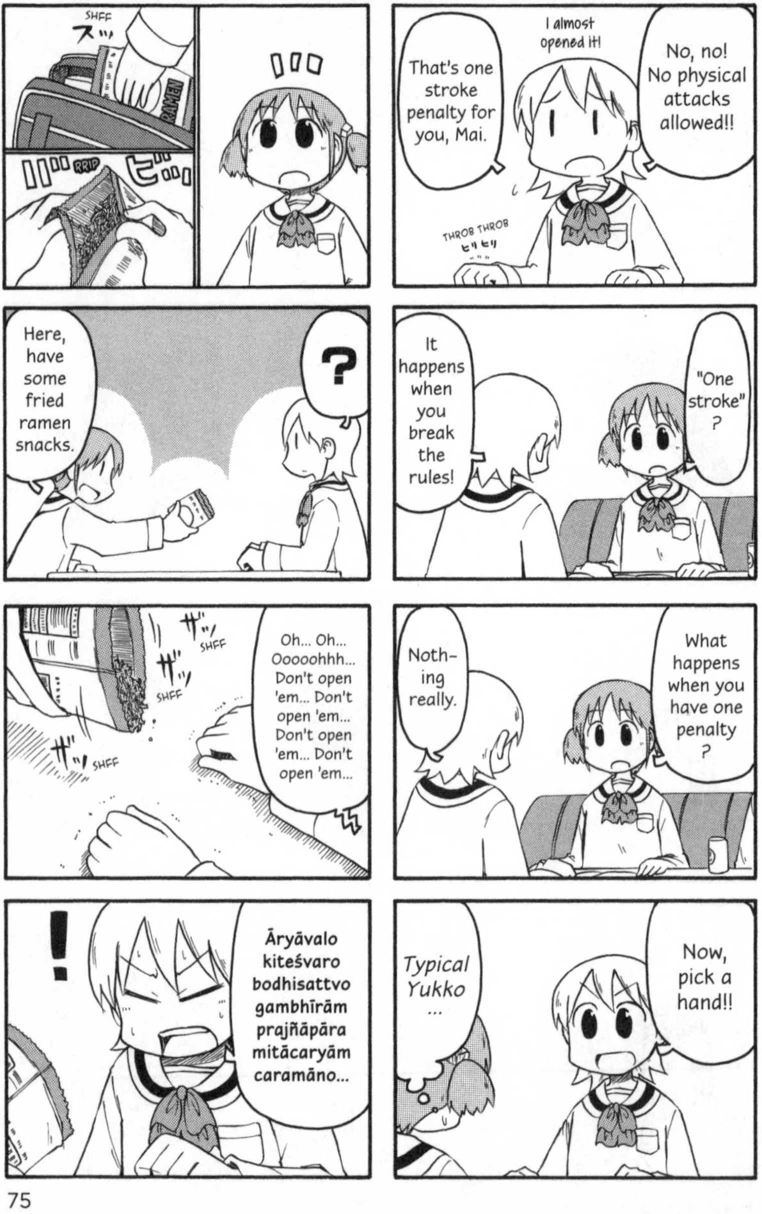

No, no! No physical attacks allowed!!
I almost opened it!
That's one stroke penalty for you, Mai.
THROB THROB
SHFF
RRIP
"One stroke"?
It happens when you break the rules!
?
Here, have some fried ramen snacks.
What happens when you have one penalty?
Noth-ing really.
Oh... Oh... Ooooohhh... Don't open 'em... Don't open 'em... Don't open 'em... Don't open 'em...
SHFF
SHFF
SHFF
Now, pick a hand!!
Typical Yukko ...
Āryāvalo kiteśvaro bodhisattvo gambhīrām prajñāpāra mitācaryām caramāno...
!

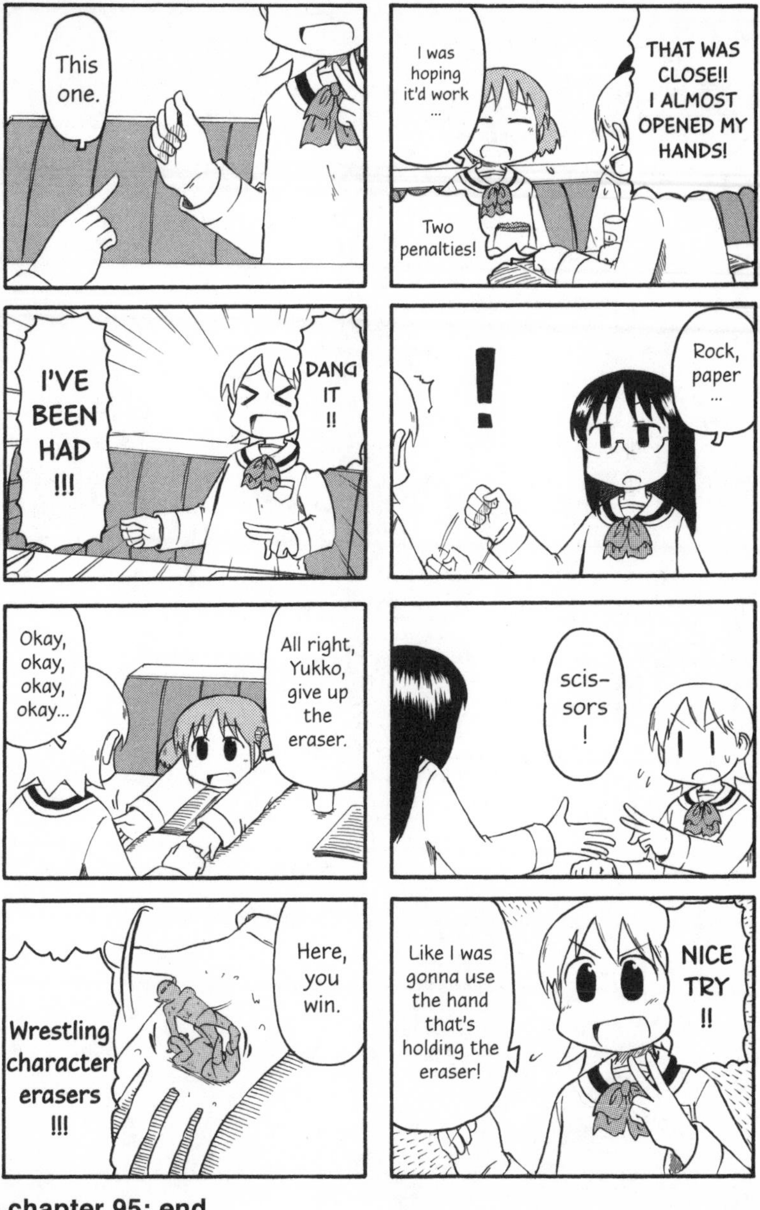
THAT WAS CLOSE!! I ALMOST OPENED MY HANDS!
I was hoping it'd work ...
Two penalties!
This one.
Rock, paper ...
!
DANG IT !!
I'VE BEEN HAD !!!
scis-sors !
All right, Yukko, give up the eraser.
Okay, okay, okay, okay...
NICE TRY !!
Like I was gonna use the hand that's holding the eraser!
Here, you win.
Wrestling character erasers !!!

chapter 95: end

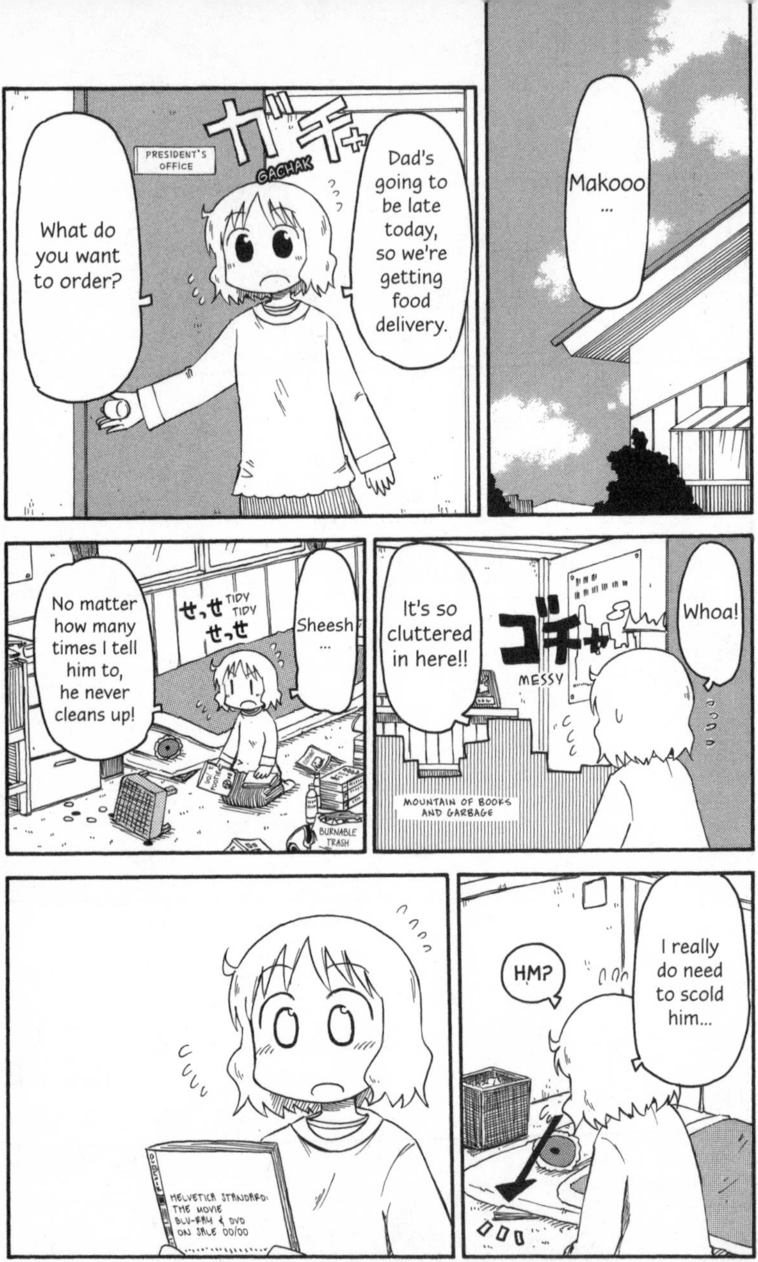
Makooo ...
Dad's going to be late today, so we're getting food delivery.
ガチャ
GACHAK
PRESIDENT'S OFFICE
What do you want to order?
Whoa!
ゴチャ
MESSY
It's so cluttered in here!!
MOUNTAIN OF BOOKS AND GARBAGE
Sheesh ...
せっせ TIDY TIDY せっせ
No matter how many times I tell him to, he never cleans up!
BURNABLE TRASH
I really do need to scold him...
HM?
HELVETICA STANDARD: THE MOVIE
BLU-RAY & DVD
ON SALE 00/00

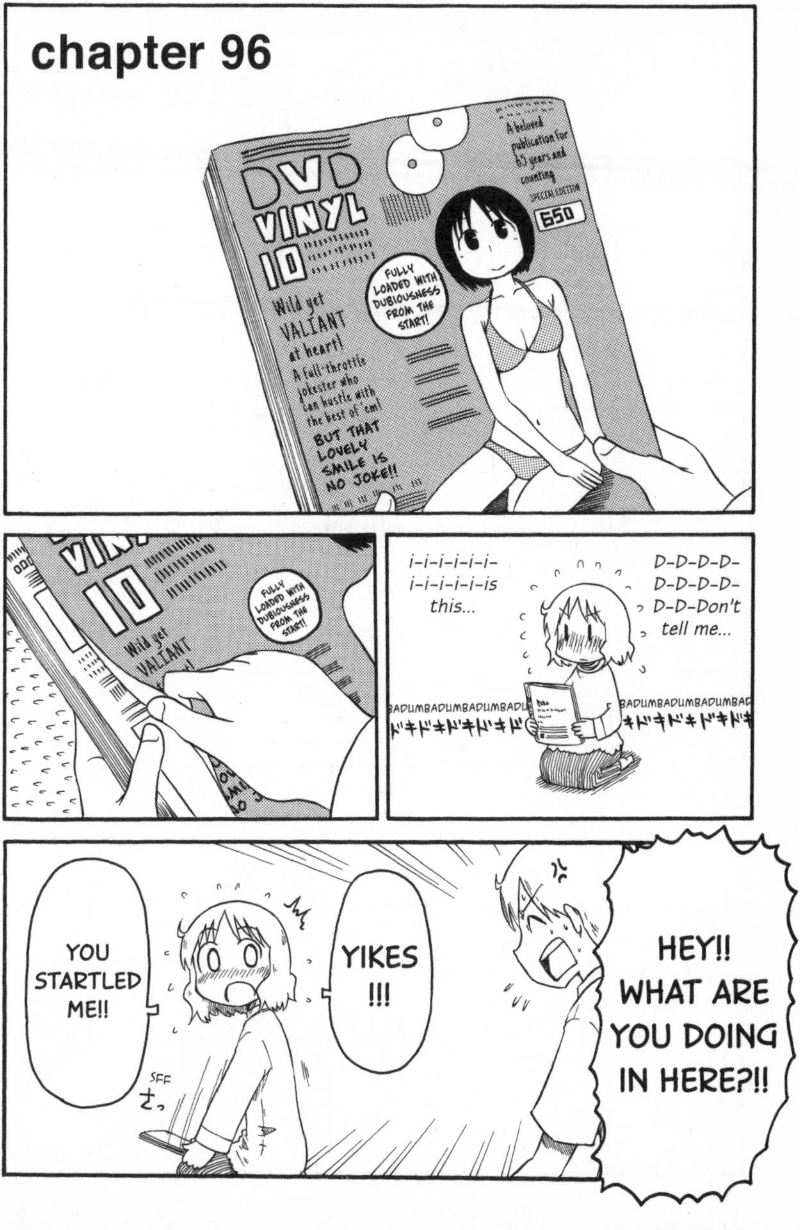
chapter 96
DVD
VINYL
10
A beloved publication for 63 years and counting
SPECIAL EDITION
650
FULLY LOADED WITH DUBIOUSNESS FROM THE START!
Wild get VALIANT at heart!
A full-throttle jokester who can hustle with the best of 'em!
BUT THAT LOVELY SMILE IS NO JOKE!!
D-D-D-D-
D-D-D-D-
D-D-Don't tell me...
i-i-i-i-i-i-
i-i-i-i-i-is this...
BADUMBADUMBADUMBADUMBADUMBADUMBAD
ドキドキドキドキドキドキドキドキ
VINYL
10
FULLY LOADED WITH DUBIOUSNESS FROM THE START!
Wild get VALIANT
HEY!! WHAT ARE YOU DOING IN HERE?!!
YIKES!!!
YOU STARTLED ME!!
SFF
さっ

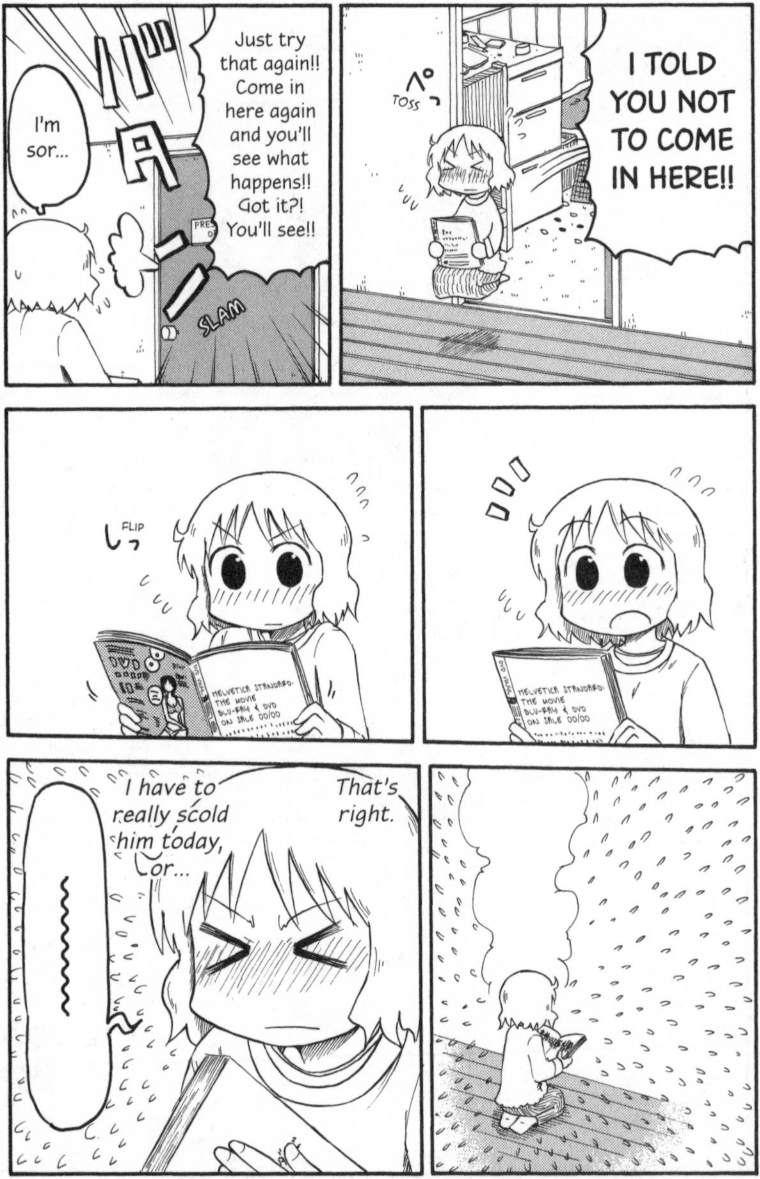

I TOLD YOU NOT TO COME IN HERE!!
TOSS
Just try that again!! Come in here again and you'll see what happens!! Got it?! You'll see!!
I'm sor...
SLAM
HELVETICA STANDARD: THE MOVIE BLU-RAY & DVD ON SALE 00/00
FLIP
DVD
HELVETICA STANDARD: THE MOVIE BLU-RAY & DVD ON SALE 00/00
That's right.
I have to really scold him today, or...

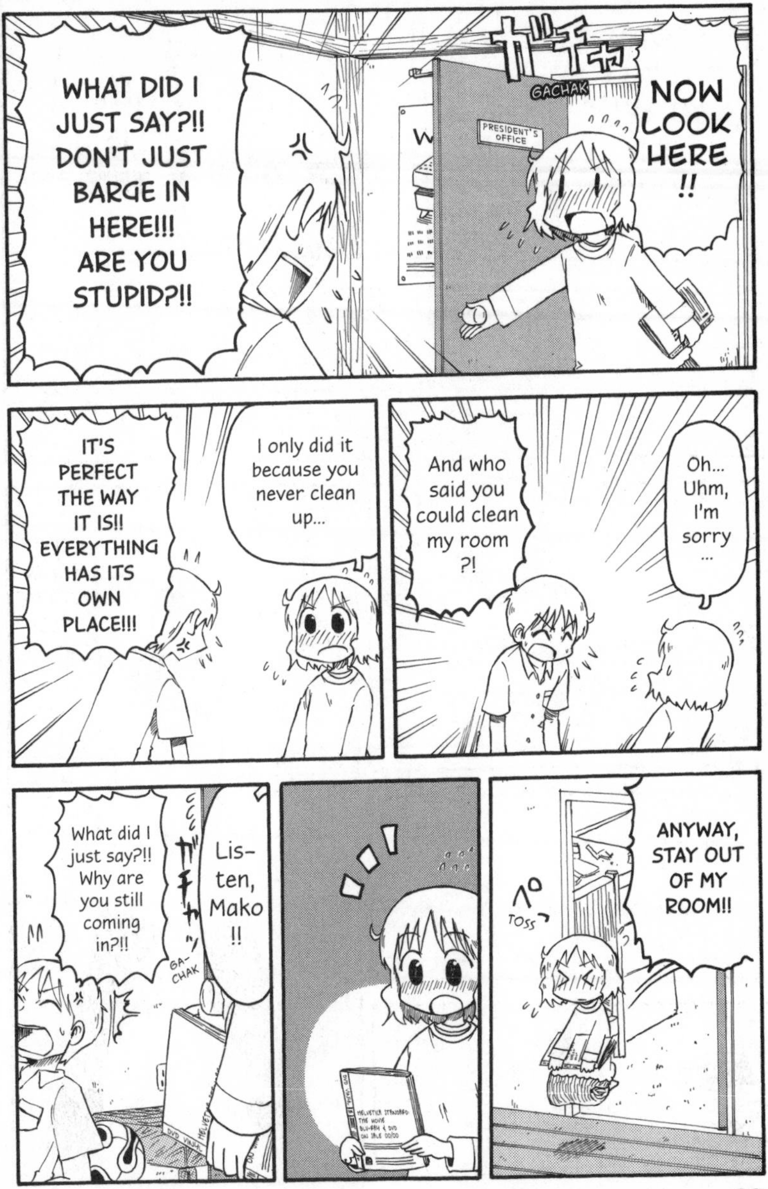
NOW LOOK HERE !!
GACHAK
PRESIDENT'S OFFICE
WHAT DID I JUST SAY?!! DON'T JUST BARGE IN HERE!!! ARE YOU STUPID?!!
Oh... Uhm, I'm sorry ...
And who said you could clean my room ?!
I only did it because you never clean up...
IT'S PERFECT THE WAY IT IS!! EVERYTHING HAS ITS OWN PLACE!!!
ANYWAY, STAY OUT OF MY ROOM!!
TOSS
Lis-ten, Mako !!
GA-CHAK
What did I just say?!! Why are you still coming in?!!

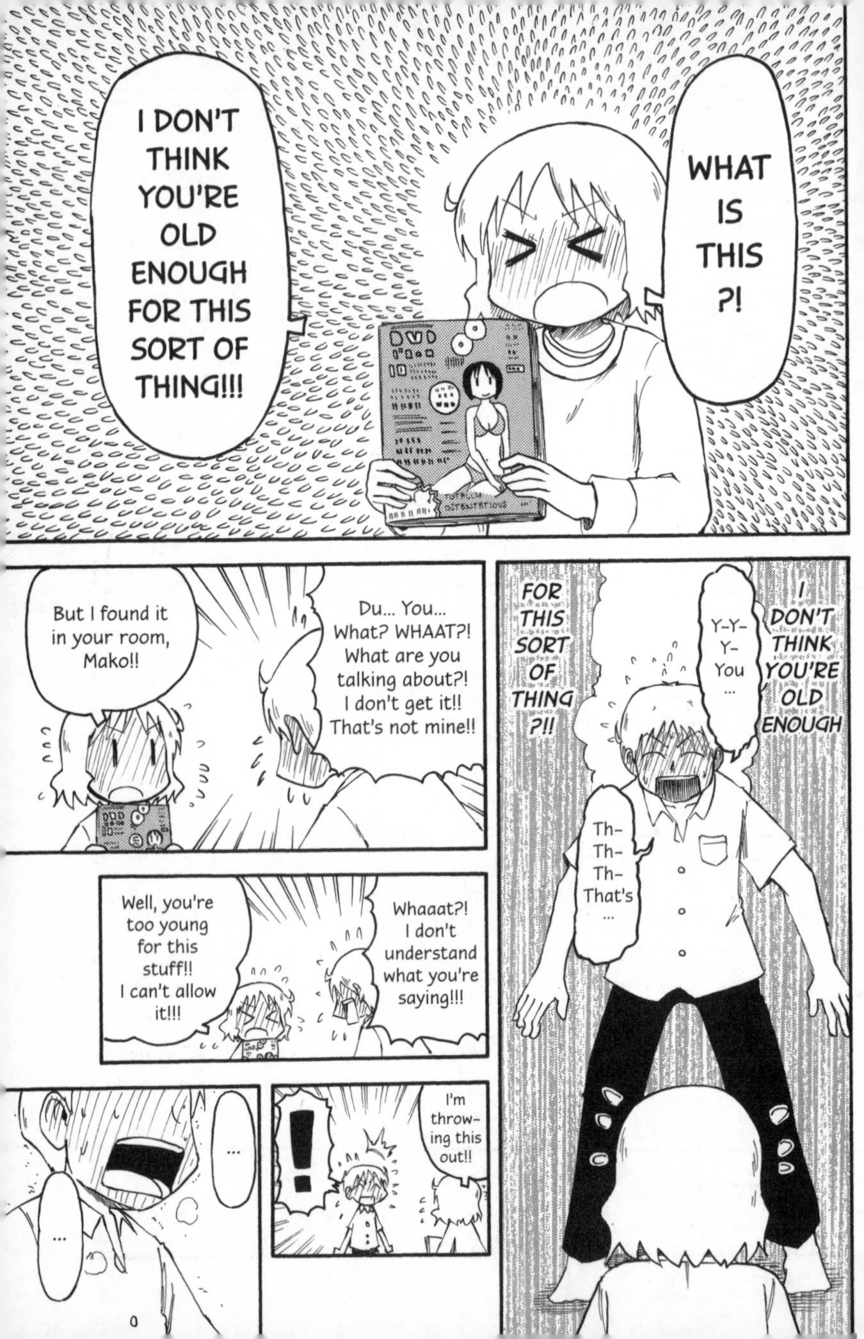
WHAT IS THIS ?!
I DON'T THINK YOU'RE OLD ENOUGH FOR THIS SORT OF THING!!!
I DON'T THINK YOU'RE OLD ENOUGH
Y-Y-Y- You ...
FOR THIS SORT OF THING ?!!
Th- Th- Th- That's ...
Du... You... What? WHAAT?! What are you talking about?! I don't get it!! That's not mine!!
But I found it in your room, Mako!!
Whaaat?! I don't understand what you're saying!!!
Well, you're too young for this stuff!! I can't allow it!!!
I'm throw- ing this out!!
!
...
...

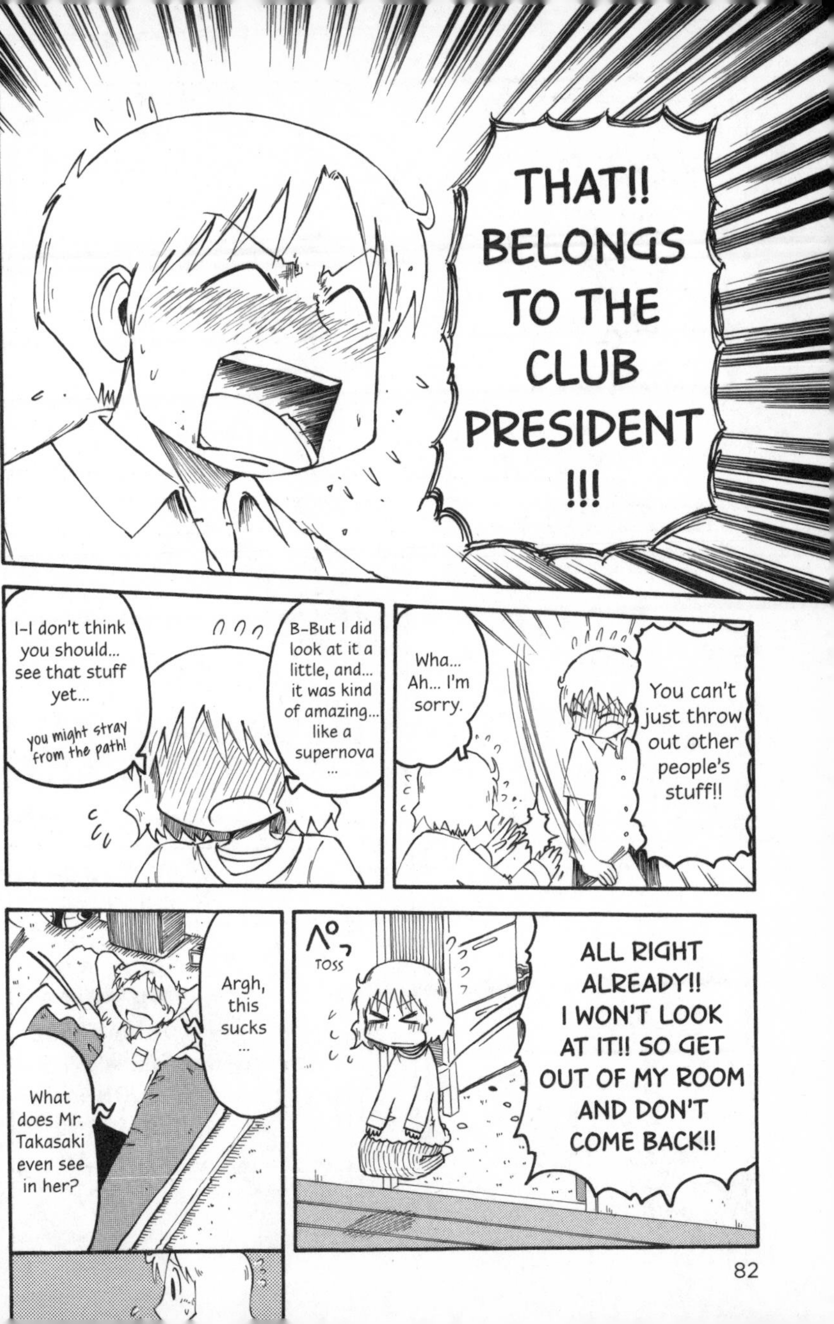
THAT!! BELONGS TO THE CLUB PRESIDENT !!!
You can't just throw out other people's stuff!!
Wha... Ah... I'm sorry.
B-But I did look at it a little, and... it was kind of amazing... like a supernova ...
I-I don't think you should... see that stuff yet...
you might stray from the path!
ペっ
TOSS
ALL RIGHT ALREADY!! I WON'T LOOK AT IT!! SO GET OUT OF MY ROOM AND DON'T COME BACK!!
Argh, this sucks ...
What does Mr. Takasaki even see in her?

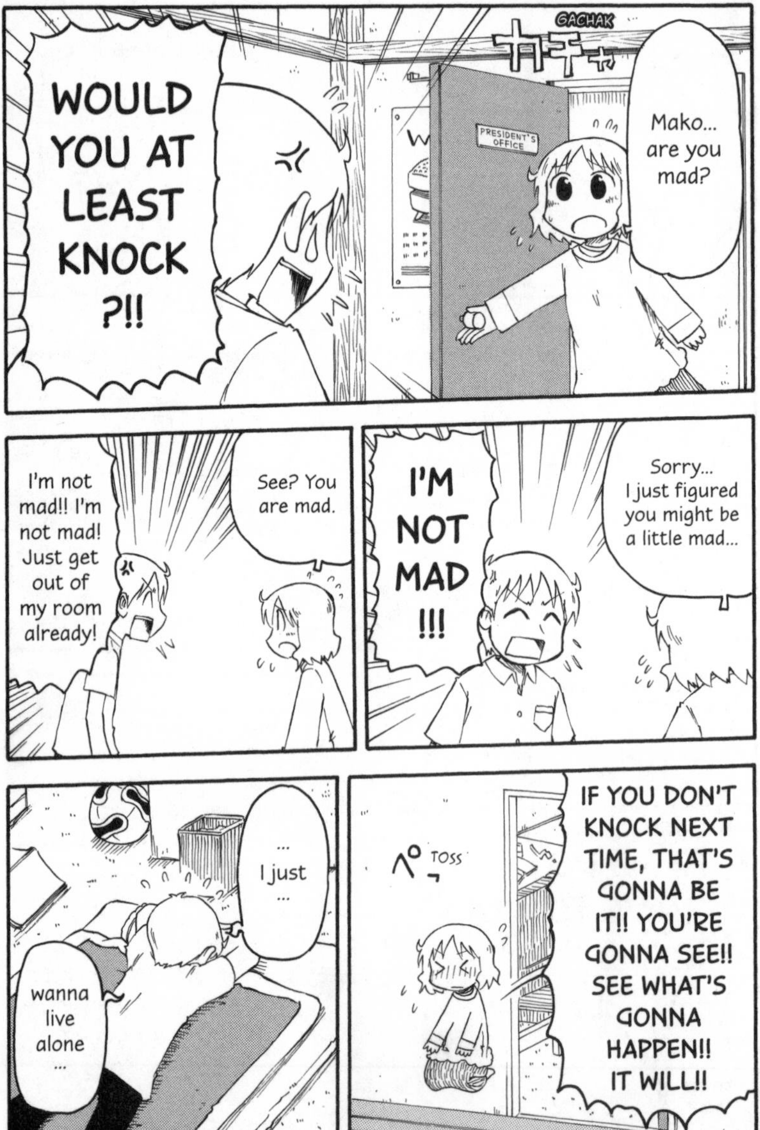
GACHAK
Mako... are you mad?
WOULD YOU AT LEAST KNOCK ?!!
Sorry... I just figured you might be a little mad...
I'M NOT MAD !!!
See? You are mad.
I'm not mad!! I'm not mad! Just get out of my room already!
IF YOU DON'T KNOCK NEXT TIME, THAT'S GONNA BE IT!! YOU'RE GONNA SEE!! SEE WHAT'S GONNA HAPPEN!! IT WILL!!
TOSS
... I just ...
wanna live alone ...

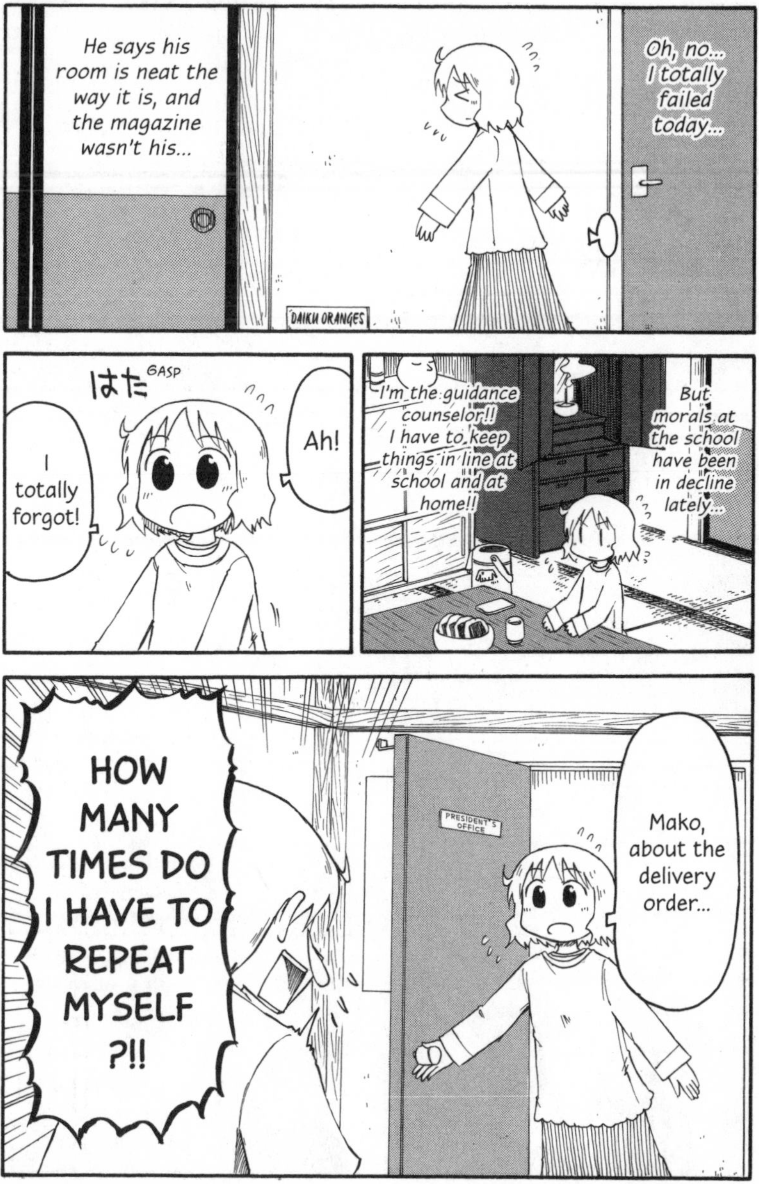
Oh, no... I totally failed today...
He says his room is neat the way it is, and the magazine wasn't his...
DAIKU ORANGES
But morals at the school have been in decline lately...
I'm the guidance counselor!! I have to keep things in line at school and at home!!
はた GASP
Ah!
I totally forgot!
Mako, about the delivery order...
PRESIDENT'S OFFICE
HOW MANY TIMES DO I HAVE TO REPEAT MYSELF ?!!

chapter 96: end

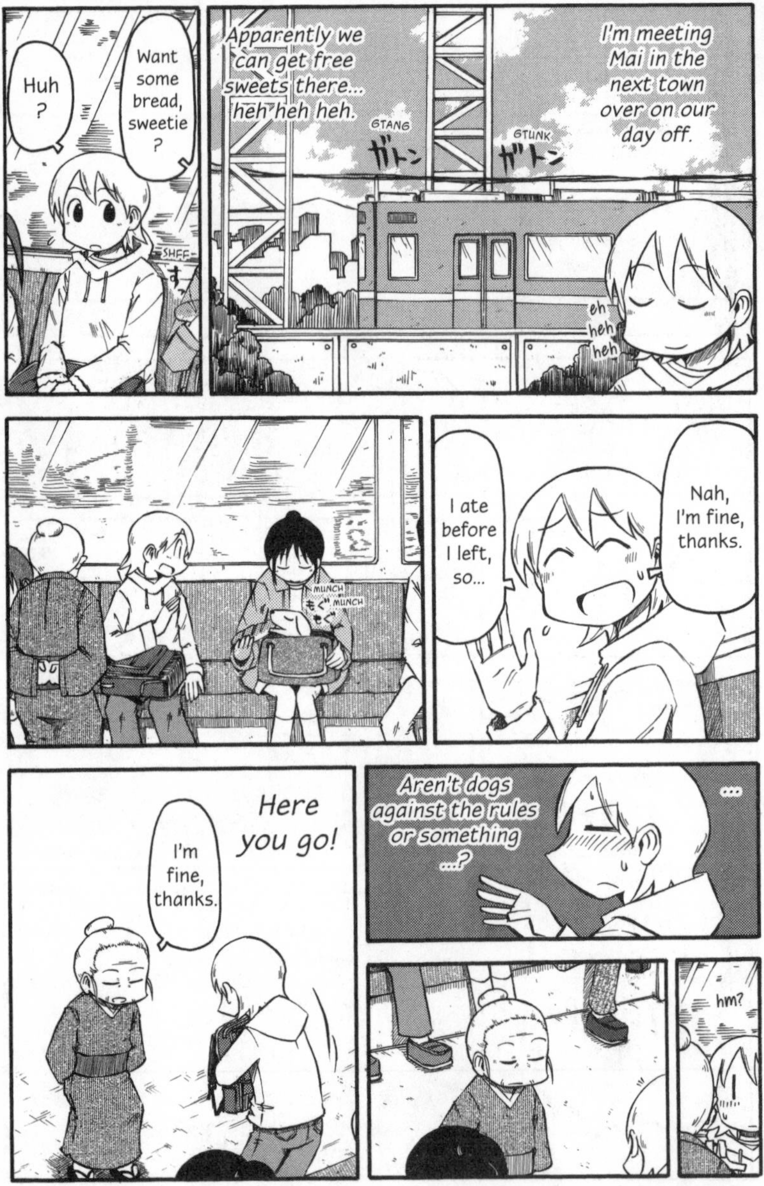
I'm meeting Mai in the next town over on our day off.
GTUNK
ガトン
GTANG
ガトン
Apparently we can get free sweets there... heh heh heh.
eh heh heh
Want some bread, sweetie?
Huh?
SHFF
す
Nah, I'm fine, thanks.
I ate before I left, so...
MUNCH MUNCH
もぐもぐ
...
Aren't dogs against the rules or something...?
hm?
Here you go!
I'm fine, thanks.

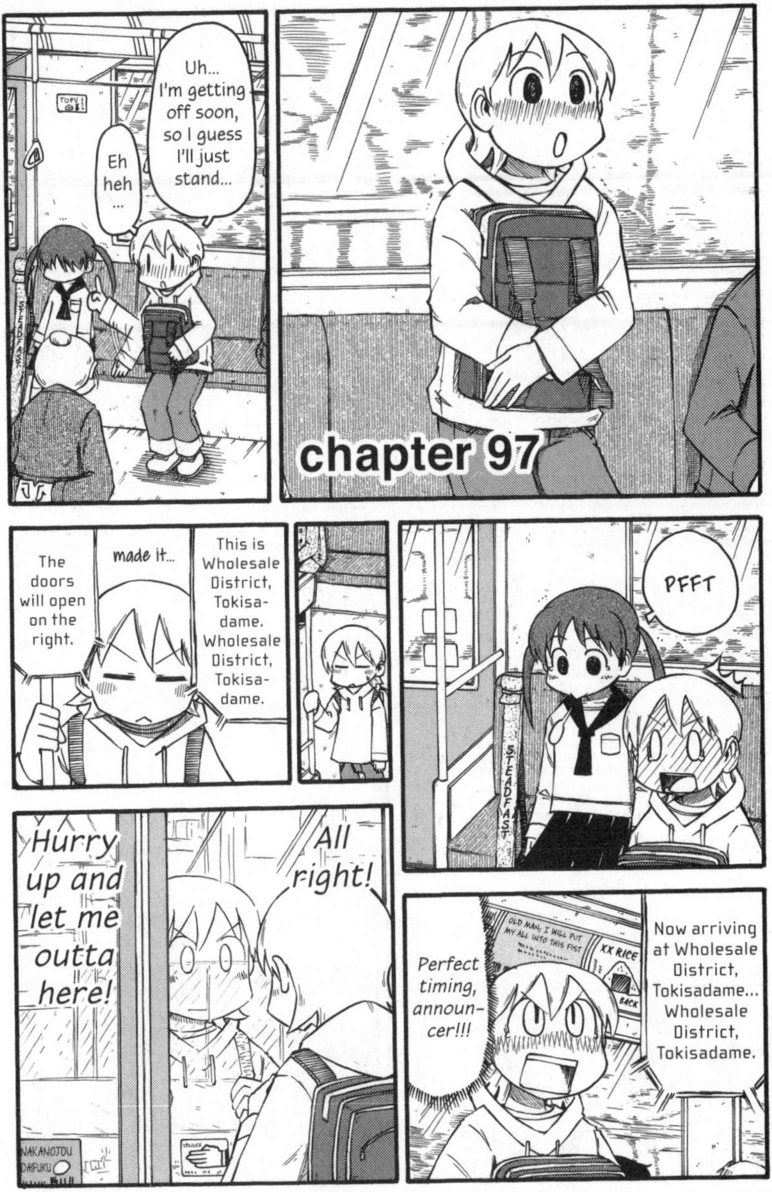
chapter 97
Uh... I'm getting off soon, so I guess I'll just stand...
Eh heh ...
STEADFAST
PFFT
STEADFAST
Now arriving at Wholesale District, Tokisadame... Wholesale District, Tokisadame.
OLD MAN, I WILL PUT MY ALL INTO THIS FIST
XX RICE
BACK
Perfect timing, announcer!!!
This is Wholesale District, Tokisadame. Wholesale District, Tokisadame.
made it...
The doors will open on the right.
Hurry up and let me outta here!
All right!
NAKANOJOU DAIFUKU
DANGER

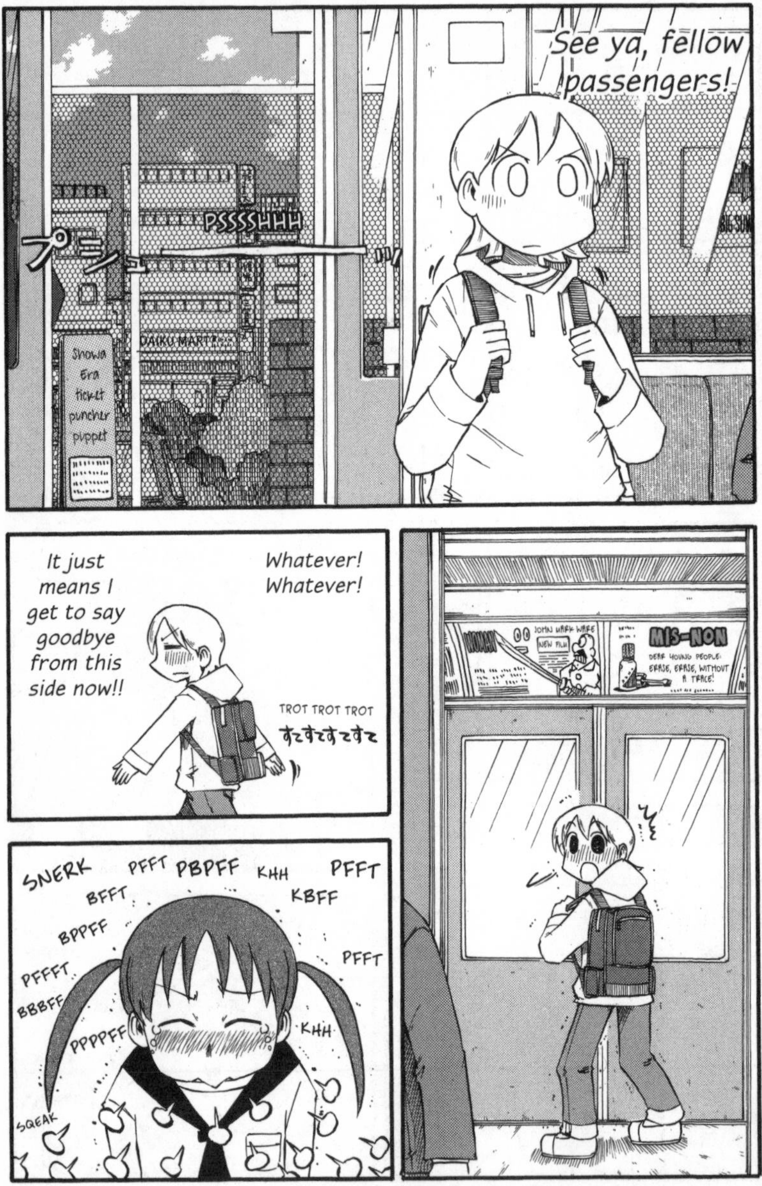
See ya, fellow passengers!
PSSSSHHH
プシュ
DAIKU MART
Showa Era ticket puncher puppet
JOHN MARK WAKE
NEW FILM
WOMAN
MIS-NON
DEAR YOUNG PEOPLE: ERASE, ERASE, WITHOUT A TRACE!
Whatever! Whatever!
It just means I get to say goodbye from this side now!!
TROT TROT TROT
すてすてすてすて
SNERK PFFT PBPFF KHH PFFT
BFFT KBFF
BPPFF
PFFFT
BBBFF
PFFT
PPPPFF
KHH
SQEAK

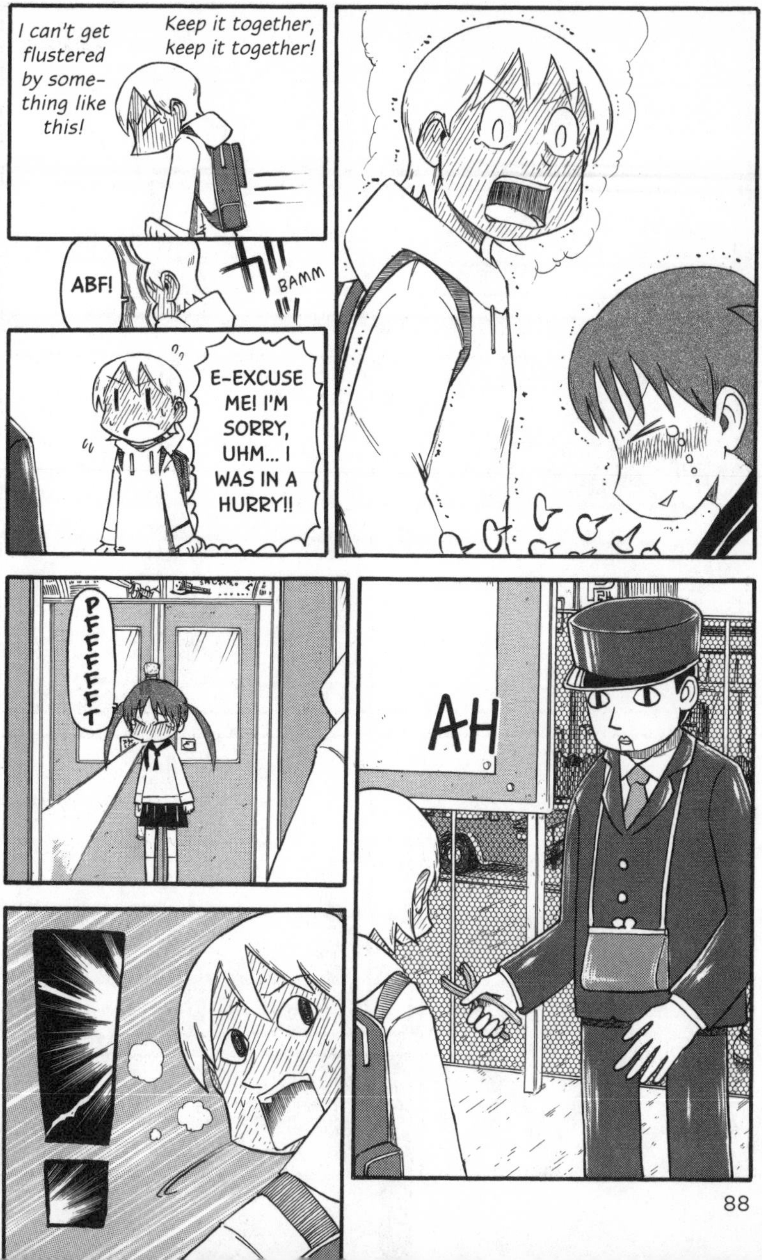
Keep it together, keep it together!
I can't get flustered by some-thing like this!
BAMM
ABF!
E-EXCUSE ME! I'M SORRY, UHM... I WAS IN A HURRY!!
AH
PFFFFFFT

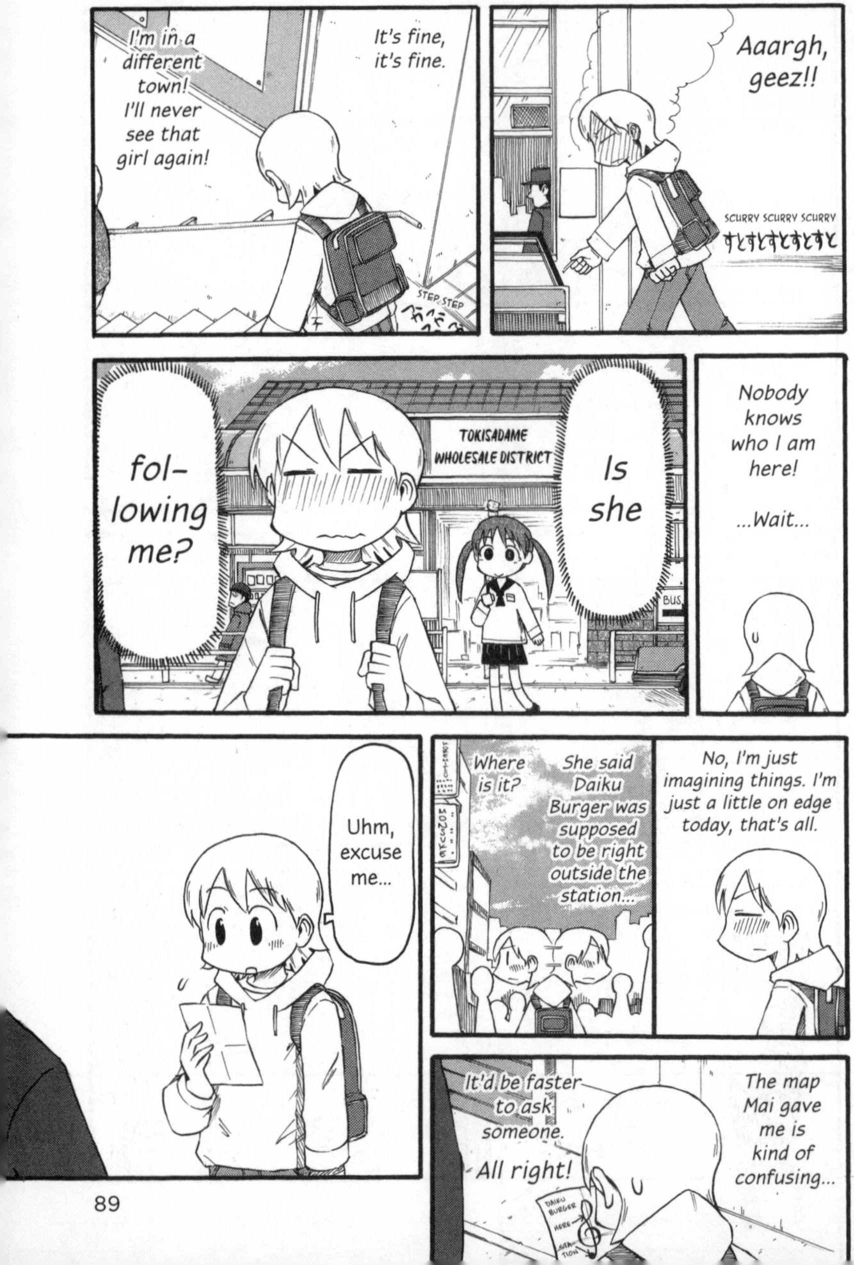
Aaargh, geez!!
SCURRY SCURRY SCURRY
すとすとすとすとすと
It's fine, it's fine.
I'm in a different town! I'll never see that girl again!
STEP STEP
Nobody knows who I am here!
...Wait...
Is she
fol- lowing me?
TOKISADAME WHOLESALE DISTRICT
BUS
No, I'm just imagining things. I'm just a little on edge today, that's all.
She said Daiku Burger was supposed to be right outside the station...
Where is it?
The map Mai gave me is kind of confusing...
It'd be faster to ask someone.
All right!
DAIKU BURGER
HERE
STA- TION
Uhm, excuse me...

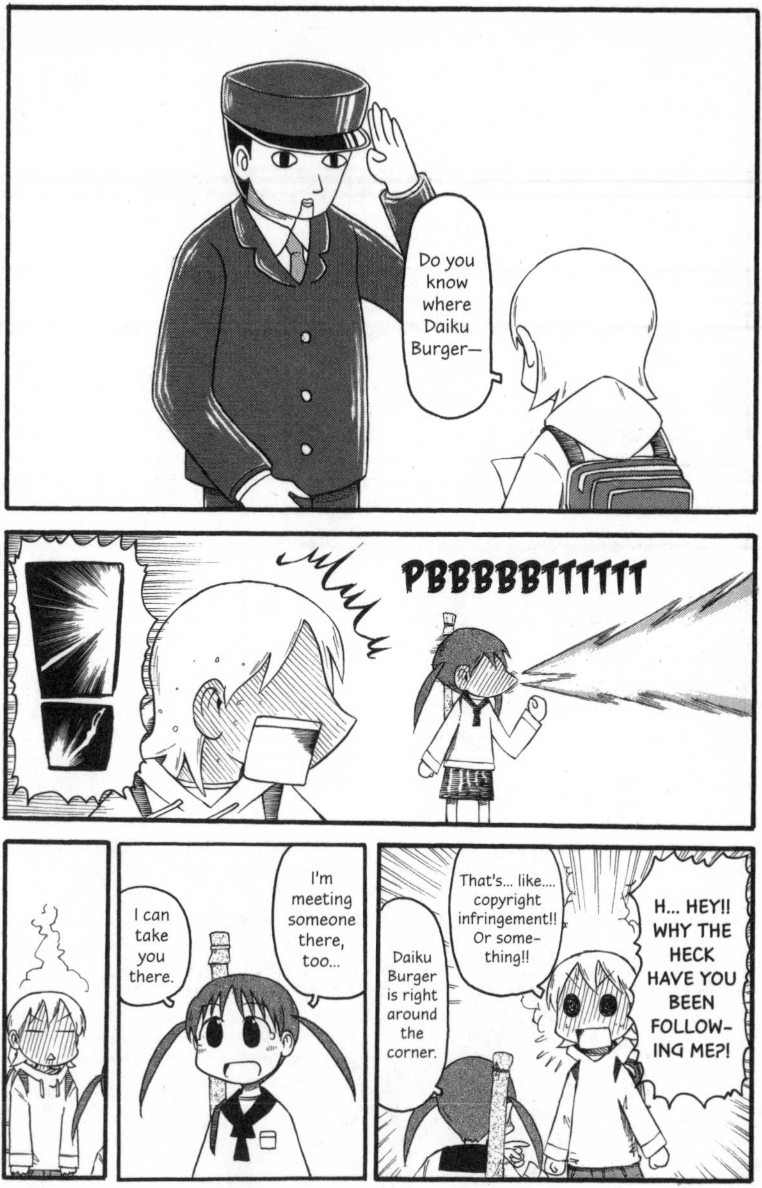
Do you know where Daiku Burger—
PBBBBBTTTTTT
H... HEY!! WHY THE HECK HAVE YOU BEEN FOLLOW-ING ME?!
That's... like.... copyright infringement!! Or some-thing!!
Daiku Burger is right around the corner.
I'm meeting someone there, too...
I can take you there.

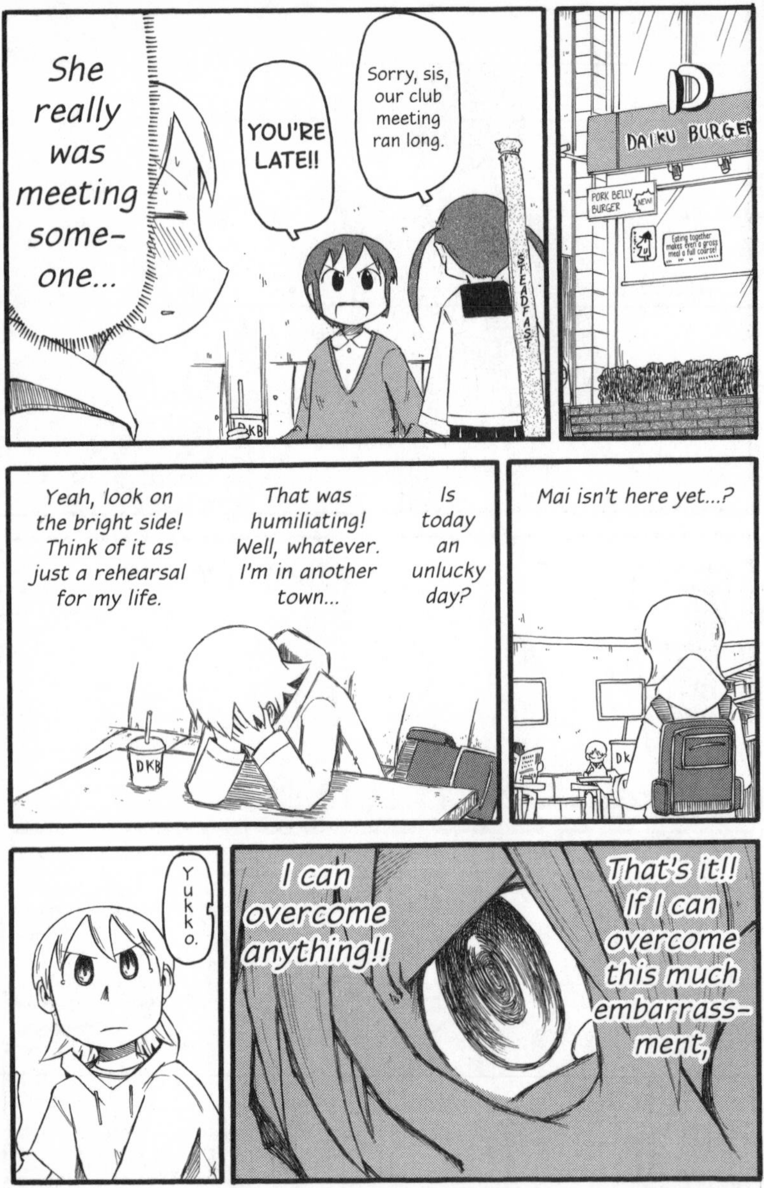
D
DAIKU BURGER
PORK BELLY BURGER
NEW
Eating together makes even a gross meal a full course!
Sorry, sis, our club meeting ran long.
YOU'RE LATE!!
STEADFAST
DKB
She really was meeting some-one...
Mai isn't here yet...?
Is today an unlucky day?
That was humiliating! Well, whatever. I'm in another town...
Yeah, look on the bright side! Think of it as just a rehearsal for my life.
DKB
That's it!! If I can overcome this much embarrass-ment,
I can overcome anything!!
Yukko.

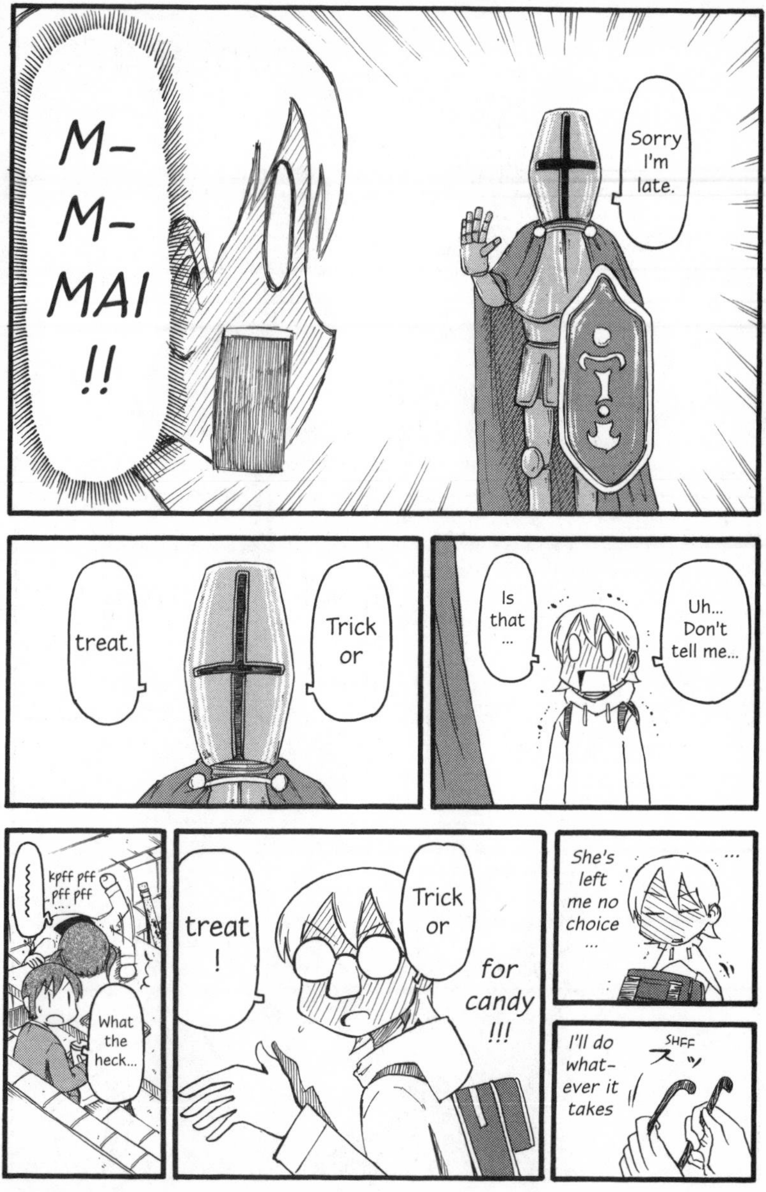
Sorry I'm late.
M-M-MAI!!
Uh... Don't tell me...
Is that ...
Trick or
treat.
...
She's left me no choice ...
SHFF
スッ
I'll do what-ever it takes
Trick or
treat!
for candy!!!
kpff pff pff pff ...
What the heck...

chapter 97: end

chapter 97.5

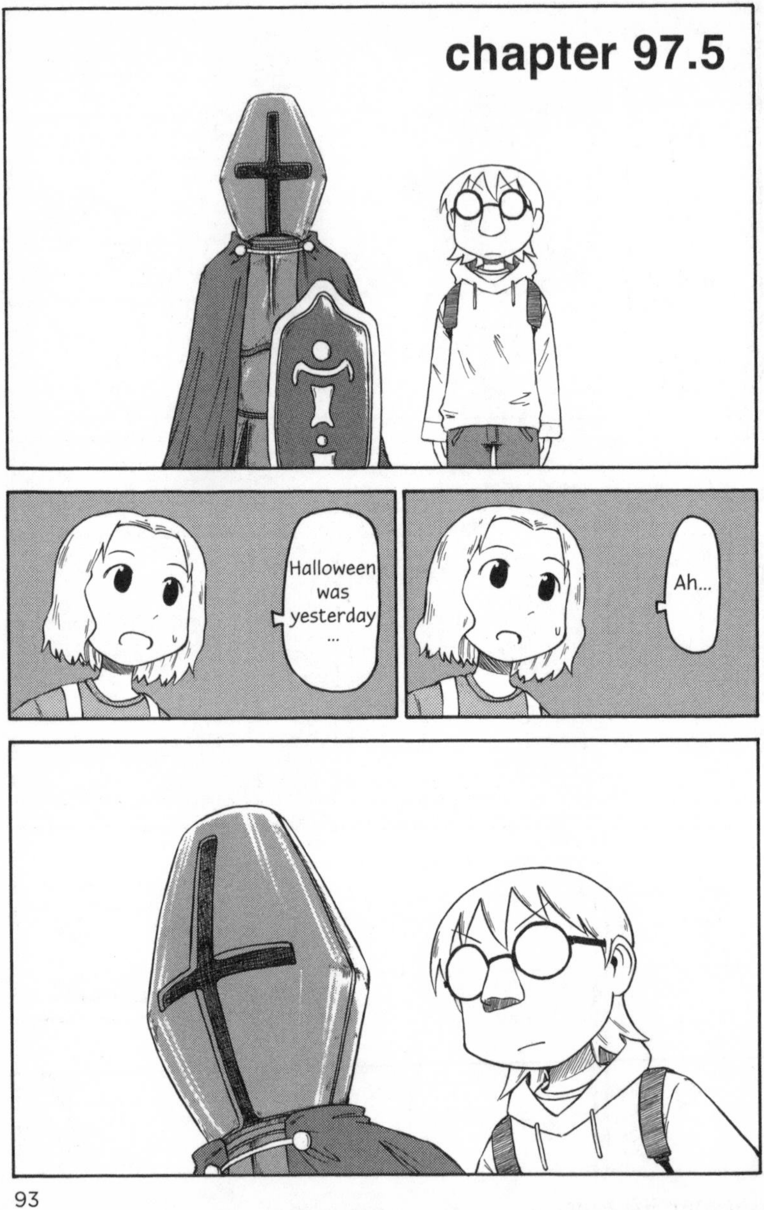
Ah...
Halloween was yesterday ...

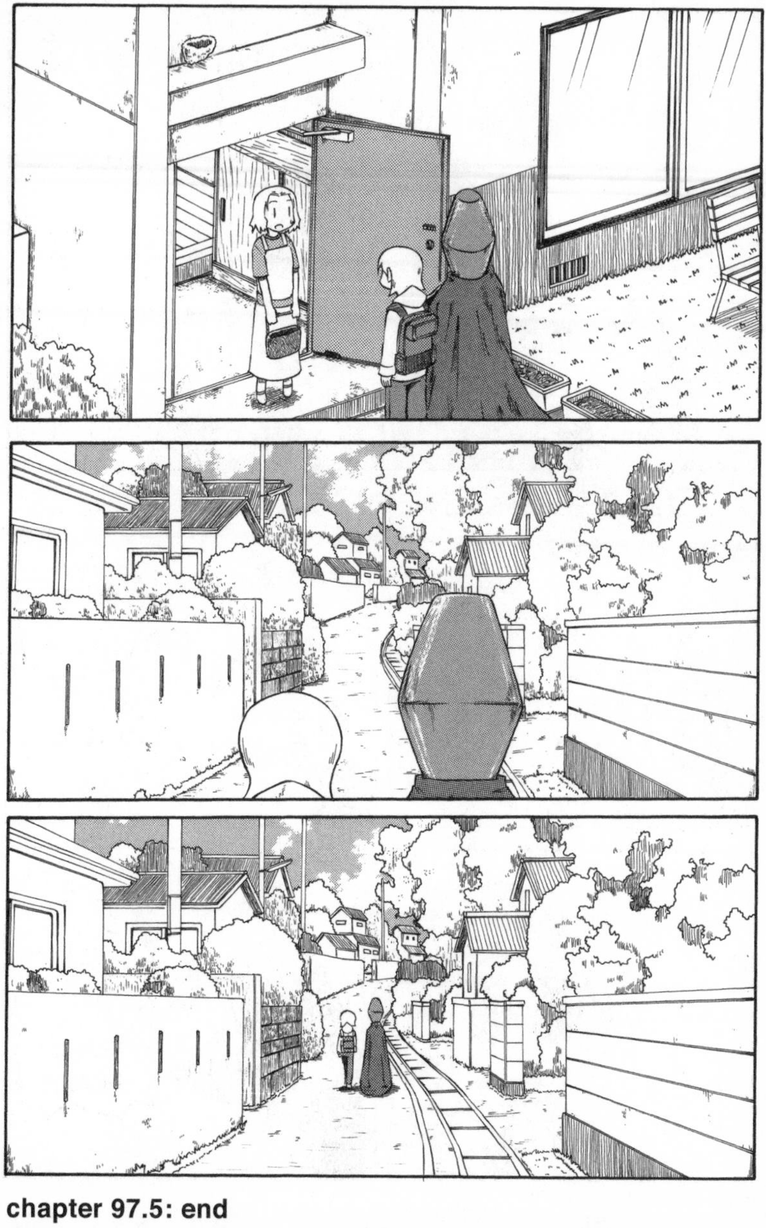

chapter 97.5: end

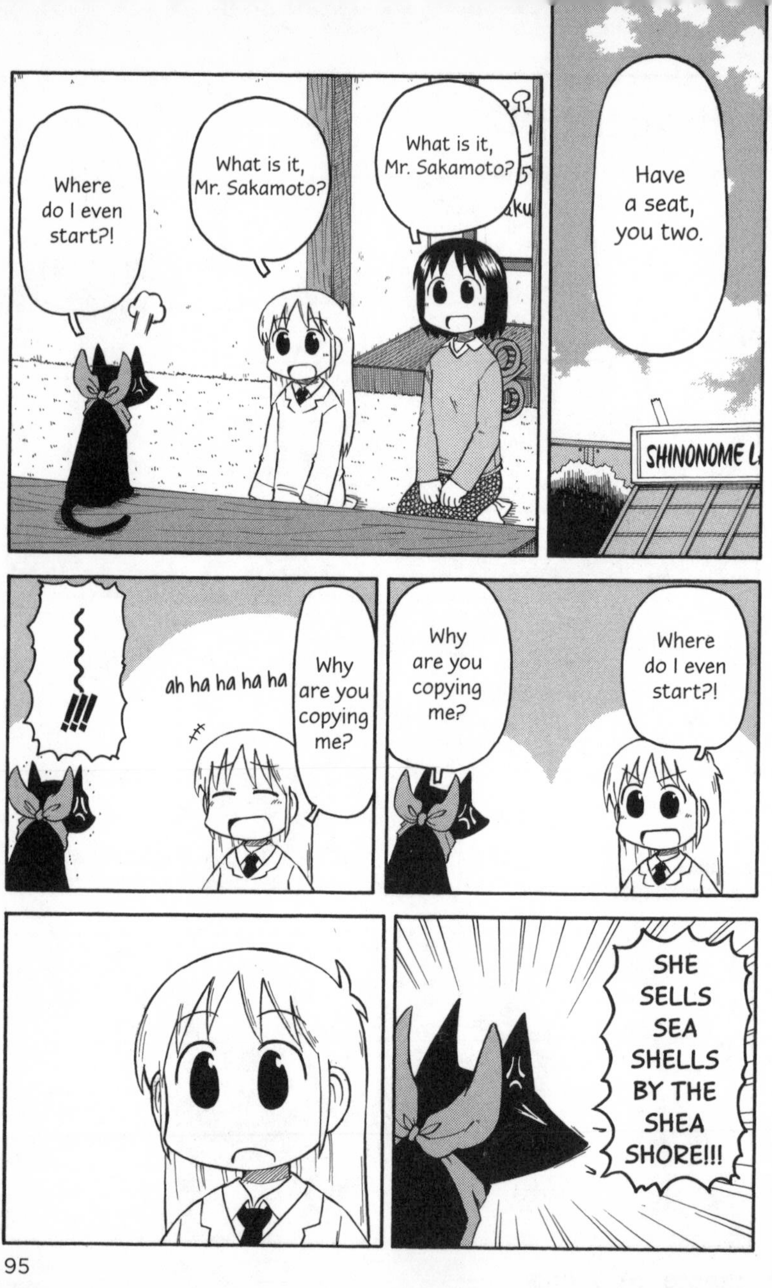
Have a seat, you two.
SHINONOME
What is it, Mr. Sakamoto?
What is it, Mr. Sakamoto?
Where do I even start?!
Where do I even start?!
Why are you copying me?
Why are you copying me?
ah ha ha ha ha
!!!
SHE SELLS SEA SHELLS BY THE SHEA SHORE!!!

chapter 98

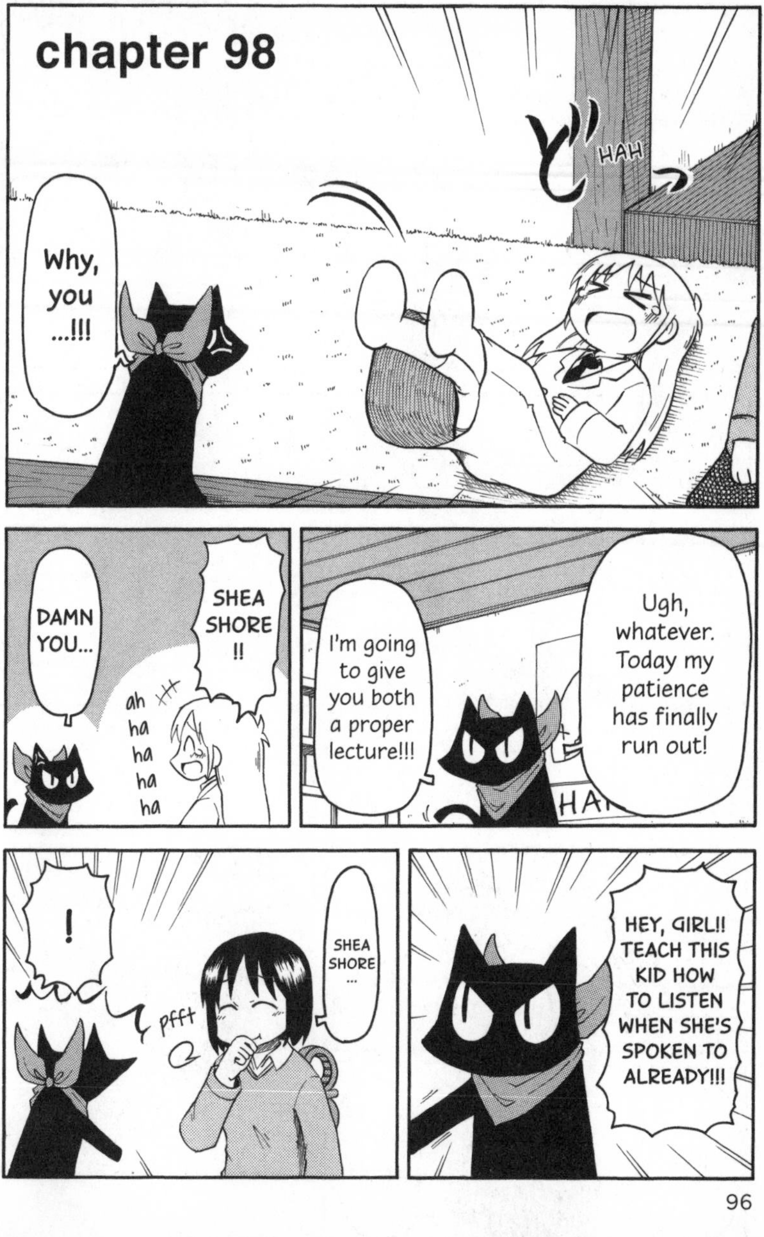
HAH
Why, you ...!!!
Ugh, whatever. Today my patience has finally run out!
I'm going to give you both a proper lecture!!!
SHEA SHORE !!
DAMN YOU...
ah ha ha ha ha
HEY, GIRL!! TEACH THIS KID HOW TO LISTEN WHEN SHE'S SPOKEN TO ALREADY!!!
SHEA SHORE ...
pfft
!

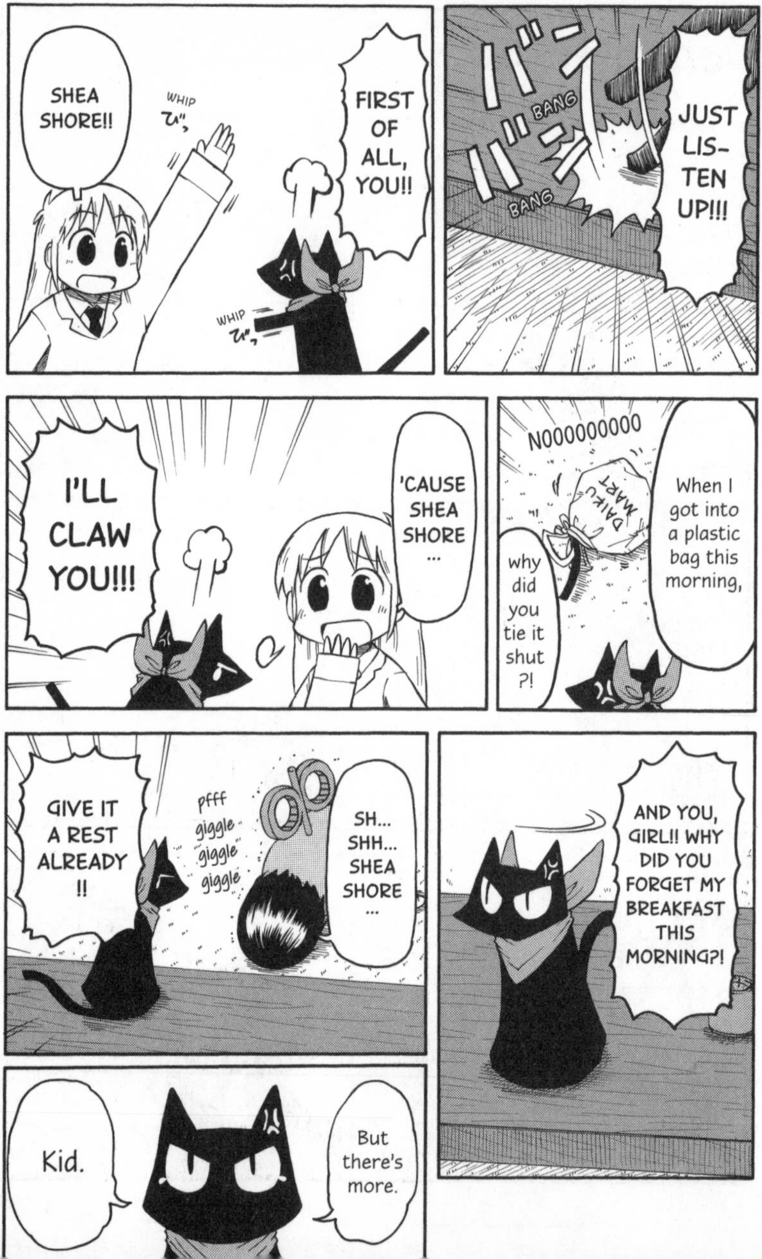
JUST LISTEN UP!!!
BANG
BANG
FIRST OF ALL, YOU!!
WHIP
SHEA SHORE!!
WHIP
When I got into a plastic bag this morning,
NOOOOOOOOO
DAIKU MART
why did you tie it shut?!
'CAUSE SHEA SHORE...
I'LL CLAW YOU!!!
AND YOU, GIRL!! WHY DID YOU FORGET MY BREAKFAST THIS MORNING?!
SH... SHH... SHEA SHORE...
pfff giggle giggle giggle
GIVE IT A REST ALREADY!!
But there's more.
Kid.

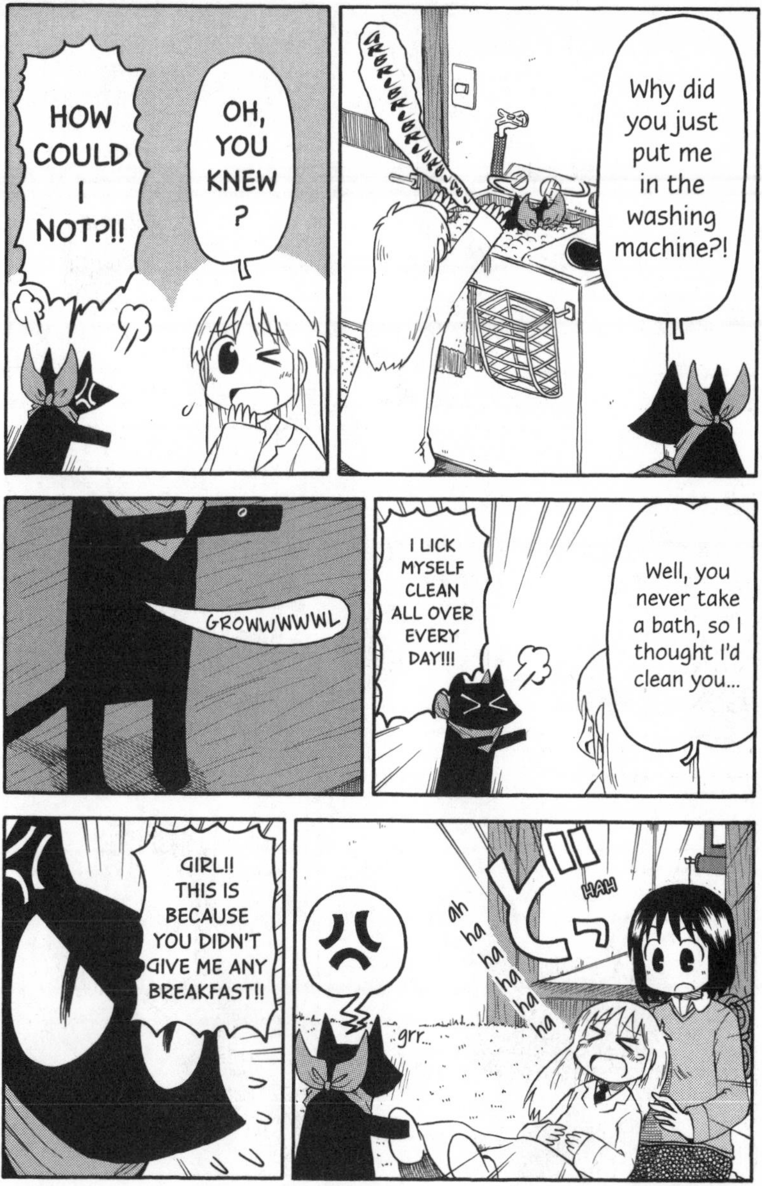
Why did you just put me in the washing machine?!
OH, YOU KNEW?
HOW COULD I NOT?!!
Well, you never take a bath, so I thought I'd clean you...
I LICK MYSELF CLEAN ALL OVER EVERY DAY!!!
GROWWWWWL
HAH
ah ha ha ha ha ha ha
grr...
GIRL!! THIS IS BECAUSE YOU DIDN'T GIVE ME ANY BREAKFAST!!

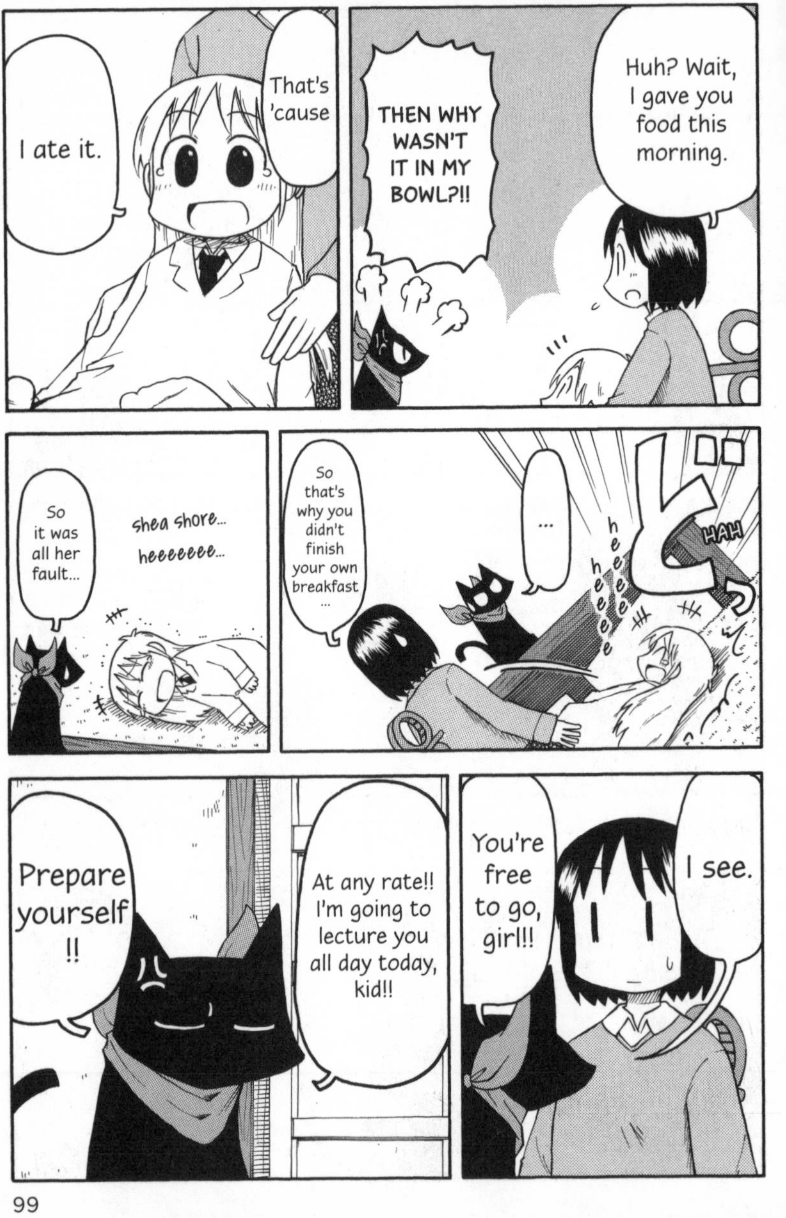
Huh? Wait, I gave you food this morning.
THEN WHY WASN'T IT IN MY BOWL?!!
That's 'cause
I ate it.
...
HAH
So that's why you didn't finish your own breakfast ...
shea shore... heeeeeee...
So it was all her fault...
I see.
You're free to go, girl!!!
At any rate!! I'm going to lecture you all day today, kid!!
Prepare yourself !!

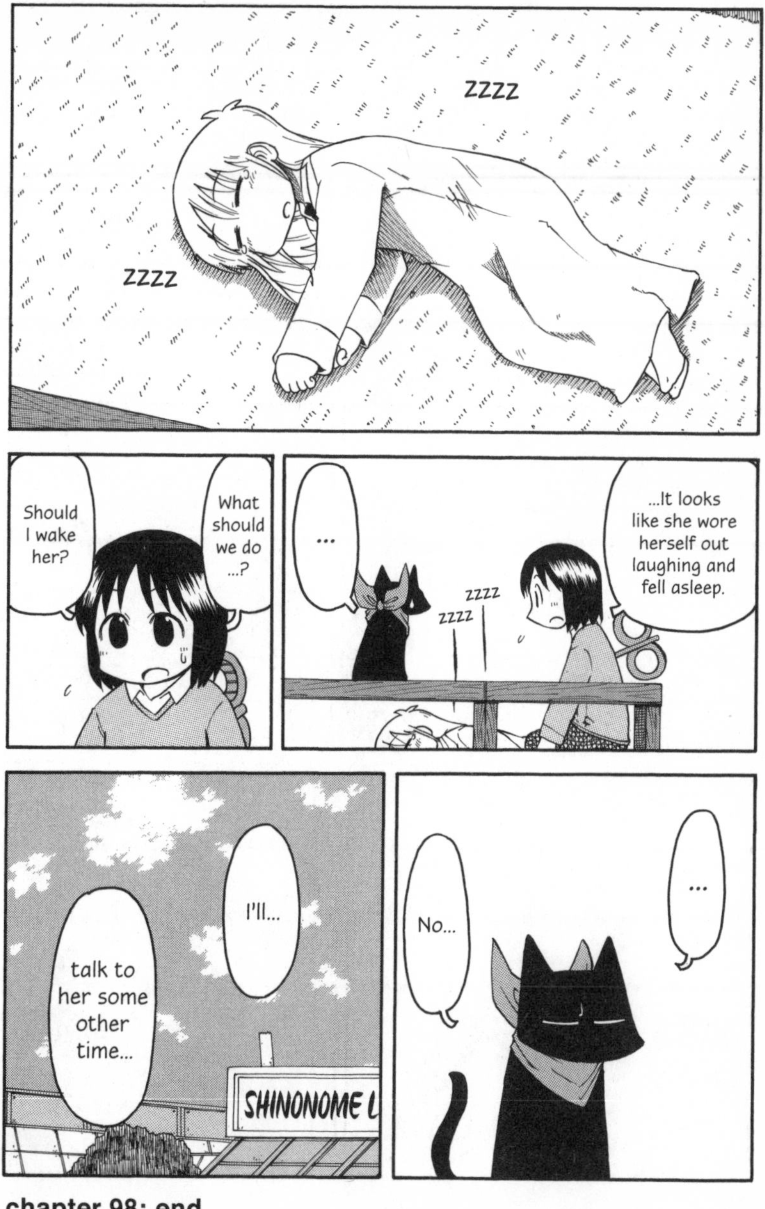
ZZZZ
ZZZZ
...It looks like she wore herself out laughing and fell asleep.
...
ZZZZ
ZZZZ
What should we do ...?
Should I wake her?
...
No...
I'll...
talk to her some other time...
SHINONOME

chapter 98: end

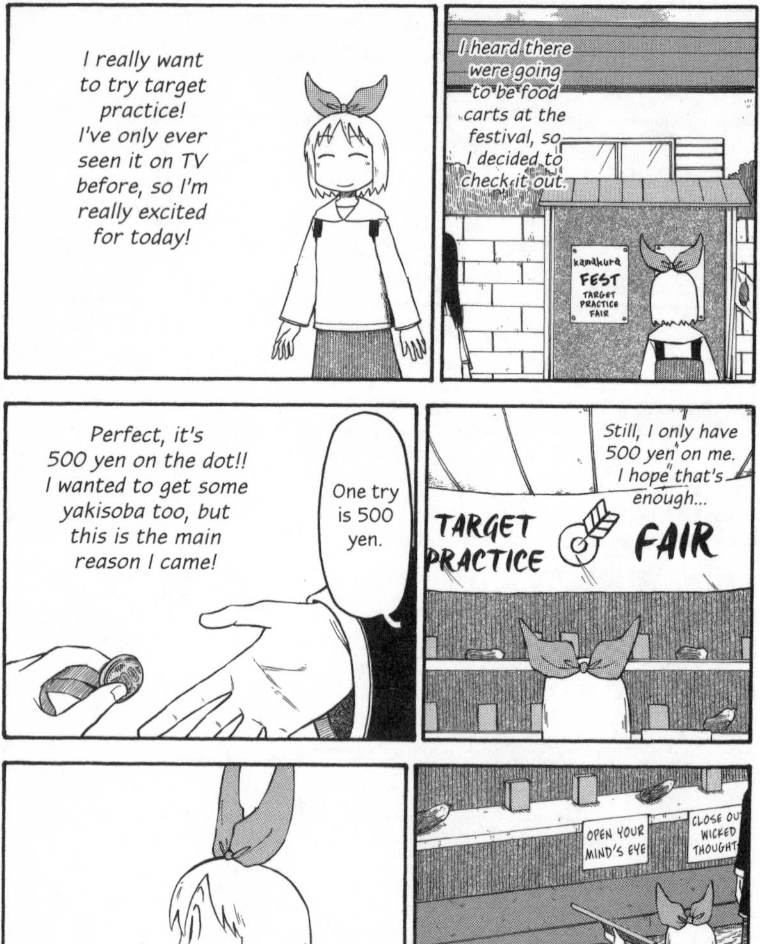
I heard there were going to be food carts at the festival, so I decided to check it out.
kamakura
FEST
TARGET PRACTICE FAIR
I really want to try target practice! I've only ever seen it on TV before, so I'm really excited for today!
Still, I only have 500 yen on me. I hope that's enough...
TARGET PRACTICE
FAIR
One try is 500 yen.
Perfect, it's 500 yen on the dot!! I wanted to get some yakisoba too, but this is the main reason I came!
CLOSE OUT WICKED THOUGHT
OPEN YOUR MIND'S EYE

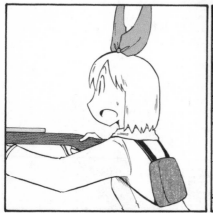

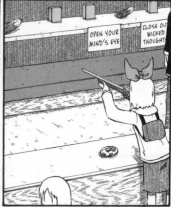

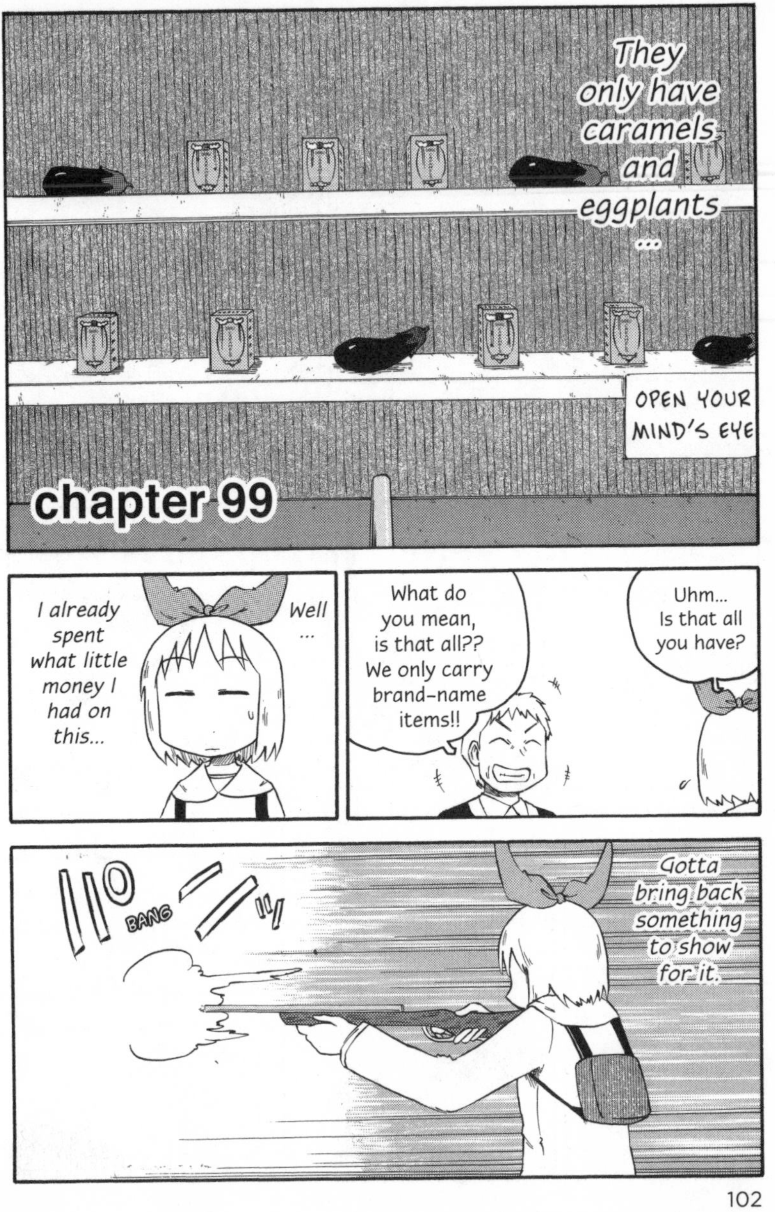
They only have caramels and eggplants ...
OPEN YOUR MIND'S EYE
chapter 99
Uhm... Is that all you have?
What do you mean, is that all?? We only carry brand-name items!!
Well ...
I already spent what little money I had on this...
Gotta bring back something to show for it.
BANG

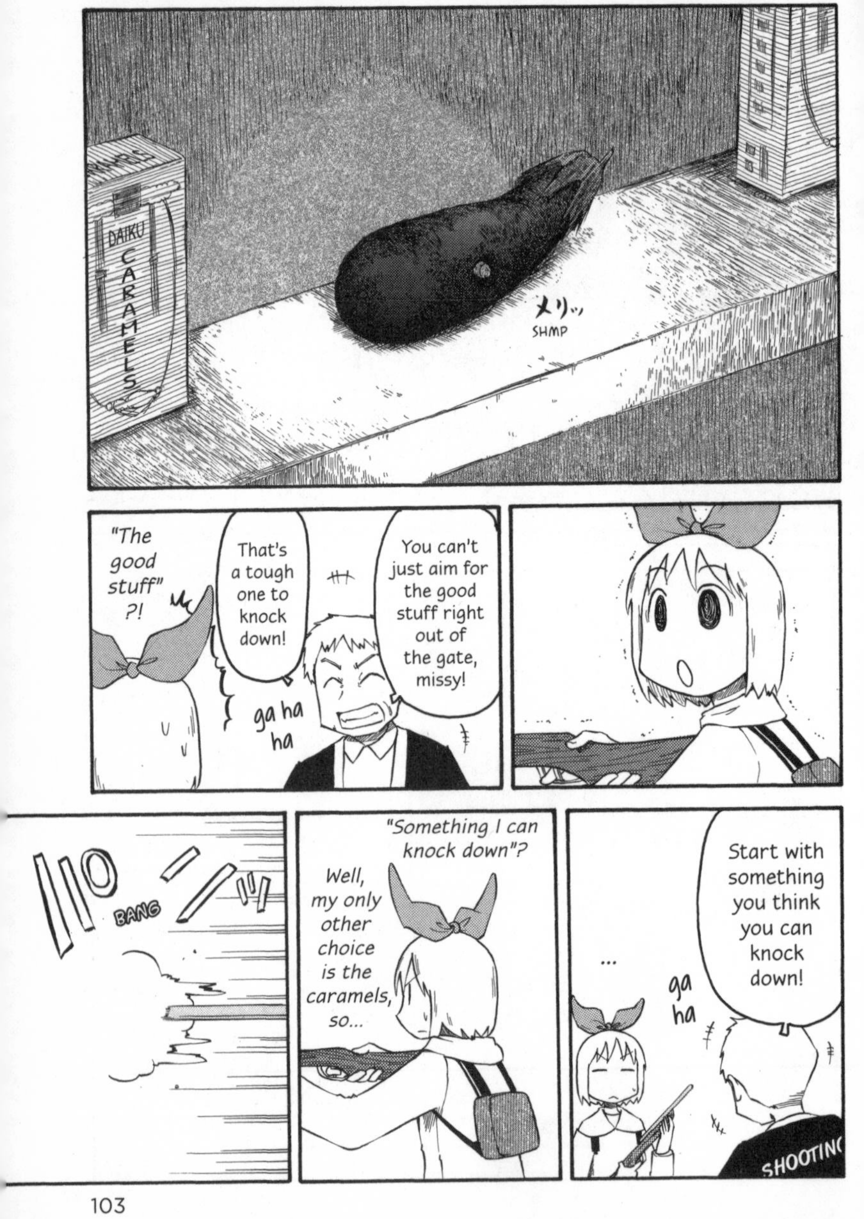
DAIKU CARAMELS
メリッ
SHMP
SHMP
You can't just aim for the good stuff right out of the gate, missy!
That's a tough one to knock down!
ga ha ha
"The good stuff"?!
Start with something you think you can knock down!
ga ha
...
SHOOTING
"Something I can knock down"?
Well, my only other choice is the caramels, so...
BANG

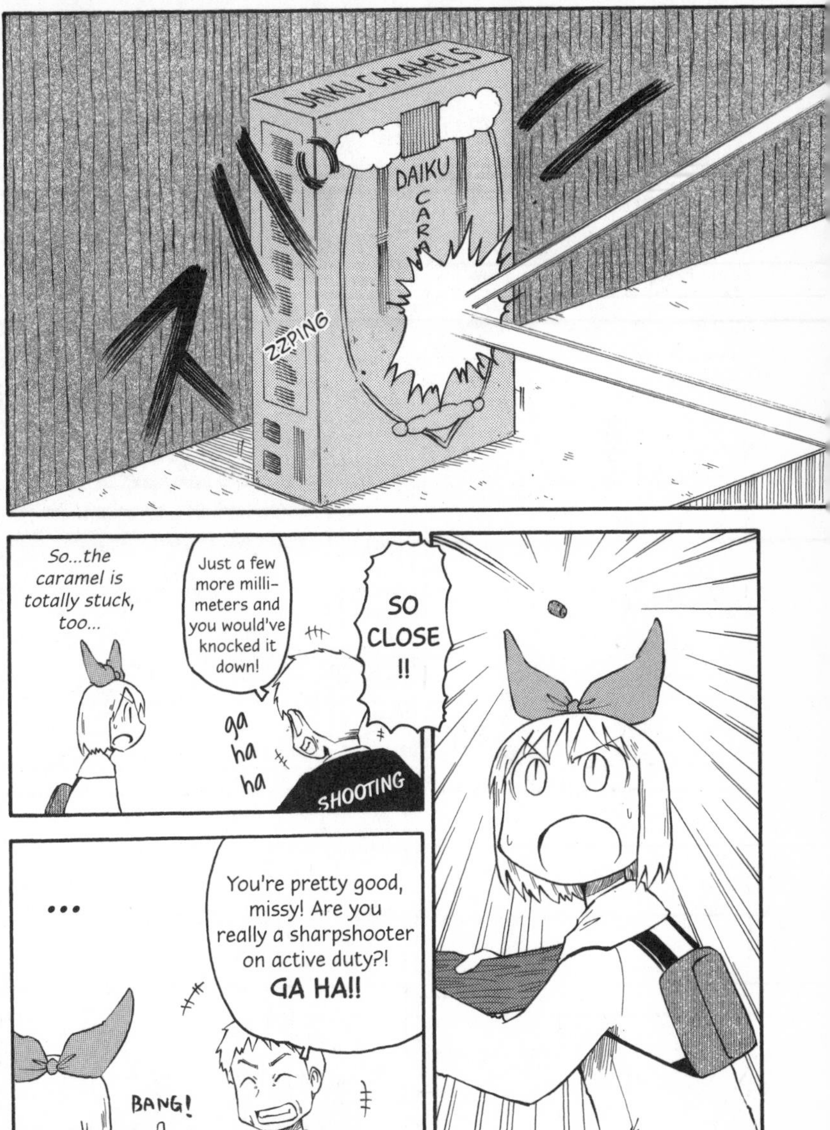
DAIKU CARAMELS
DAIKU CARA
ZZPING
SO CLOSE !!
Just a few more milli- meters and you would've knocked it down!
So...the caramel is totally stuck, too...
ga ha ha
SHOOTING
You're pretty good, missy! Are you really a sharpshooter on active duty?! GA HA!!
...
BANG!

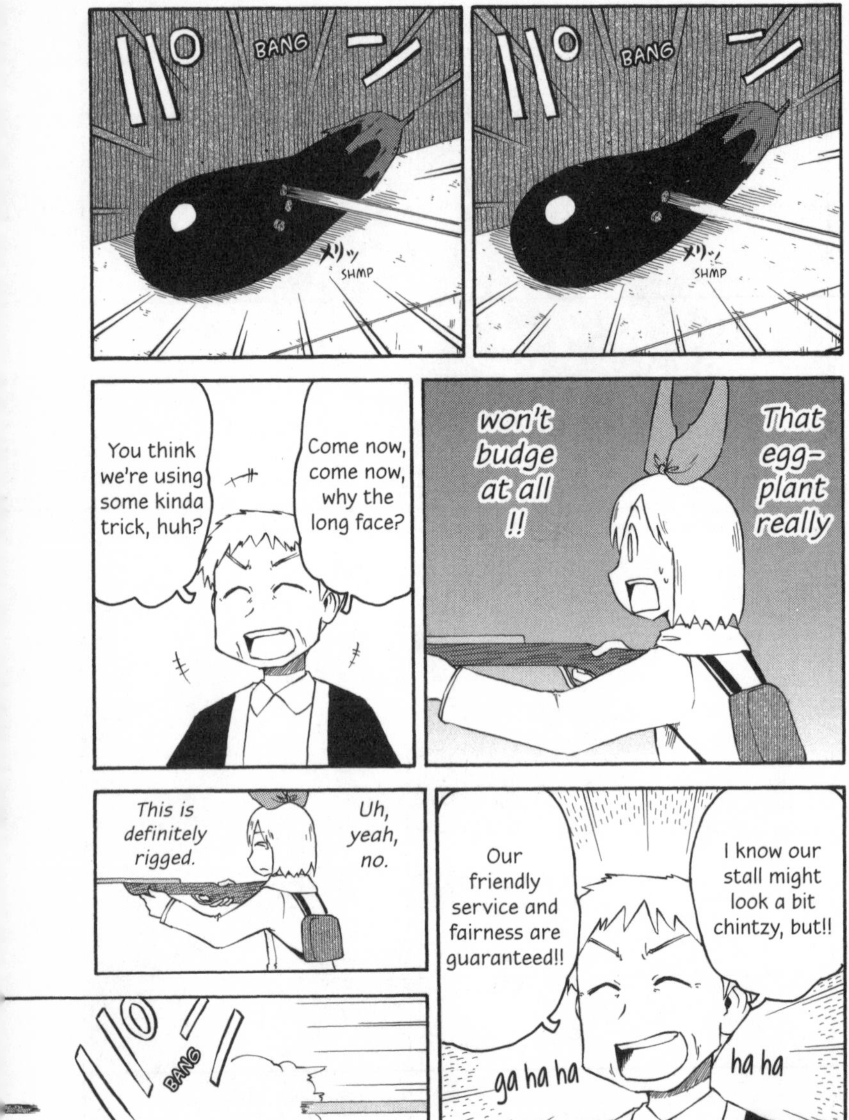

BANG
メリッ
SHMP
BANG
メリッ
SHMP
That egg-plant really
won't budge at all !!
Come now, come now, why the long face?
You think we're using some kinda trick, huh?
I know our stall might look a bit chintzy, but!!
Our friendly service and fairness are guaranteed!!
ha ha
ga ha ha
Uh, yeah, no.
This is definitely rigged.
BANG

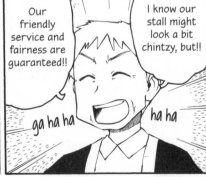

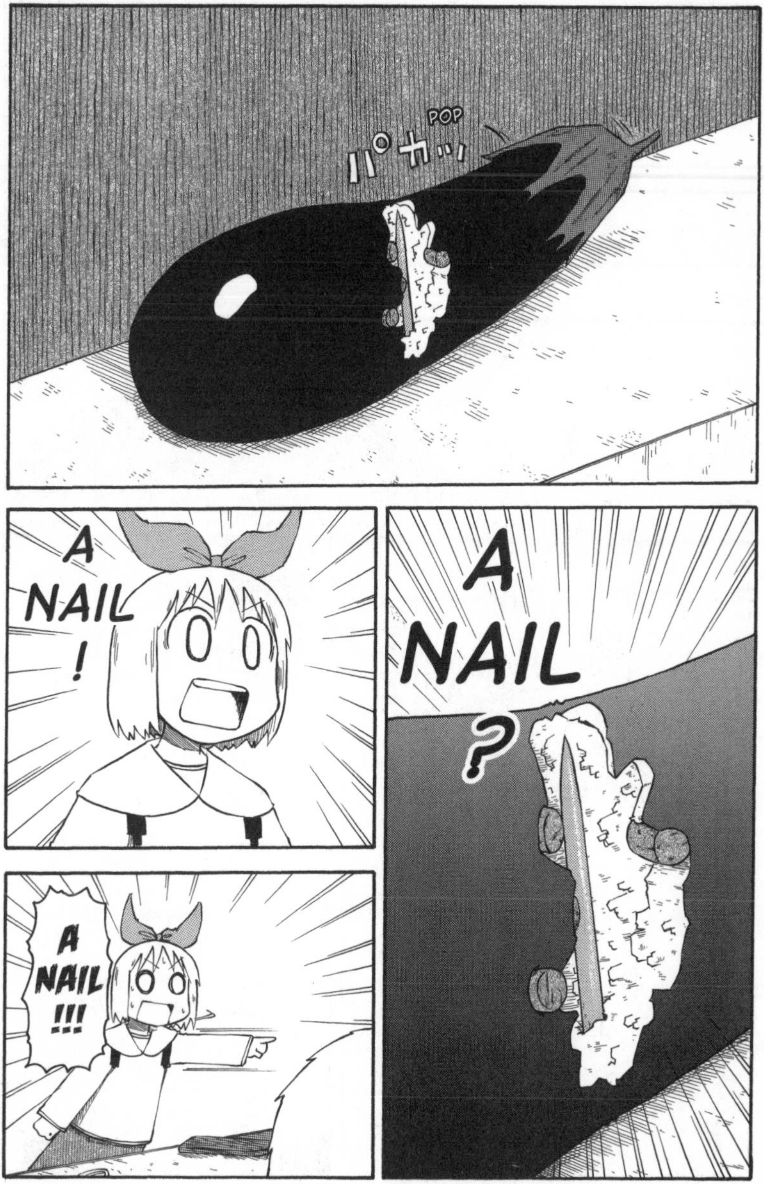
POP
パカッ
A NAIL?
A NAIL!
A NAIL!!!

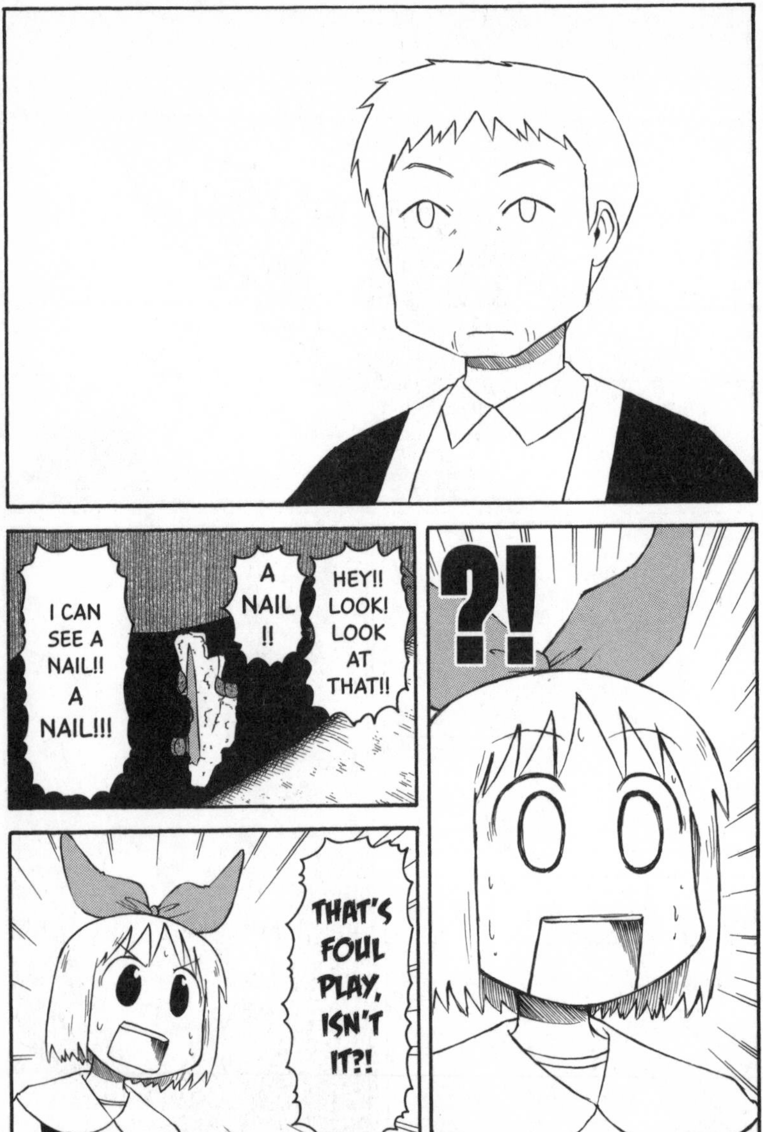
?!
HEY!! LOOK! LOOK AT THAT!!
A NAIL!!
I CAN SEE A NAIL!! A NAIL!!!
THAT'S FOUL PLAY, ISN'T IT?!

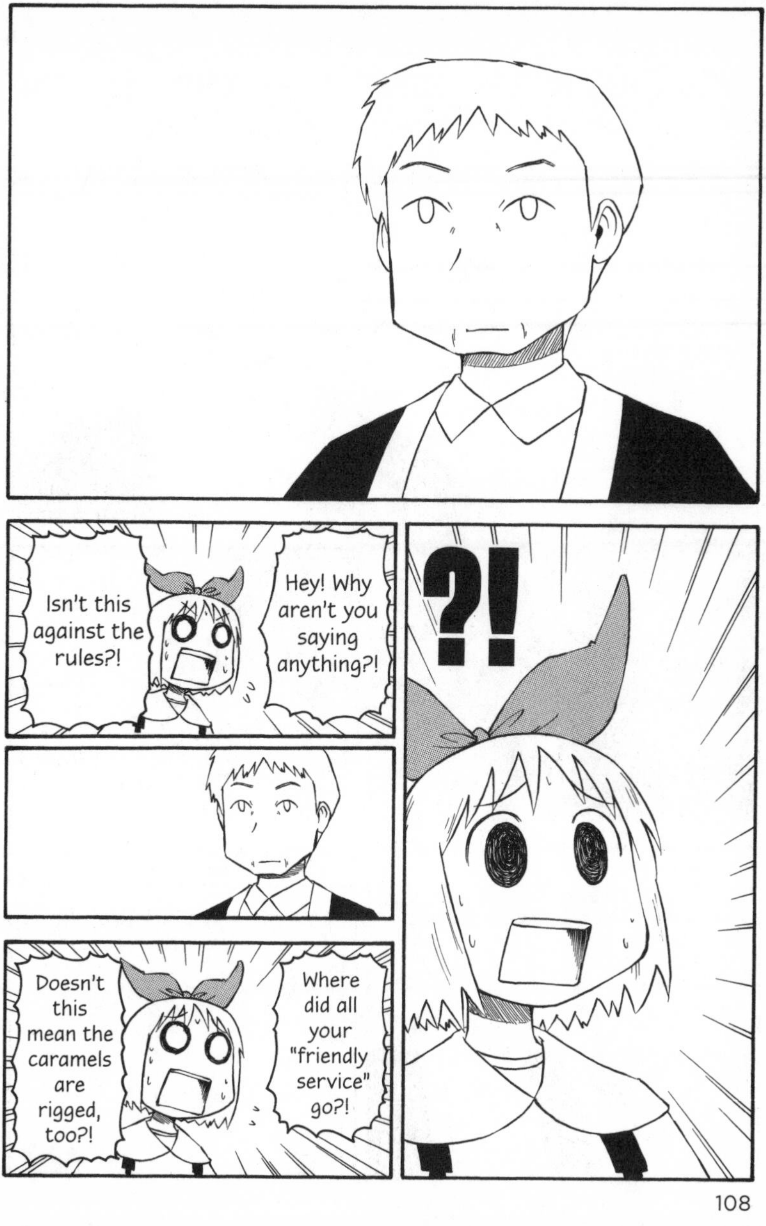
?!
Hey! Why aren't you saying anything?!
Isn't this against the rules?!
Where did all your "friendly service" go?!
Doesn't this mean the caramels are rigged, too?!

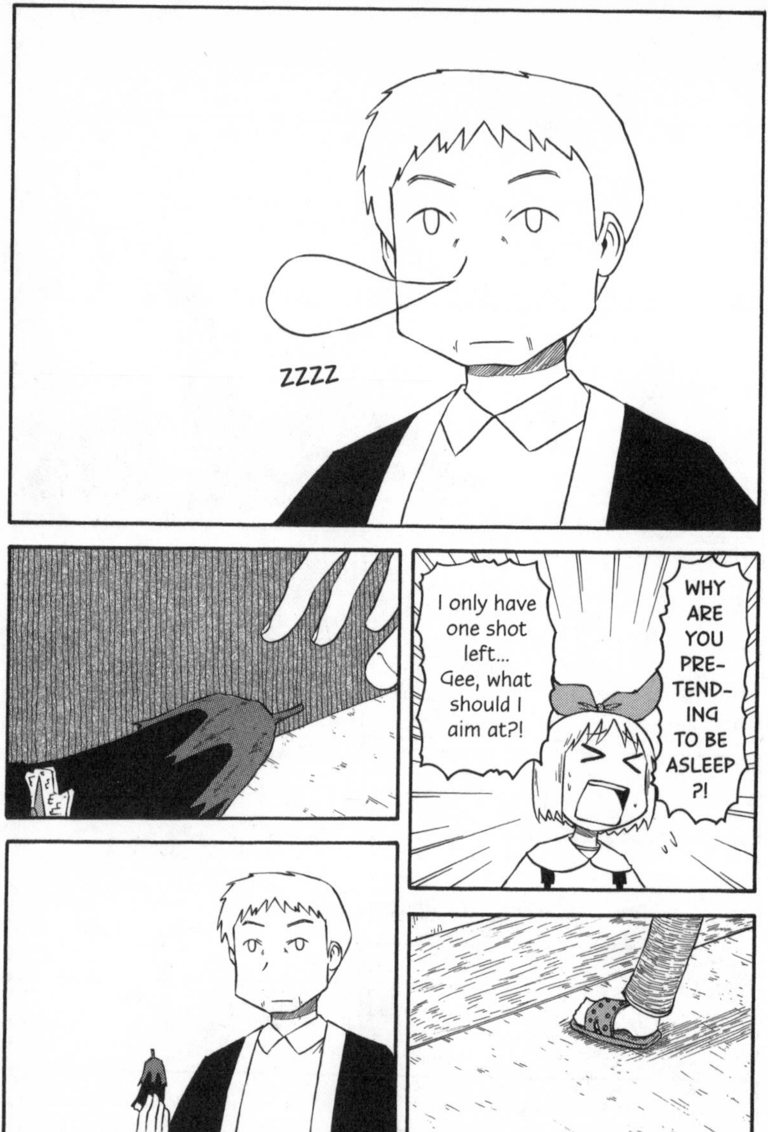
ZZZZ
WHY ARE YOU PRE-TEND-ING TO BE ASLEEP?!
I only have one shot left... Gee, what should I aim at?!

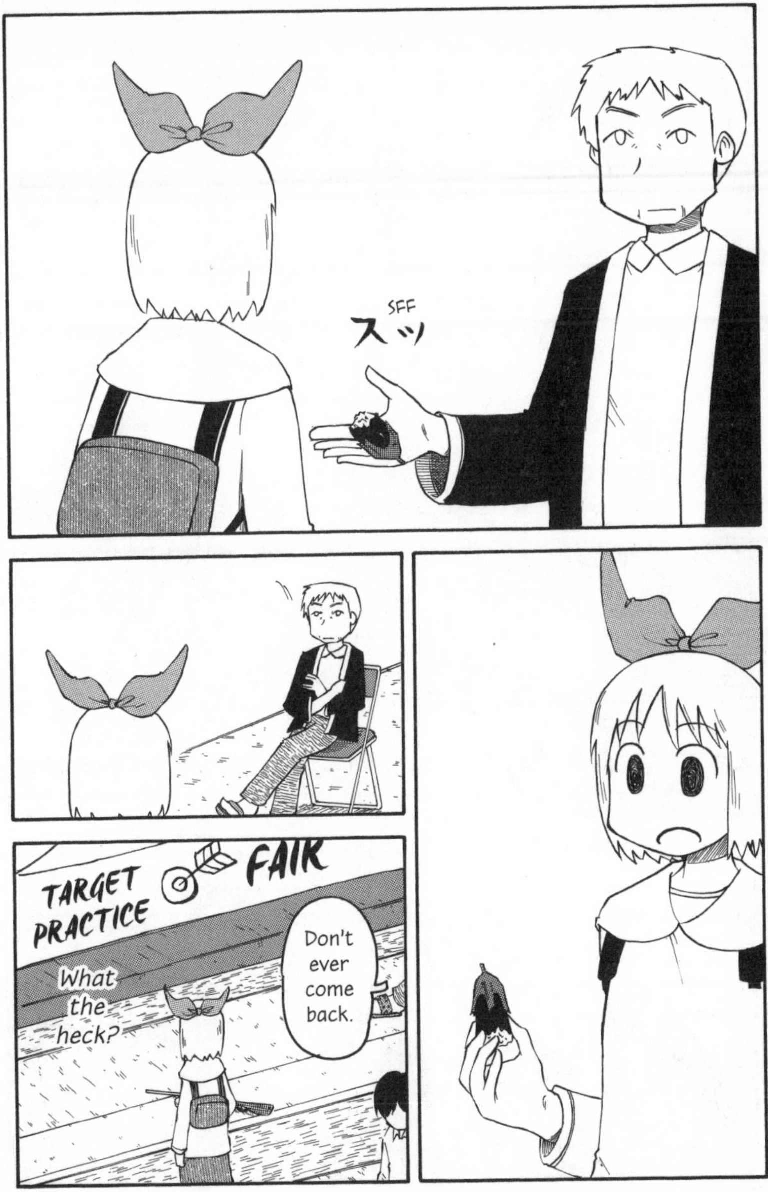
スッ
SFF
TARGET PRACTICE
FAIR
Don't ever come back.
What the heck?

chapter 99: end

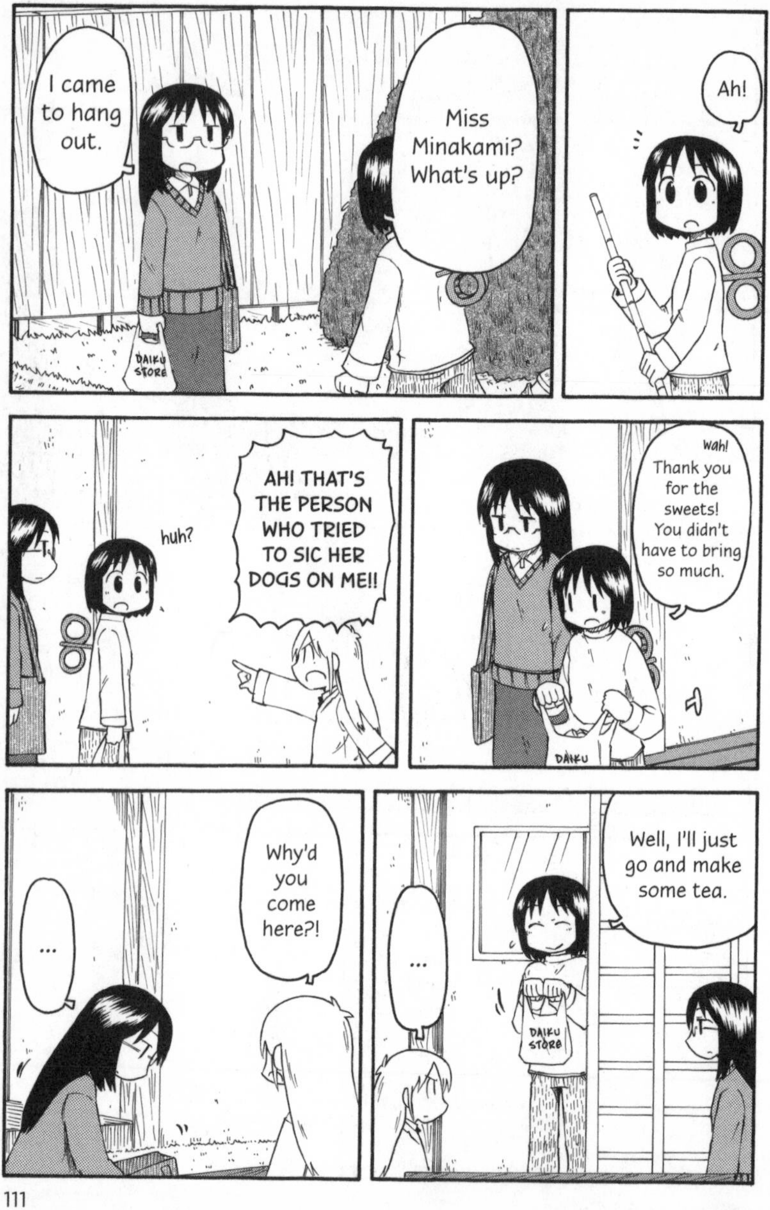
Ah!
Miss Minakami? What's up?
I came to hang out.
DAIKU STORE
Wah! Thank you for the sweets! You didn't have to bring so much.
DAIKU
AH! THAT'S THE PERSON WHO TRIED TO SIC HER DOGS ON ME!!
huh?
Well, I'll just go and make some tea.
DAIKU STORE
...
Why'd you come here?!
...

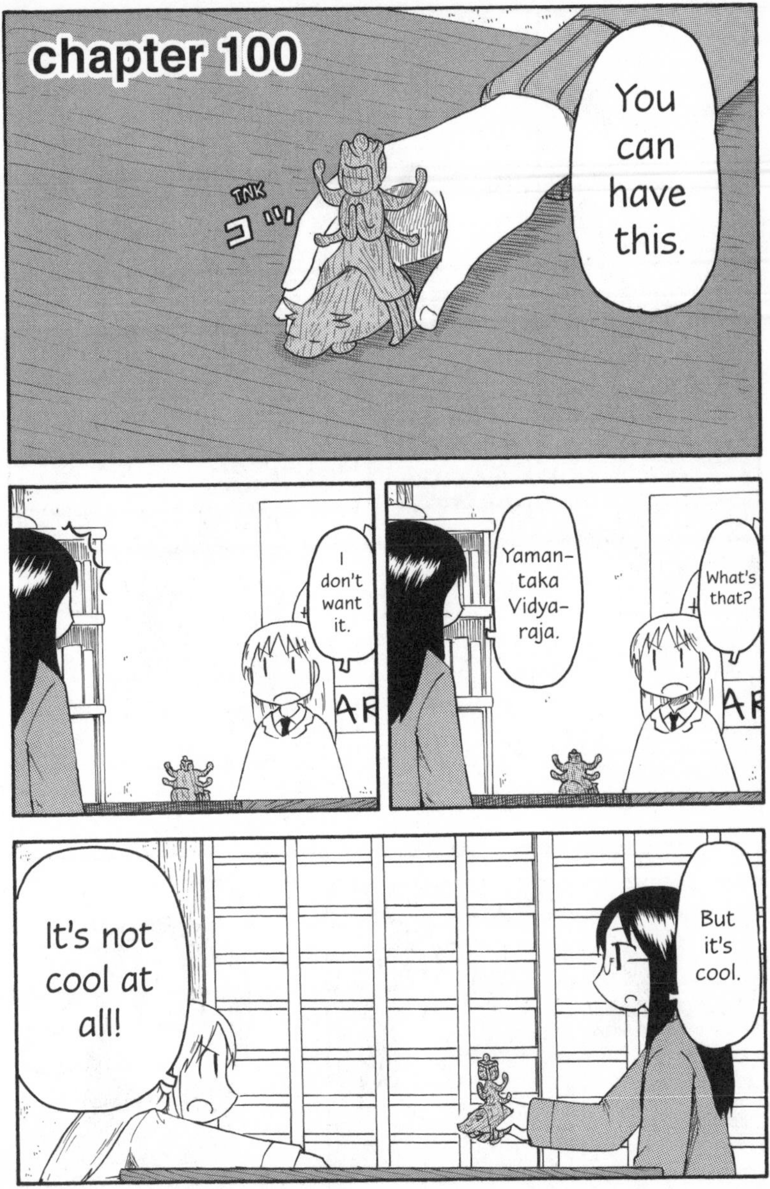
chapter 100
TNK
コッ
You can have this.
What's that?
Yaman-taka Vidya-raja.
I don't want it.
But it's cool.
It's not cool at all!

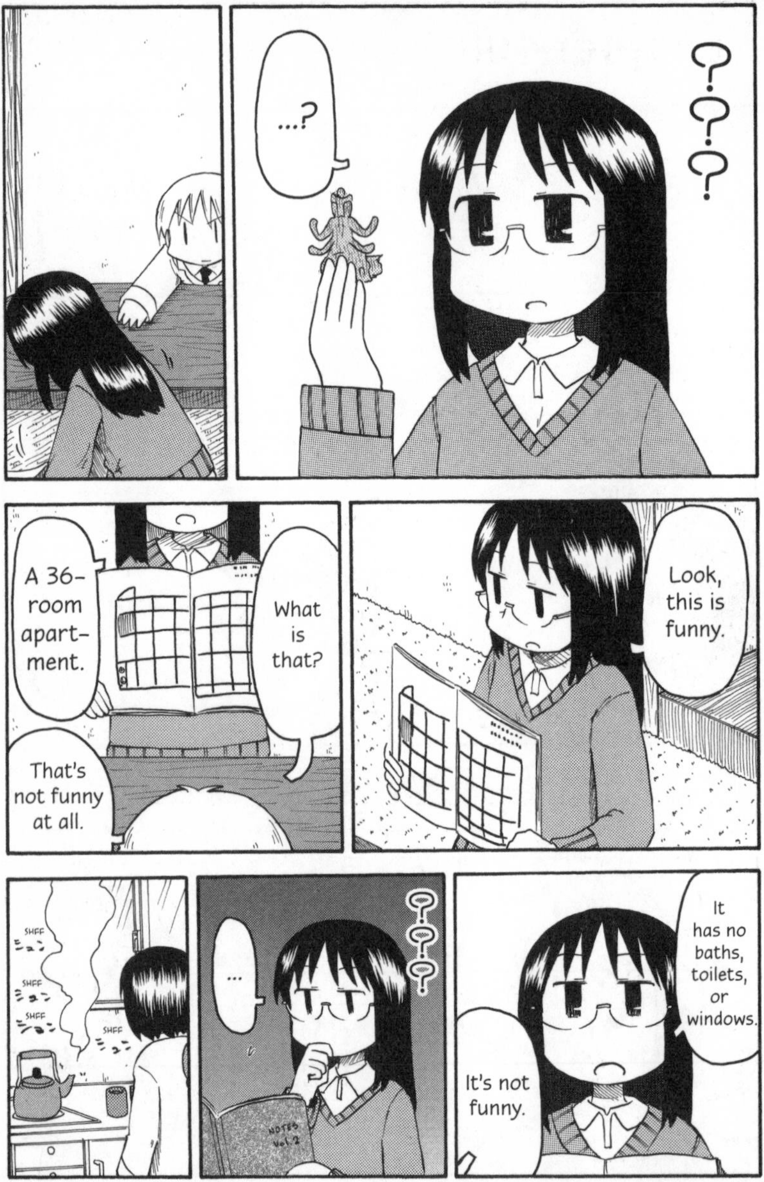
???
...?
Look, this is funny.
What is that?
A 36-room apartment.
That's not funny at all.
It has no baths, toilets, or windows.
It's not funny.
...
SHFF
SHFF
SHFF
SHFF

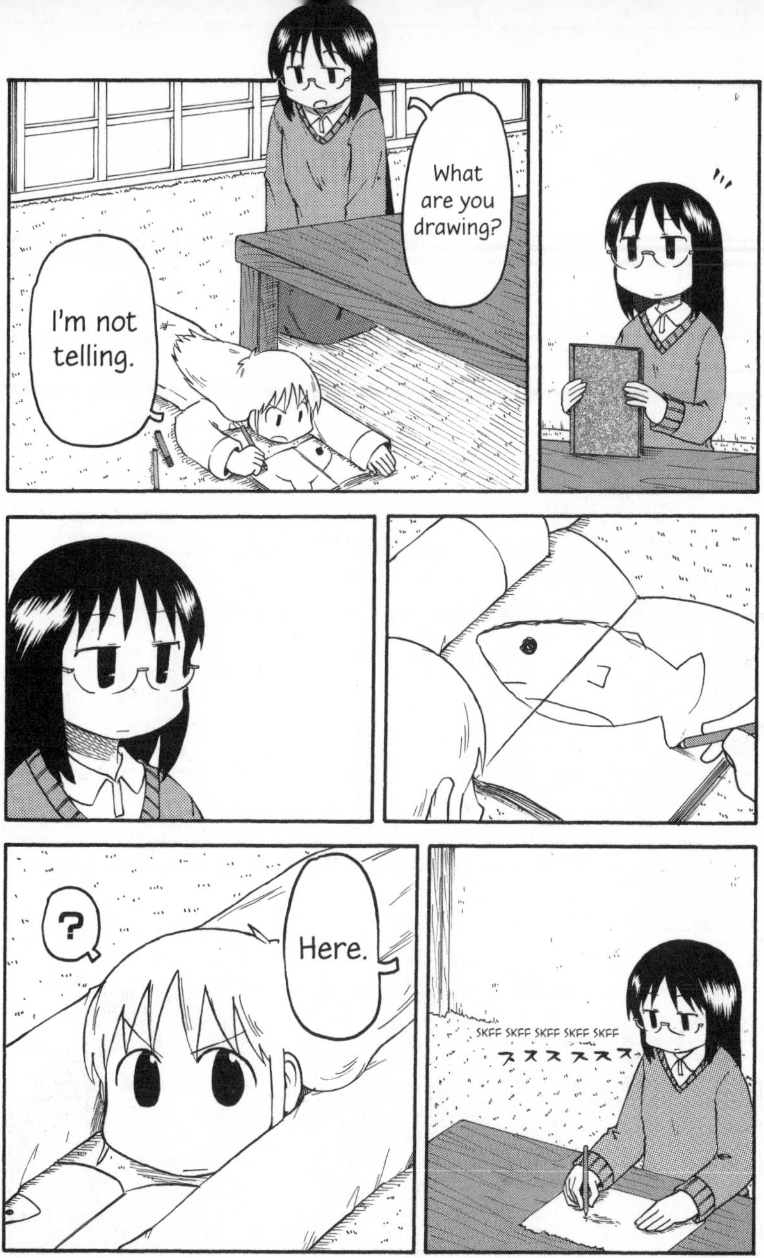
What are you drawing?
I'm not telling.
SKFF SKFF SKFF SKFF SKFF
Here.
?

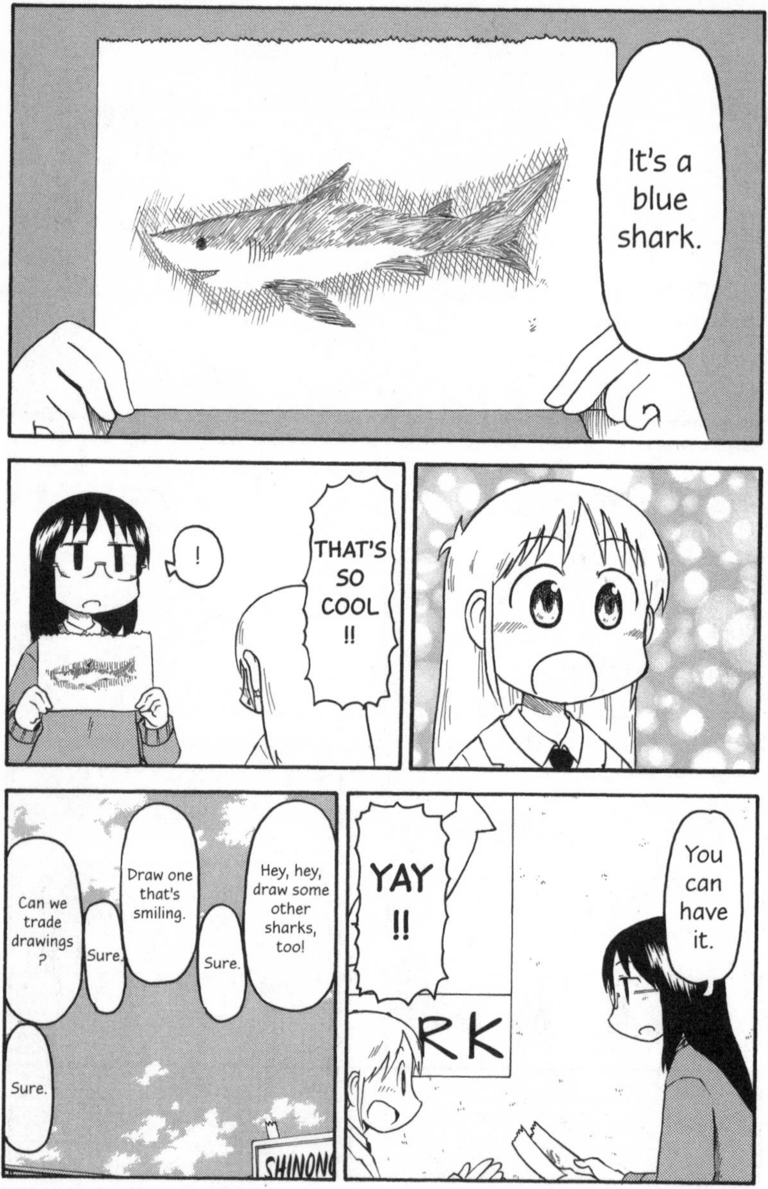

It's a blue shark.
THAT'S SO COOL !!
!
You can have it.
YAY !!
RK
Hey, hey, draw some other sharks, too!
Sure.
Draw one that's smiling.
Sure.
Can we trade drawings ?
Sure.
SHINONO

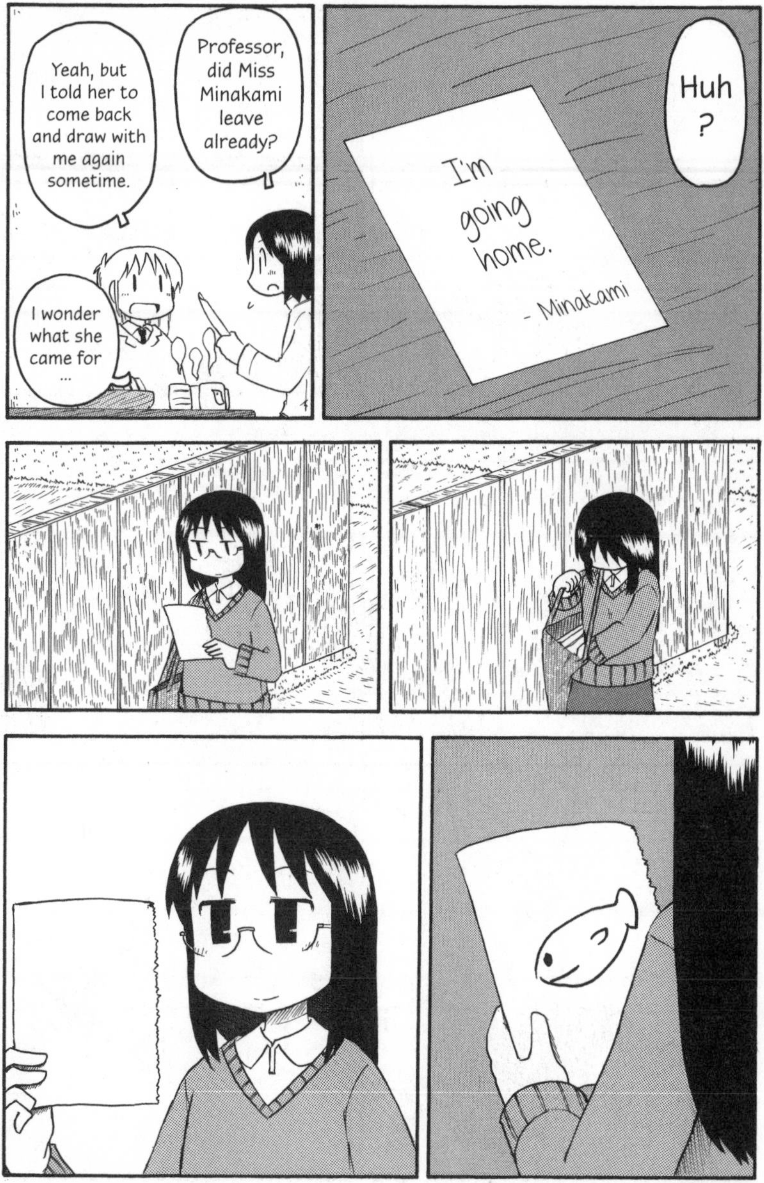
Huh ?
I'm going home. - Minakami
Professor, did Miss Minakami leave already?
Yeah, but I told her to come back and draw with me again sometime.
I wonder what she came for ...

chapter 100: end

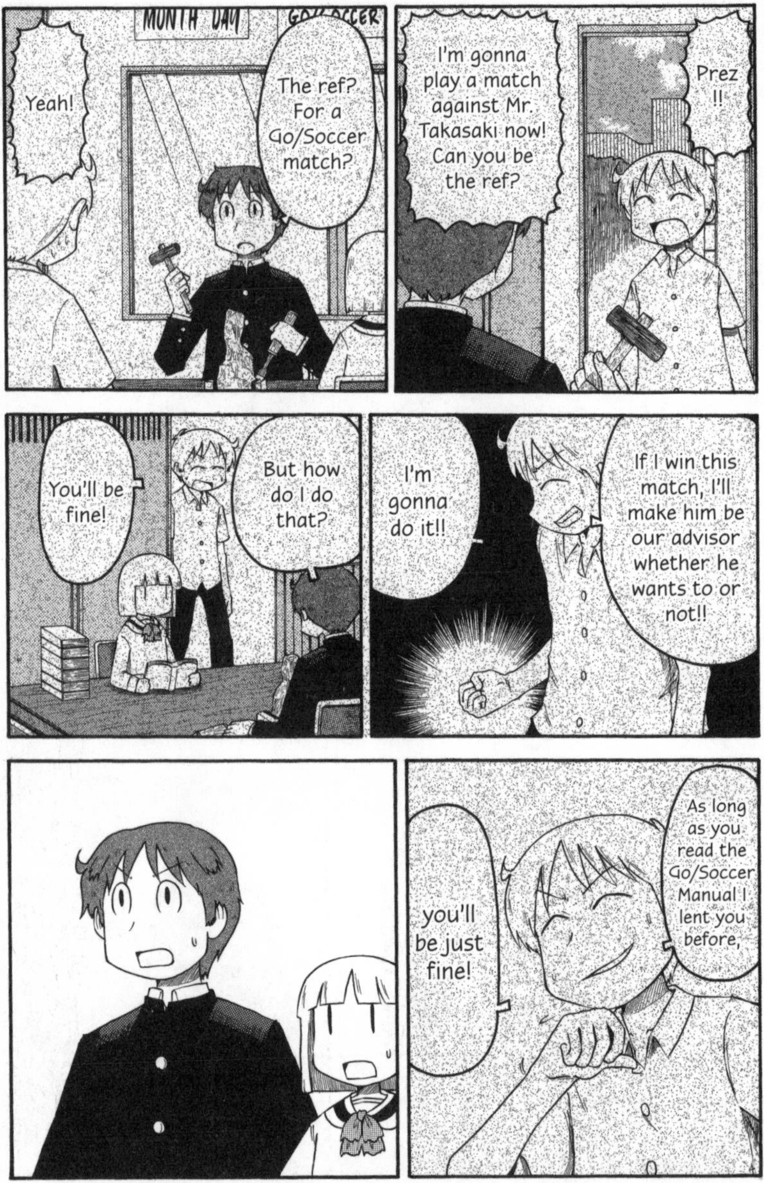
Prez !!
I'm gonna play a match against Mr. Takasaki now! Can you be the ref?
MONTH DAY
The ref? For a Go/Soccer match?
Yeah!
If I win this match, I'll make him be our advisor whether he wants to or not!!
I'm gonna do it!!
But how do I do that?
You'll be fine!
As long as you read the Go/Soccer Manual I lent you before,
you'll be just fine!

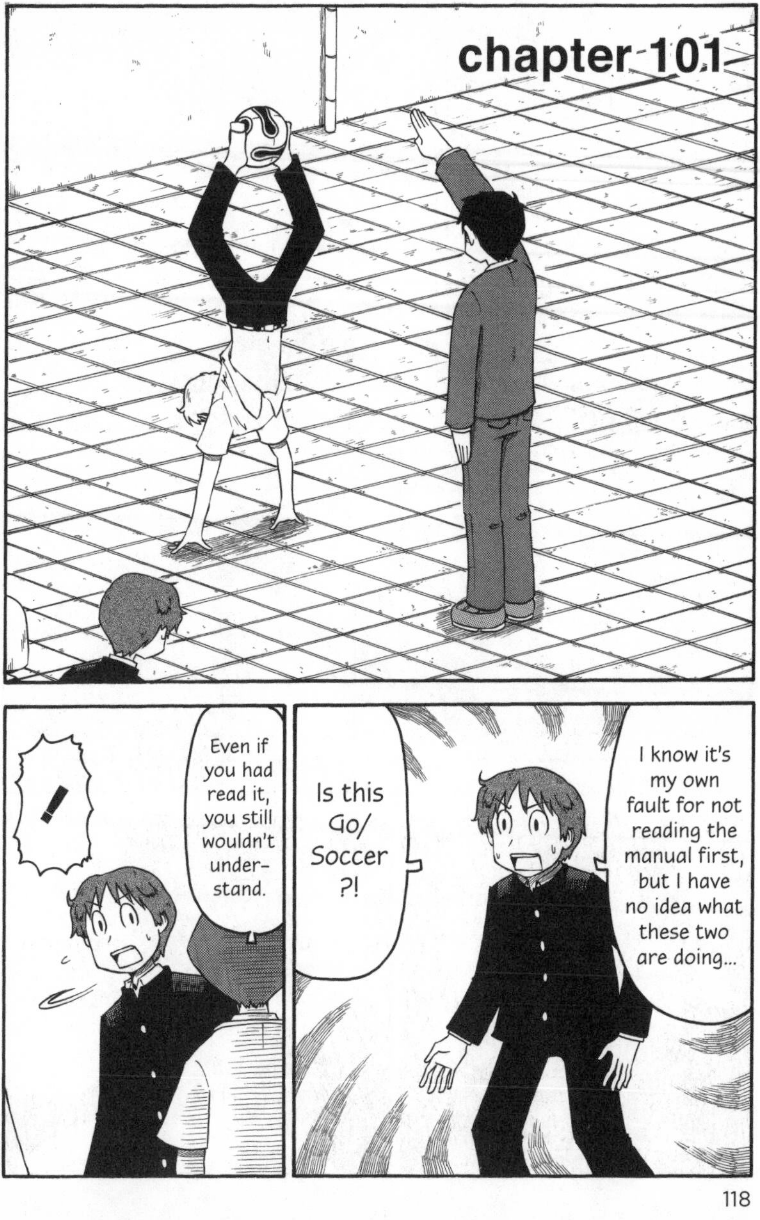
chapter 101
I know it's my own fault for not reading the manual first, but I have no idea what these two are doing...
Is this Go/ Soccer ?!
Even if you had read it, you still wouldn't under-stand.
!

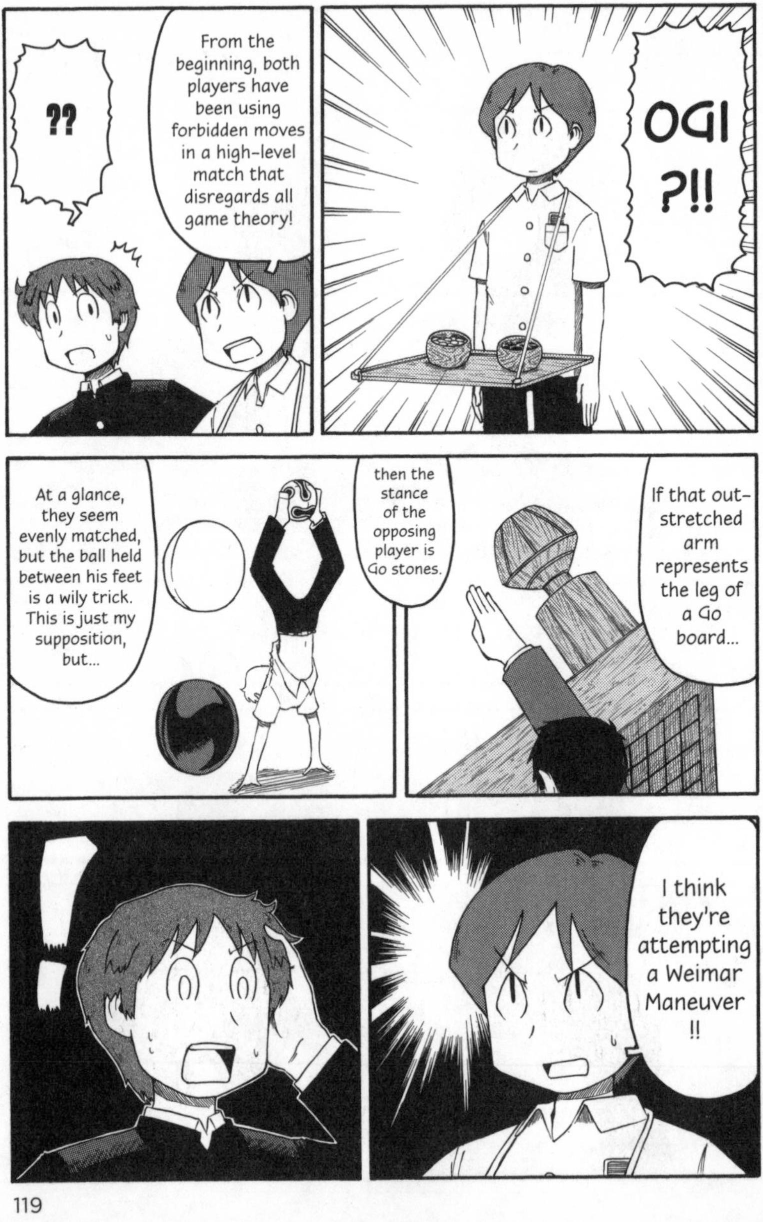
OGI ?!!
From the beginning, both players have been using forbidden moves in a high-level match that disregards all game theory!
??
If that out-stretched arm represents the leg of a Go board...
then the stance of the opposing player is Go stones.
At a glance, they seem evenly matched, but the ball held between his feet is a wily trick. This is just my supposition, but...
I think they're attempting a Weimar Maneuver !!
!

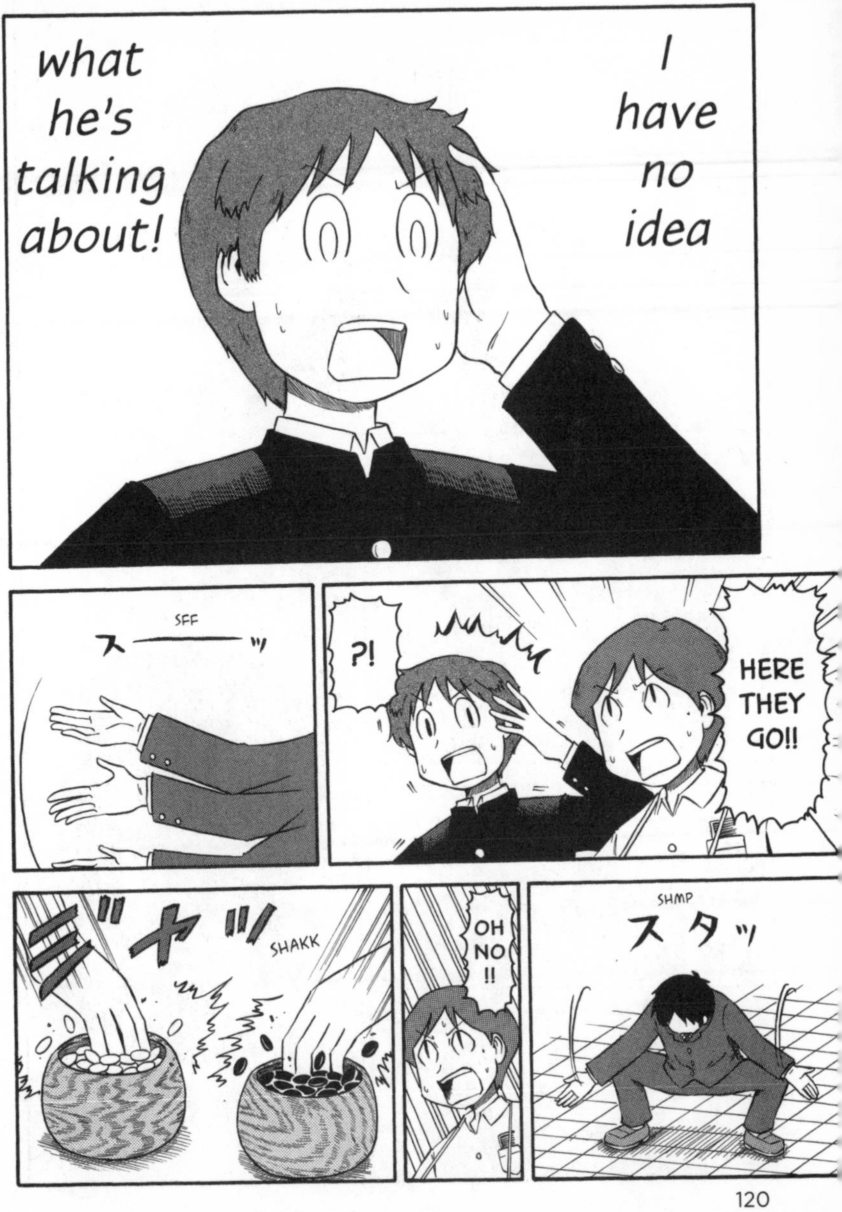
I have no idea
what he's talking about!
HERE THEY GO!!
?!
SFF
スーーーッ
SHMP
スタッ
OH NO !!
SHAKK

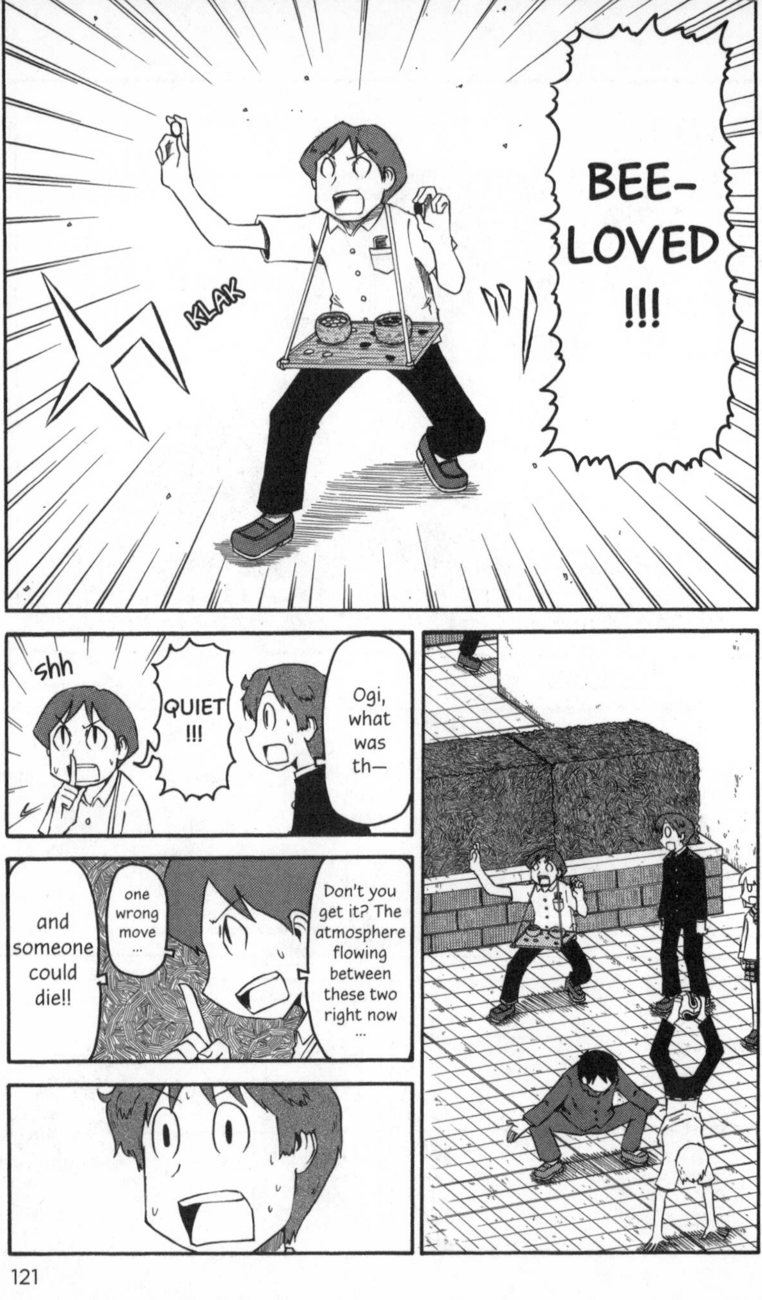
BEE-LOVED !!!
KLAK
Ogi, what was th—
QUIET !!!
shh
Don't you get it? The atmosphere flowing between these two right now ...
one wrong move ...
and someone could die!!

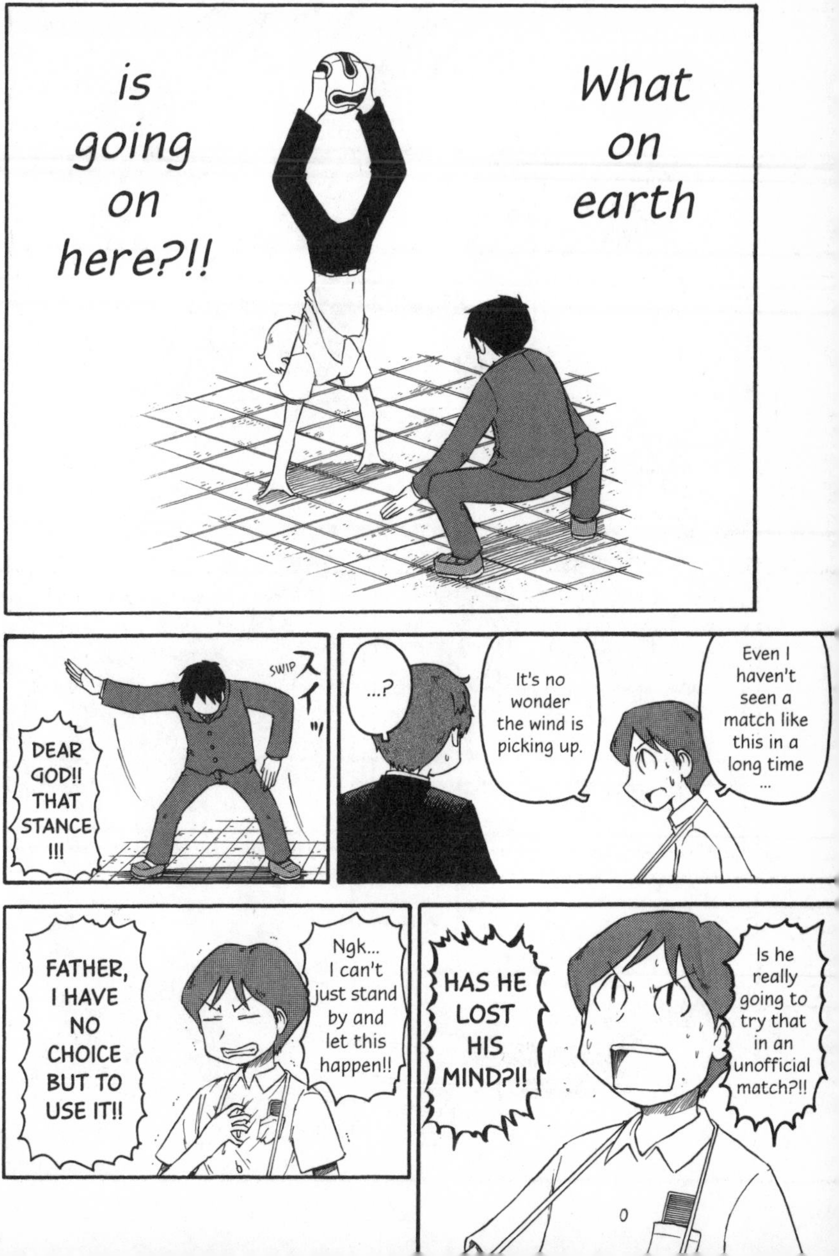
What on earth
is going on here?!!
Even I haven't seen a match like this in a long time ...
It's no wonder the wind is picking up.
...?
SWIP スイッ
DEAR GOD!! THAT STANCE!!!
Is he really going to try that in an unofficial match?!!
HAS HE LOST HIS MIND?!!
Ngk... I can't just stand by and let this happen!!
FATHER, I HAVE NO CHOICE BUT TO USE IT!!

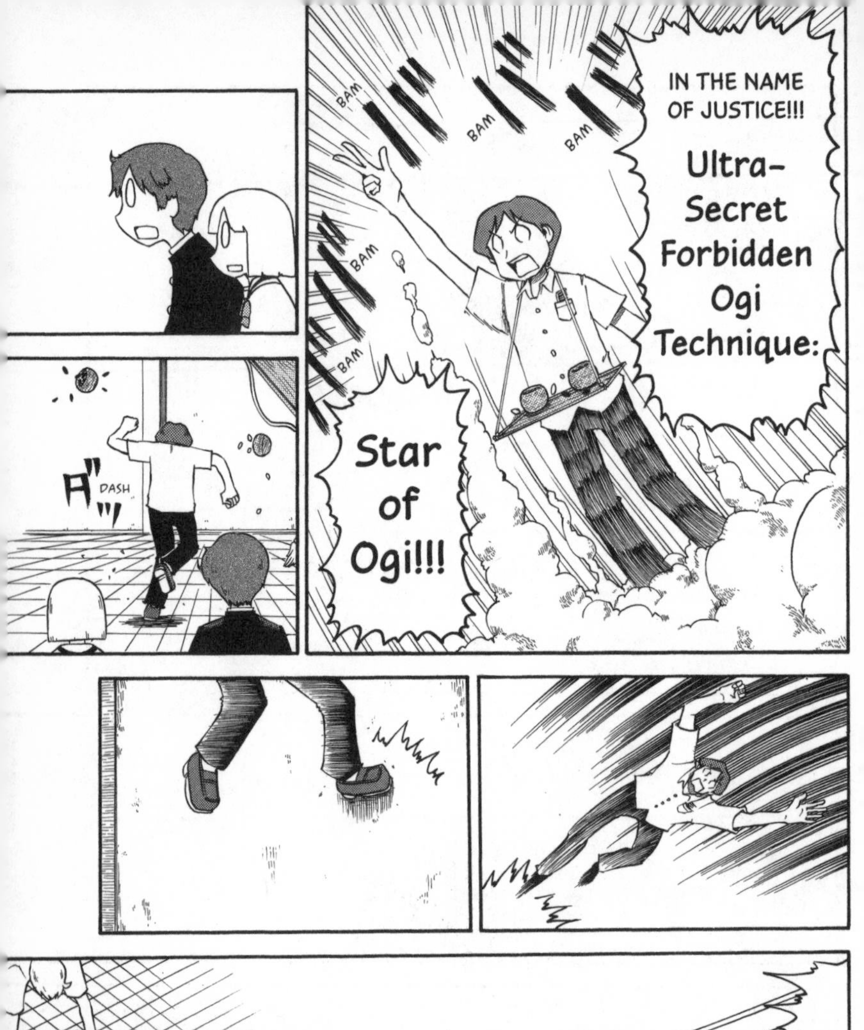
IN THE NAME OF JUSTICE!!!
Ultra-Secret Forbidden Ogi Technique:
BAM
BAM
BAM
BAM
BAM
Star of Ogi!!!
DASH

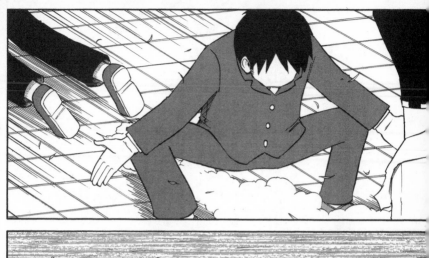

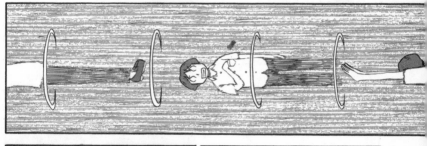

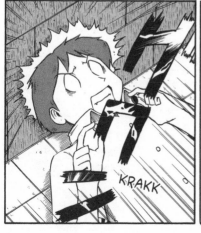

KRAKK

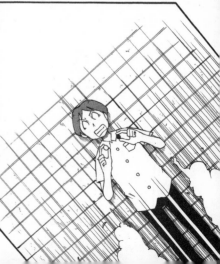

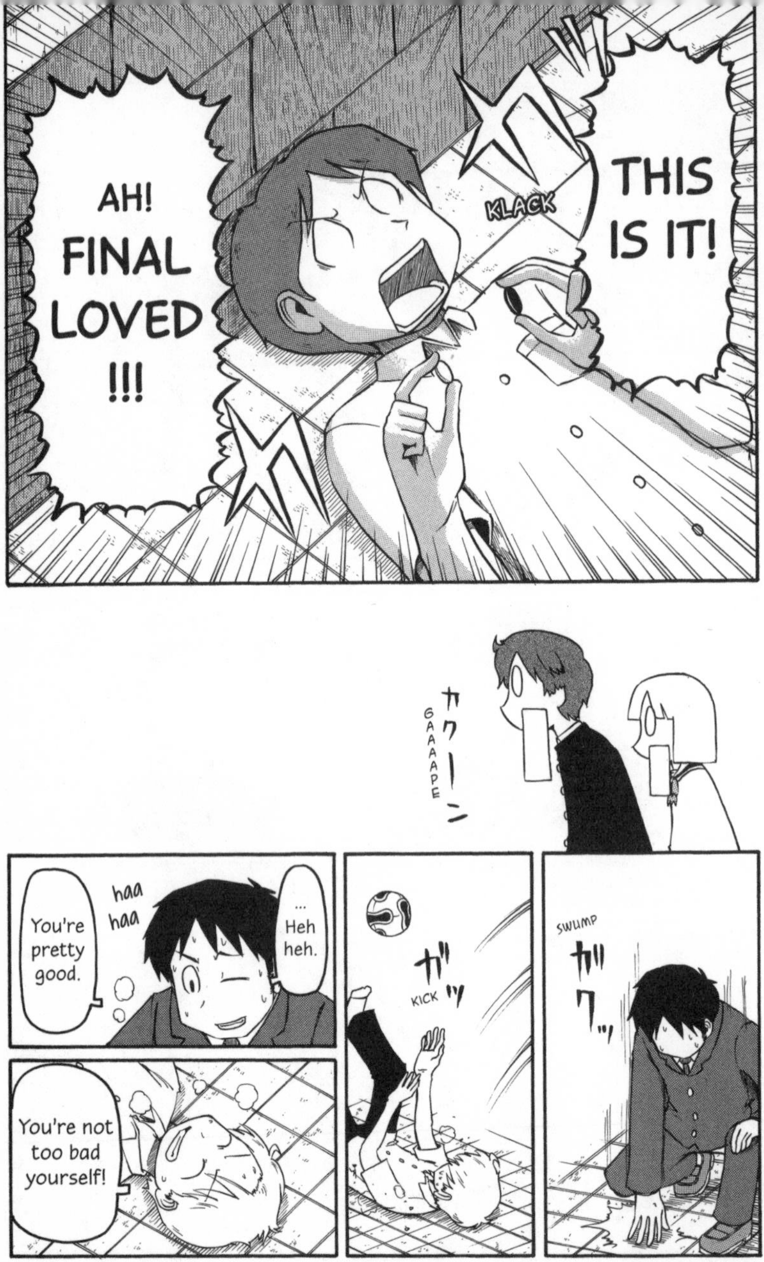
THIS IS IT!
KLACK
AH! FINAL LOVED !!!
カクーン
GAAAAAPE
ガクッ
SWUMP
ガッ
KICK
... Heh heh.
haa haa
You're pretty good.
You're not too bad yourself!

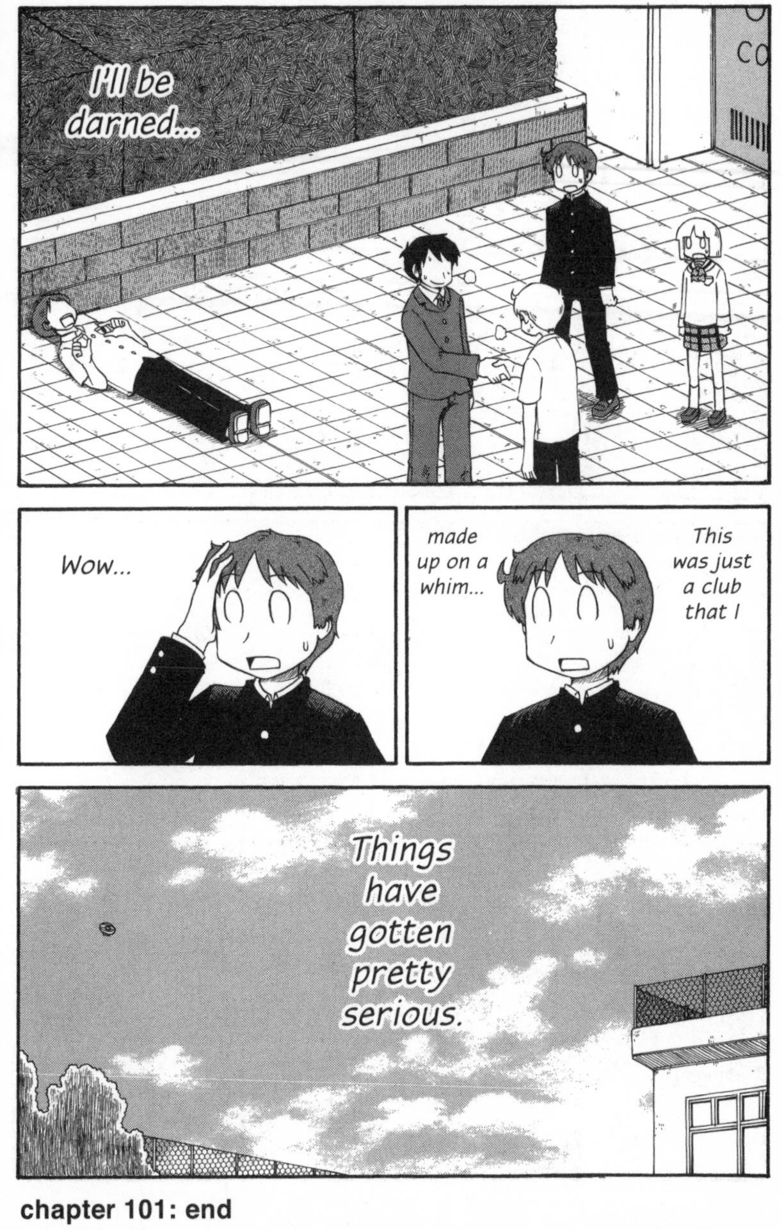
I'll be darned...
This was just a club that I
made up on a whim...
Wow...
Things have gotten pretty serious.

chapter 101: end

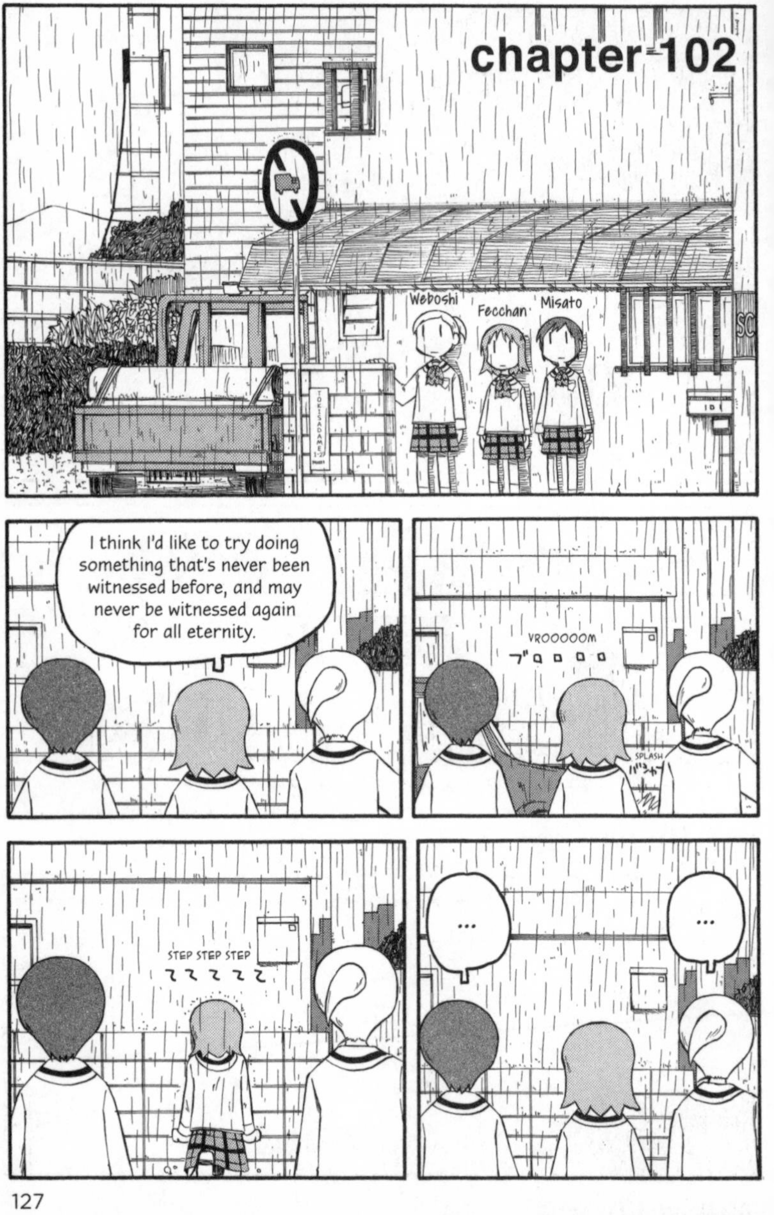
chapter 102
Weboshi
Fecchan
Misato
VROOOOOM
SPLASH
I think I'd like to try doing something that's never been witnessed before, and may never be witnessed again for all eternity.
...
...
STEP STEP STEP

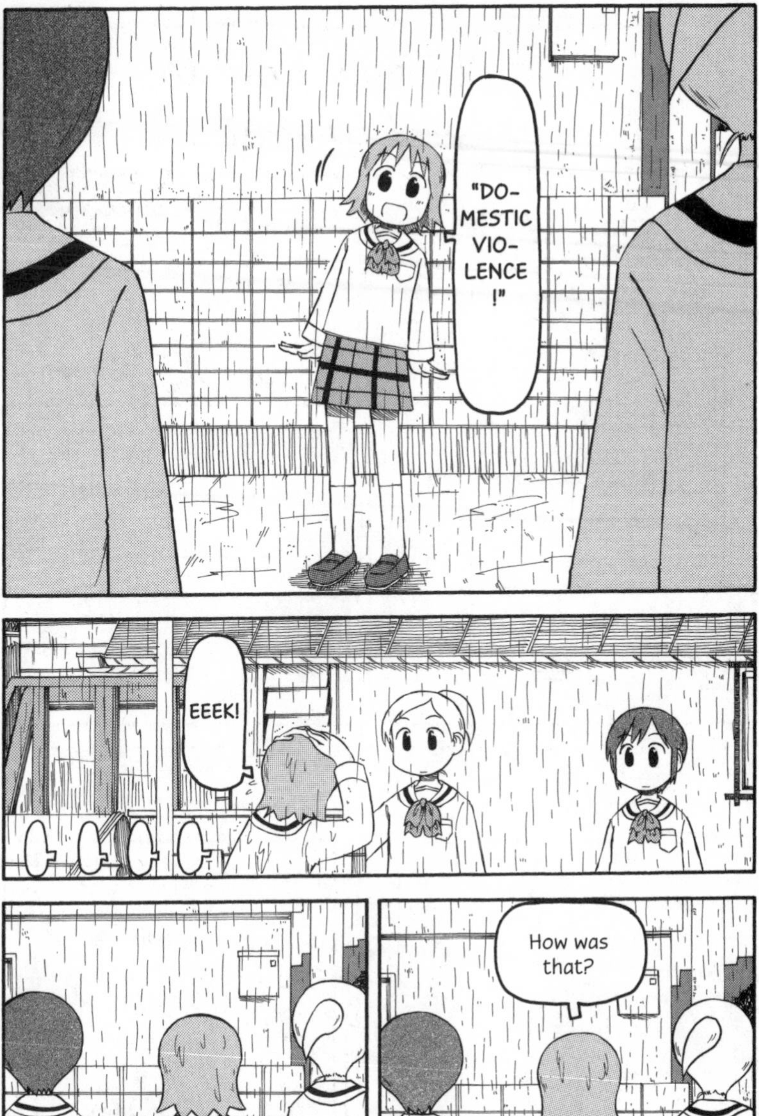
"DO-MESTIC VIO-LENCE!"
EEEK!
How was that?

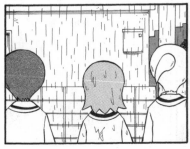

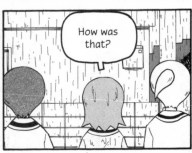

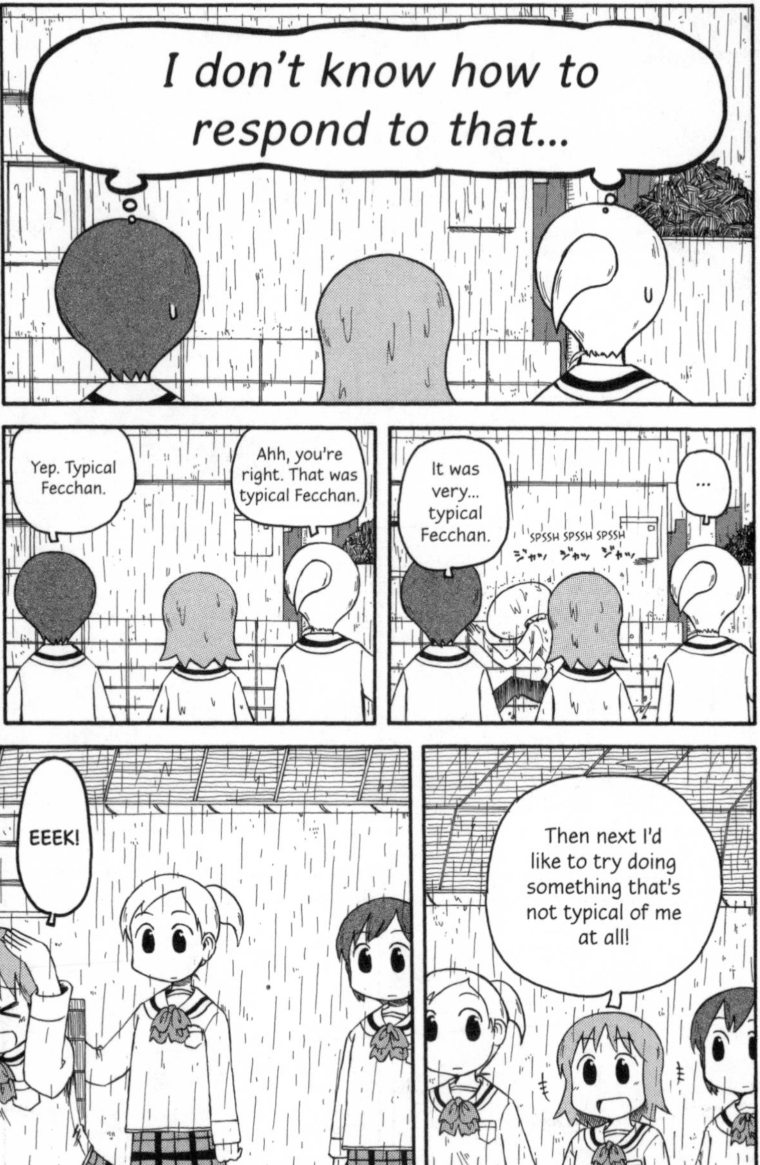
I don't know how to respond to that...
...
It was very... typical Fecchan.
SPSSH SPSSH SPSSH
Ahh, you're right. That was typical Fecchan.
Yep. Typical Fecchan.
Then next I'd like to try doing something that's not typical of me at all!
EEEK!

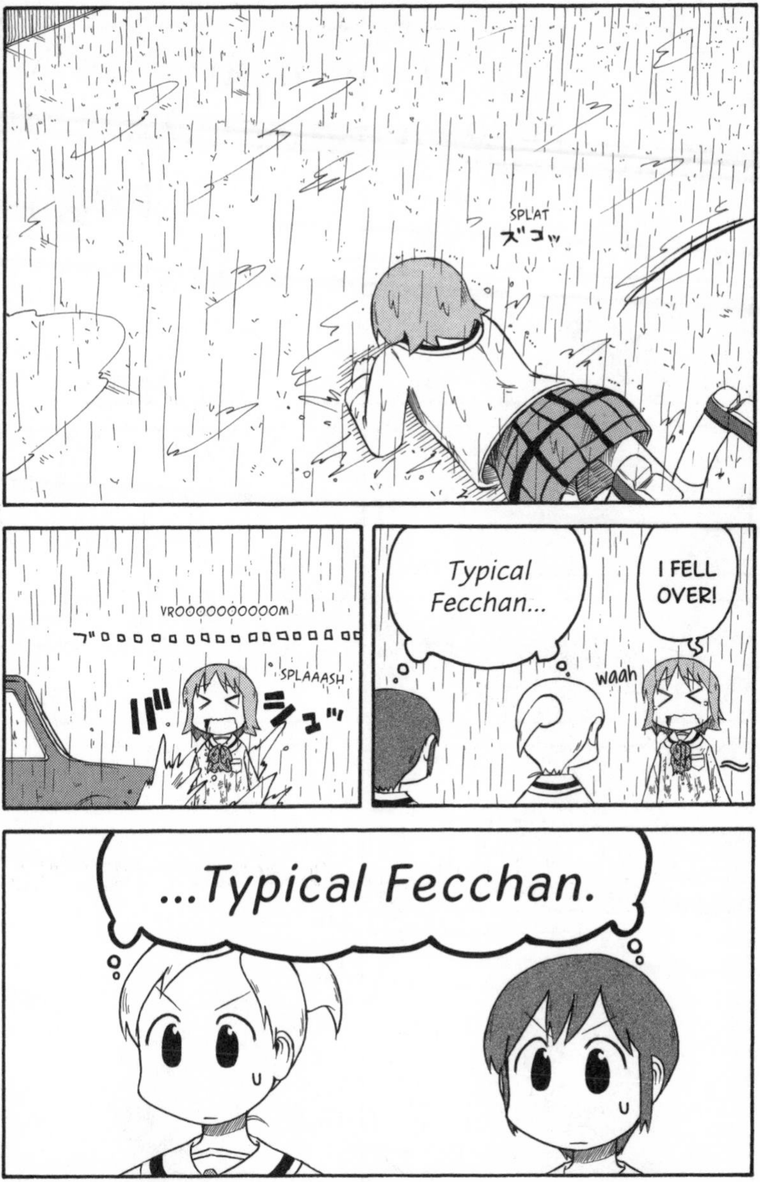
SPLAT
ズゴッ
I FELL OVER!
Typical Fecchan...
waah
VROOOOOOOOOOM
SPLAAASH
バシュッ
...Typical Fecchan.

chapter 102: end

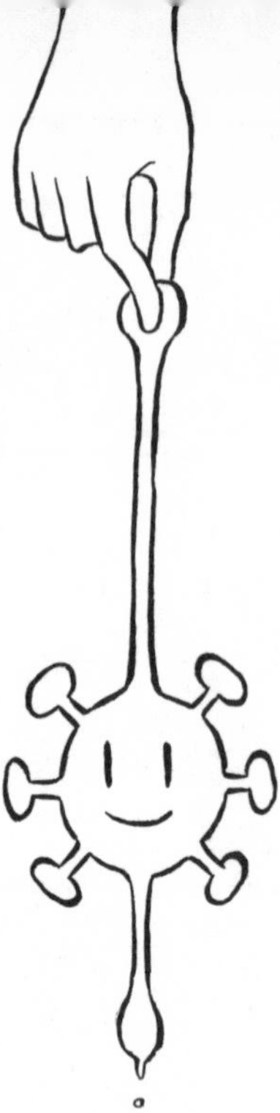

ordinary shorts 9

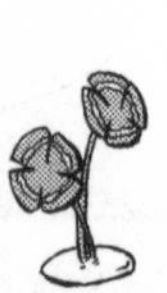

today's special

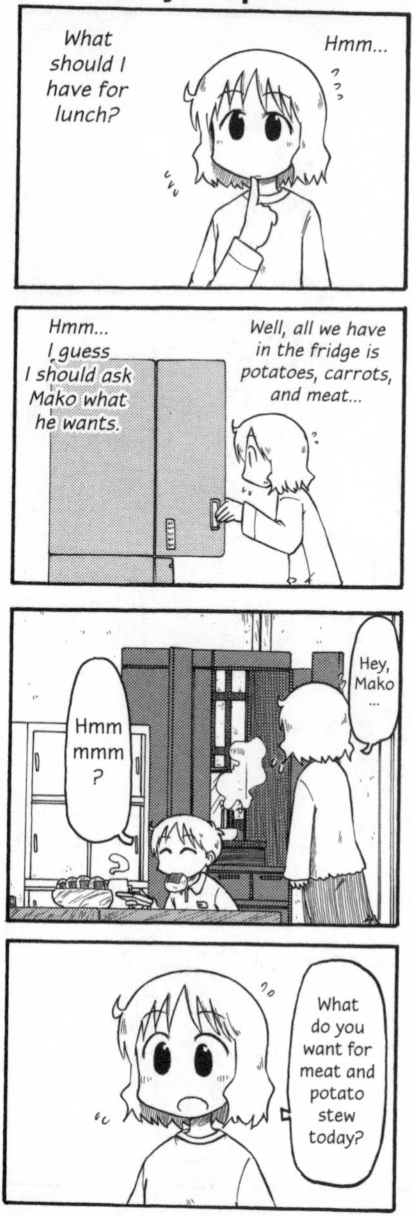
Hmm...
What should I have for lunch?
Well, all we have in the fridge is potatoes, carrots, and meat...
Hmm... I guess I should ask Mako what he wants.
Hey, Mako...
Hmm mmm ?
What do you want for meat and potato stew today?

reverse skill

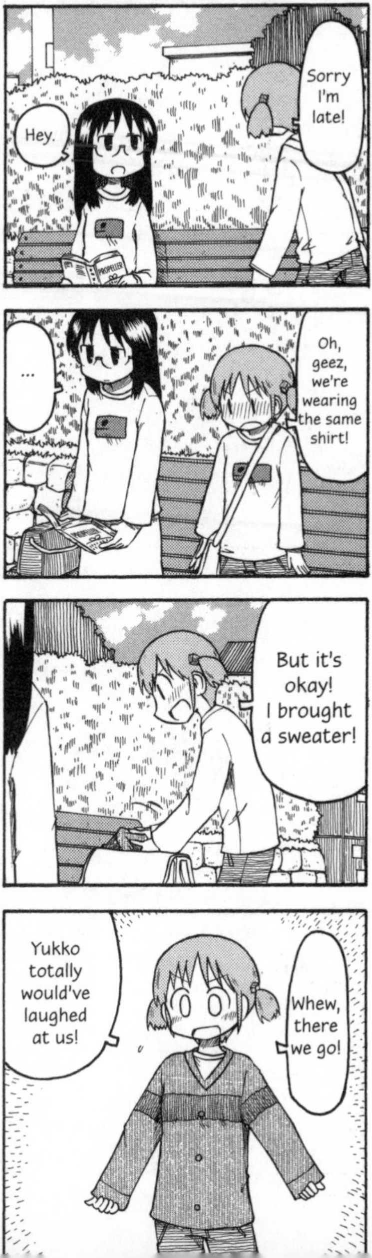
Sorry I'm late!
Hey.
Oh, geez, we're wearing the same shirt!
...
But it's okay! I brought a sweater!
Whew, there we go!
Yukko totally would've laughed at us!

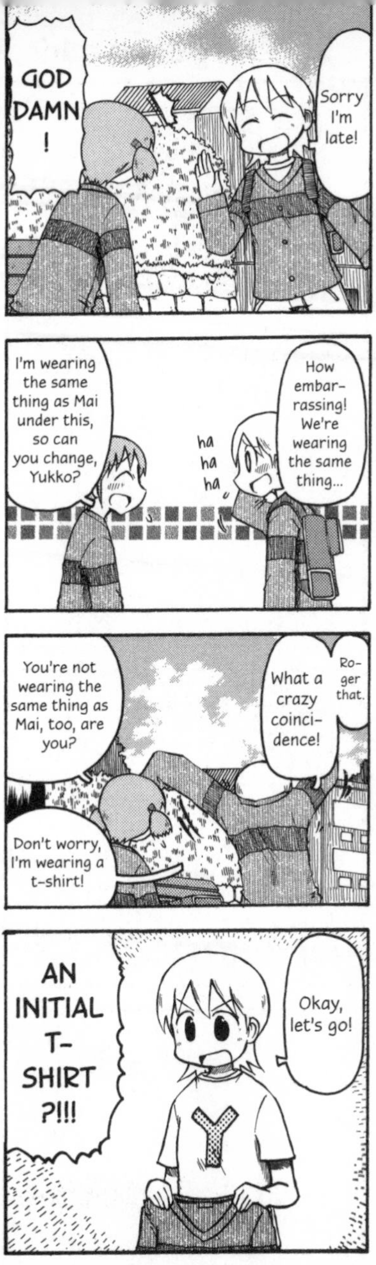
Sorry I'm late!
GOD DAMN!
How embarrassing! We're wearing the same thing...
ha ha ha
I'm wearing the same thing as Mai under this, so can you change, Yukko?
Roger that.
What a crazy coincidence!
You're not wearing the same thing as Mai, too, are you?
Don't worry, I'm wearing a t-shirt!
Okay, let's go!
AN INITIAL T-SHIRT?!!!

school gear solid

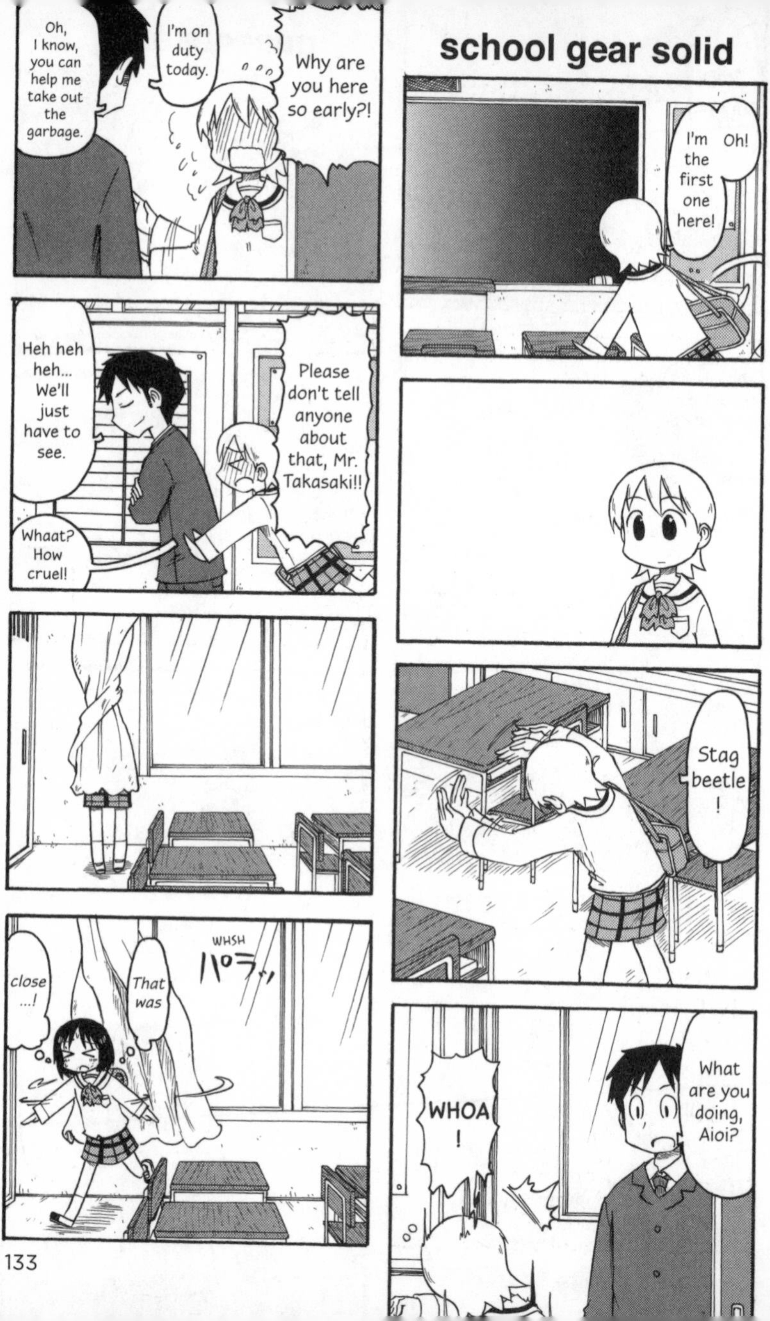
Oh!
I'm the first one here!
Stag beetle!
WHOA!
What are you doing, Aioi?
Why are you here so early?!
I'm on duty today.
Oh, I know, you can help me take out the garbage.
Please don't tell anyone about that, Mr. Takasaki!!
Heh heh heh... We'll just have to see.
Whaat? How cruel!
WHSH
パラッ
That was
close...!

peacock king

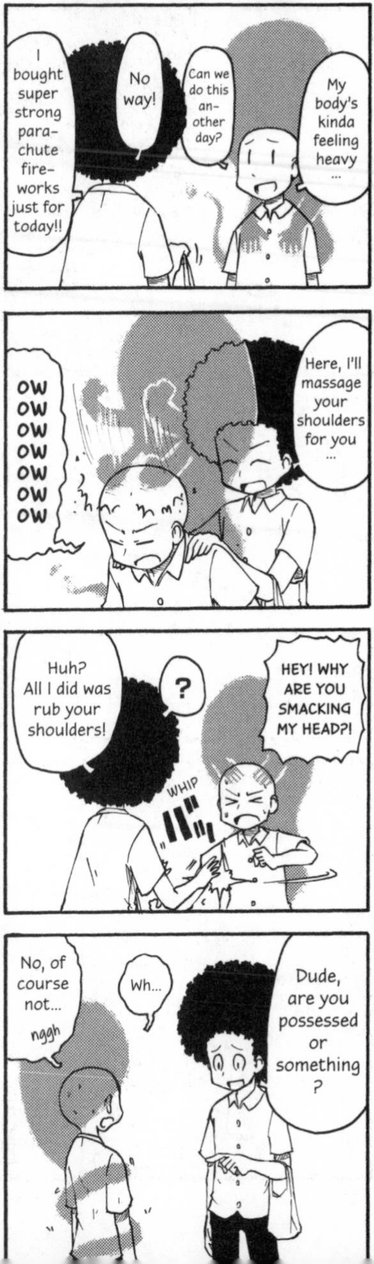
My body's kinda feeling heavy ...
Can we do this an-other day?
No way!
I bought super strong para-chute fire-works just for today!!
Here, I'll massage your shoulders for you ...
OW OW OW OW OW OW OW
HEY! WHY ARE YOU SMACKING MY HEAD?!
?
Huh? All I did was rub your shoulders!
WHIP
Dude, are you possessed or something ?
Wh...
No, of course not...
nggh

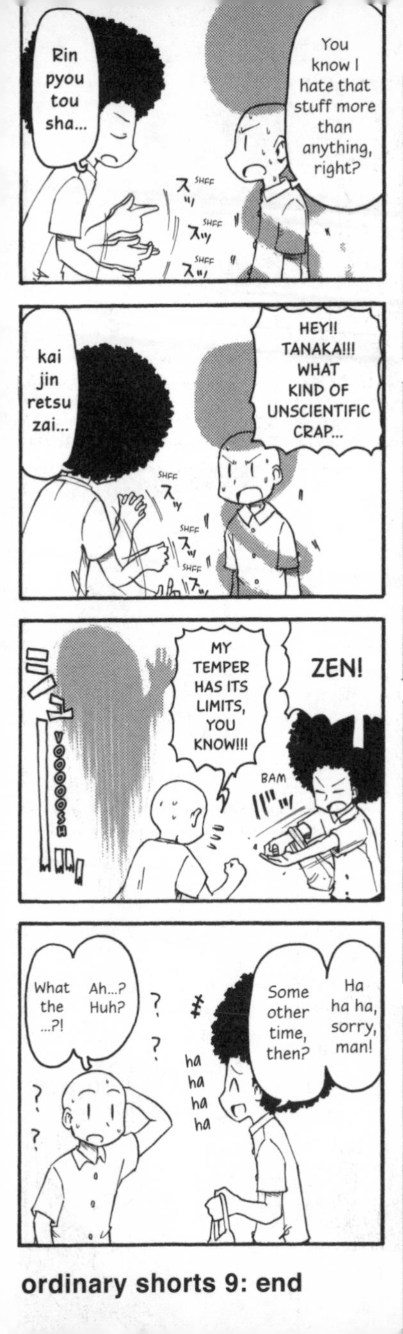
You know I hate that stuff more than anything, right?
Rin pyou tou sha...
SHFF
スッ
SHFF
スッ
SHFF
スッ
HEY!! TANAKA!!! WHAT KIND OF UNSCIENTIFIC CRAP...
kai jin retsu zai...
SHFF
スッ
SHFF
スッ
SHFF
スッ
ZEN!
MY TEMPER HAS ITS LIMITS, YOU KNOW!!!
BAM
VOOOOOOSH
Ha ha ha, sorry, man!
Some other time, then?
ha ha ha ha
Ah...? Huh?
What the ...?!
? ? ? ?

ordinary shorts 9: end

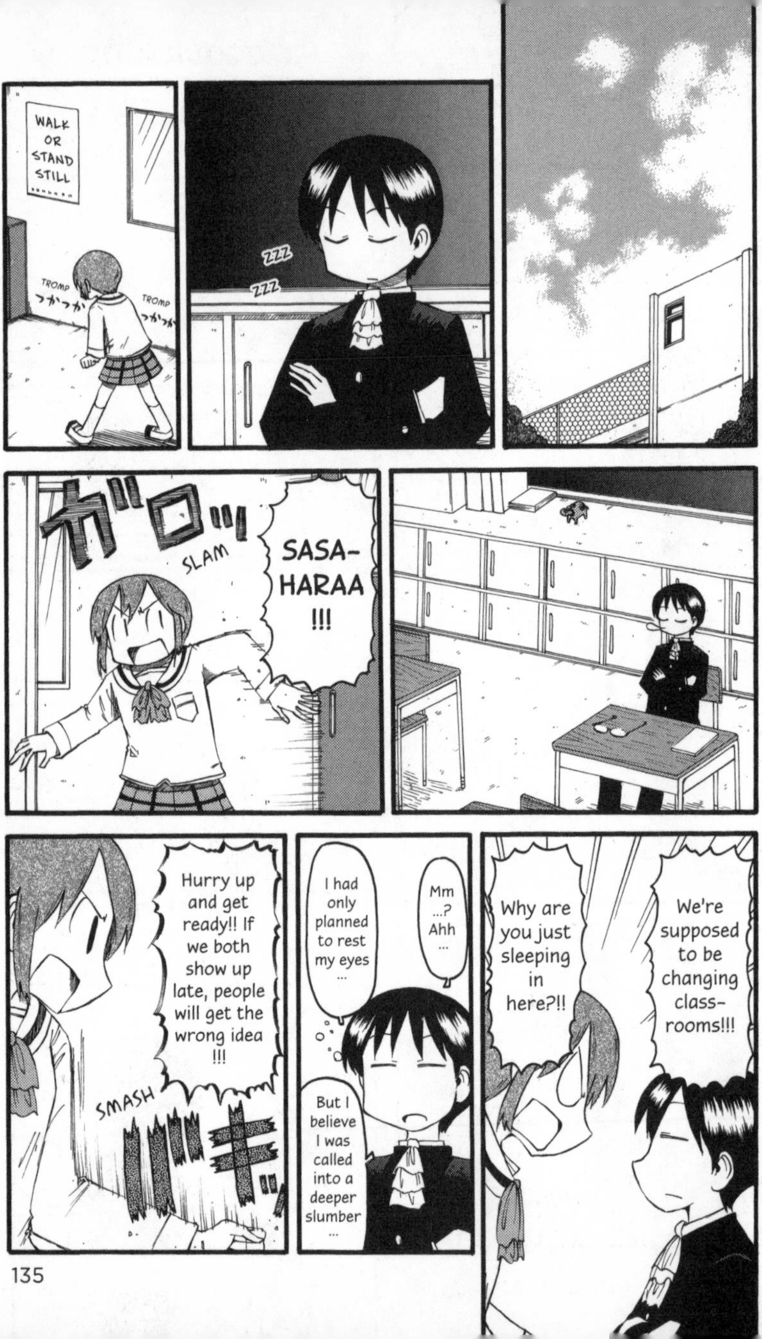
ZZZ
ZZZ
WALK OR STAND STILL
TROMP
つかつか
TROMP
つかつか
SASA-HARAA !!!
ガロッ
SLAM
We're supposed to be changing class-rooms!!!
Why are you just sleeping in here?!!
Mm ...? Ahh ...
I had only planned to rest my eyes ...
But I believe I was called into a deeper slumber ...
Hurry up and get ready!! If we both show up late, people will get the wrong idea !!!
SMASH

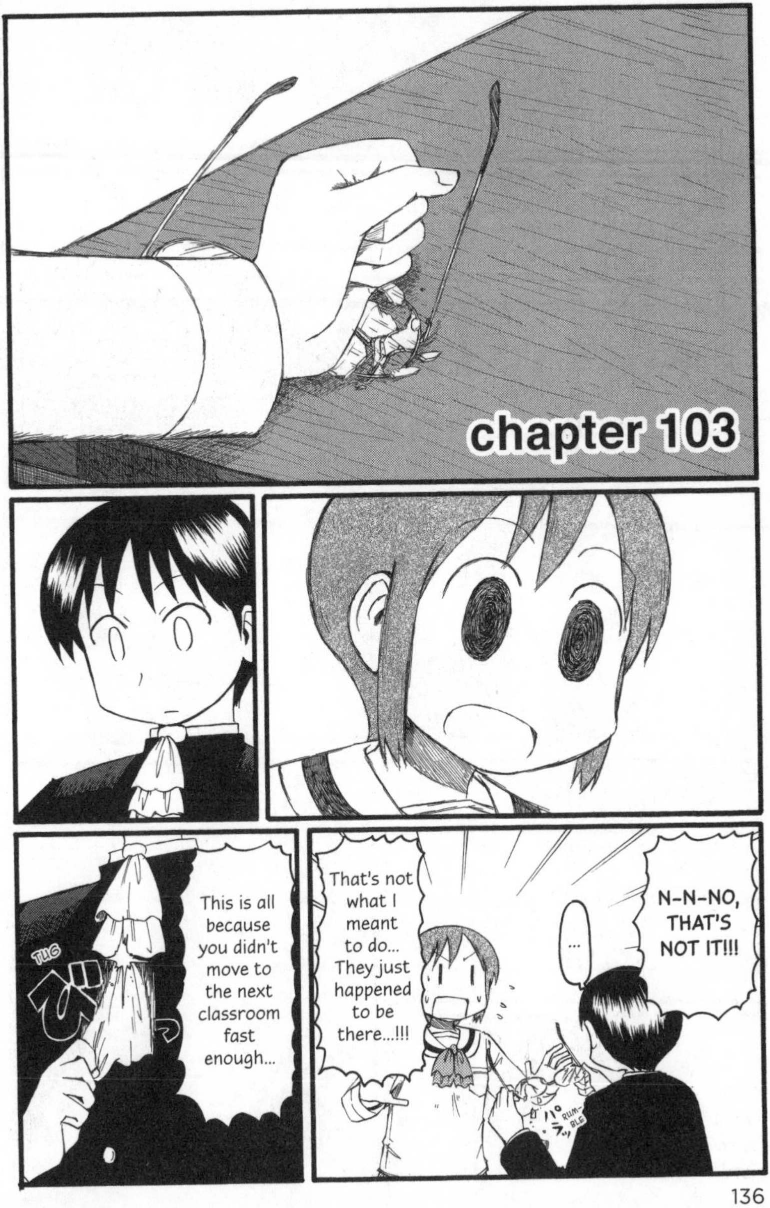
chapter 103
N-N-NO, THAT'S NOT IT!!!
...
That's not what I meant to do... They just happened to be there...!!!
RUMBLE
This is all because you didn't move to the next classroom fast enough...
TUG

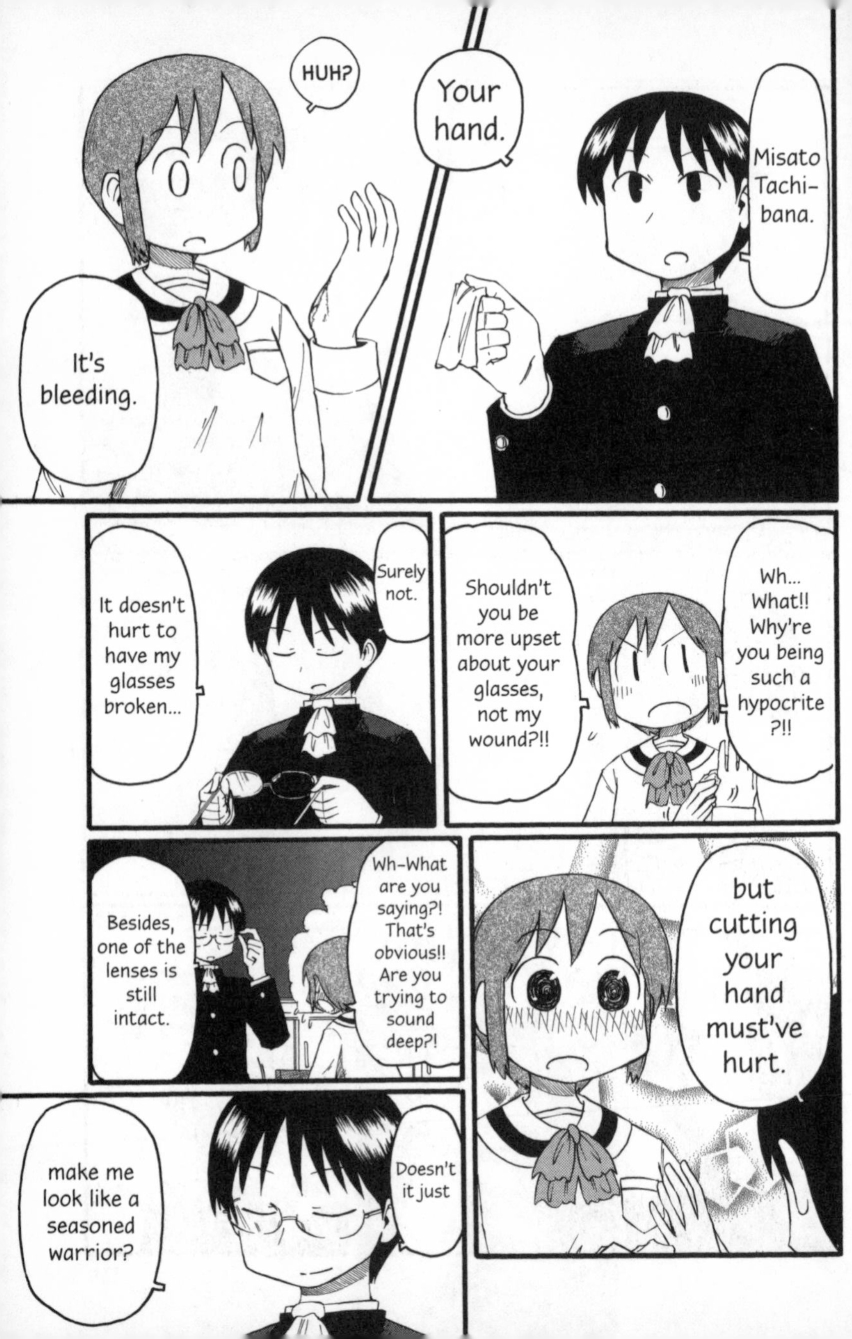
Misato Tachibana.
Your hand.
HUH?
It's bleeding.
Wh... What!! Why're you being such a hypocrite?!!
Shouldn't you be more upset about your glasses, not my wound?!!
Surely not.
It doesn't hurt to have my glasses broken...
but cutting your hand must've hurt.
Wh-What are you saying?! That's obvious!! Are you trying to sound deep?!
Besides, one of the lenses is still intact.
Doesn't it just
make me look like a seasoned warrior?

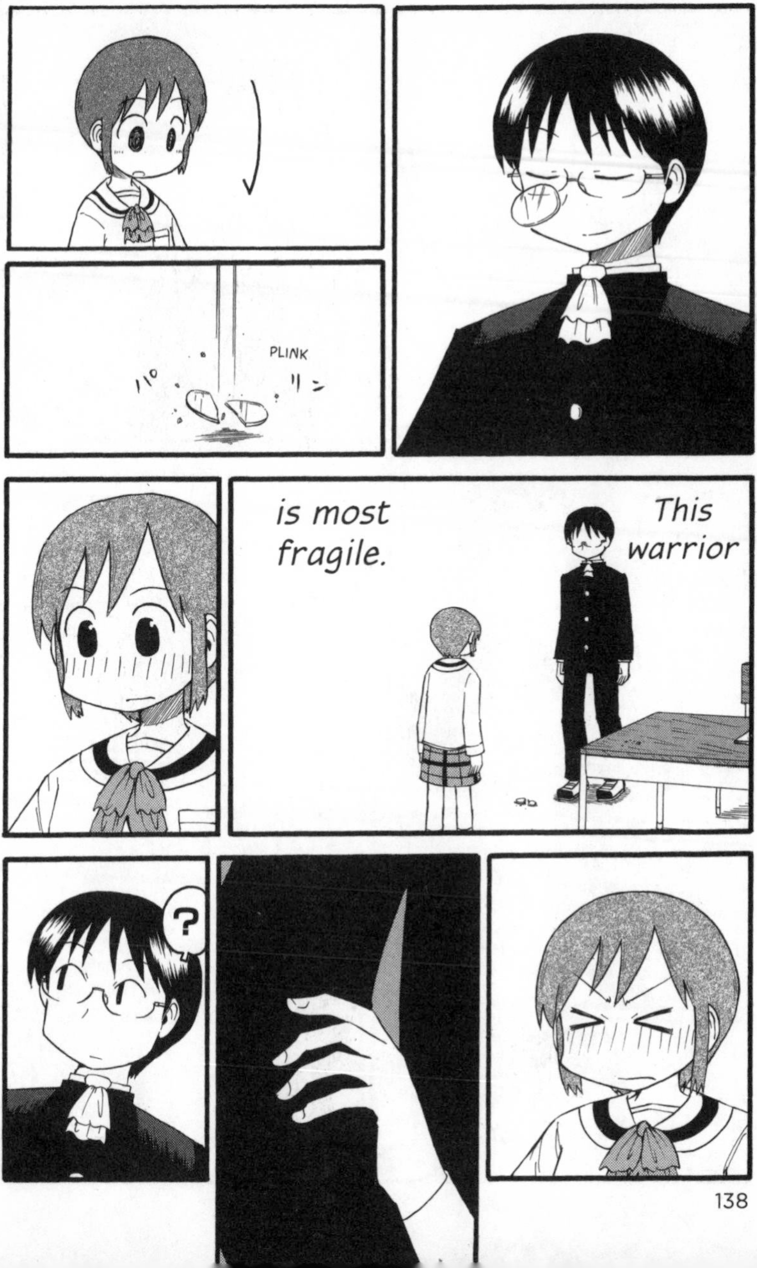
PLINK
This warrior is most fragile.
?

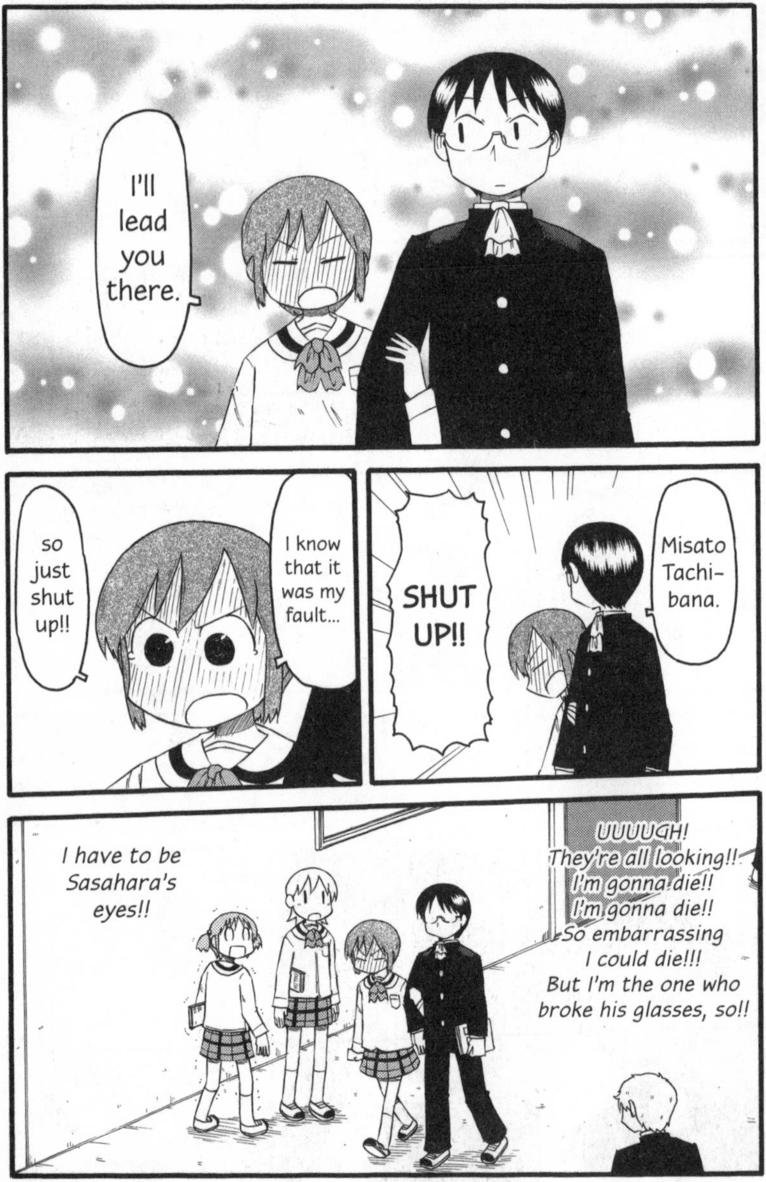
I'll lead you there.
Misato Tachibana.
SHUT UP!!
I know that it was my fault...
so just shut up!!
UUUUGH! They're all looking!! I'm gonna die!! I'm gonna die!! So embarrassing I could die!!! But I'm the one who broke his glasses, so!!
I have to be Sasahara's eyes!!

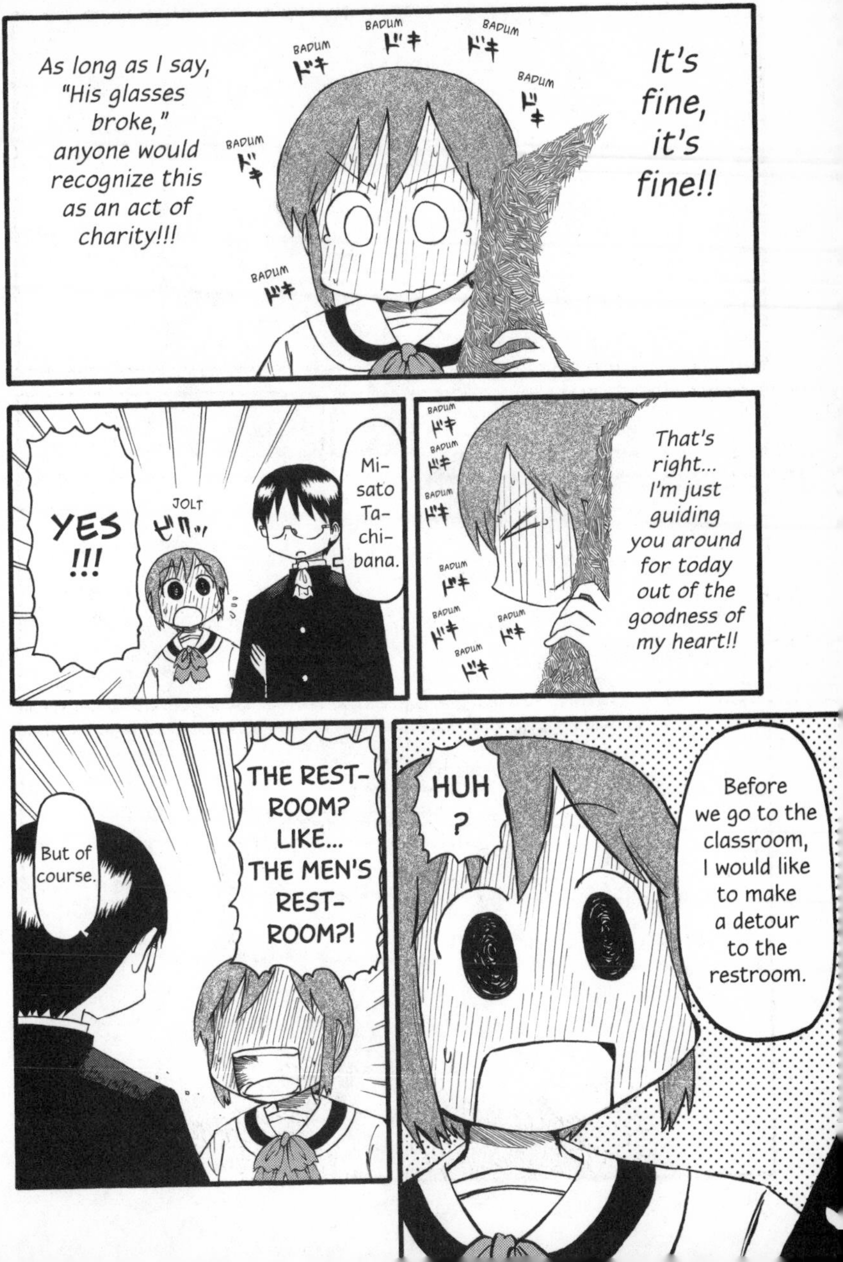
It's fine, it's fine!!
BADUM ドキ
BADUM ドキ
BADUM ドキ
BADUM ドキ
BADUM ドキ
BADUM ドキ
As long as I say, "His glasses broke," anyone would recognize this as an act of charity!!!
That's right... I'm just guiding you around for today out of the goodness of my heart!!
BADUM ドキ
BADUM ドキ
BADUM ドキ
BADUM ドキ
BADUM ドキ
BADUM ドキ
BADUM ドキ
Mi-sato Ta-chi-bana.
JOLT ビクッ
YES !!!
Before we go to the classroom, I would like to make a detour to the restroom.
HUH ?
THE REST-ROOM? LIKE... THE MEN'S REST-ROOM?!
But of course.

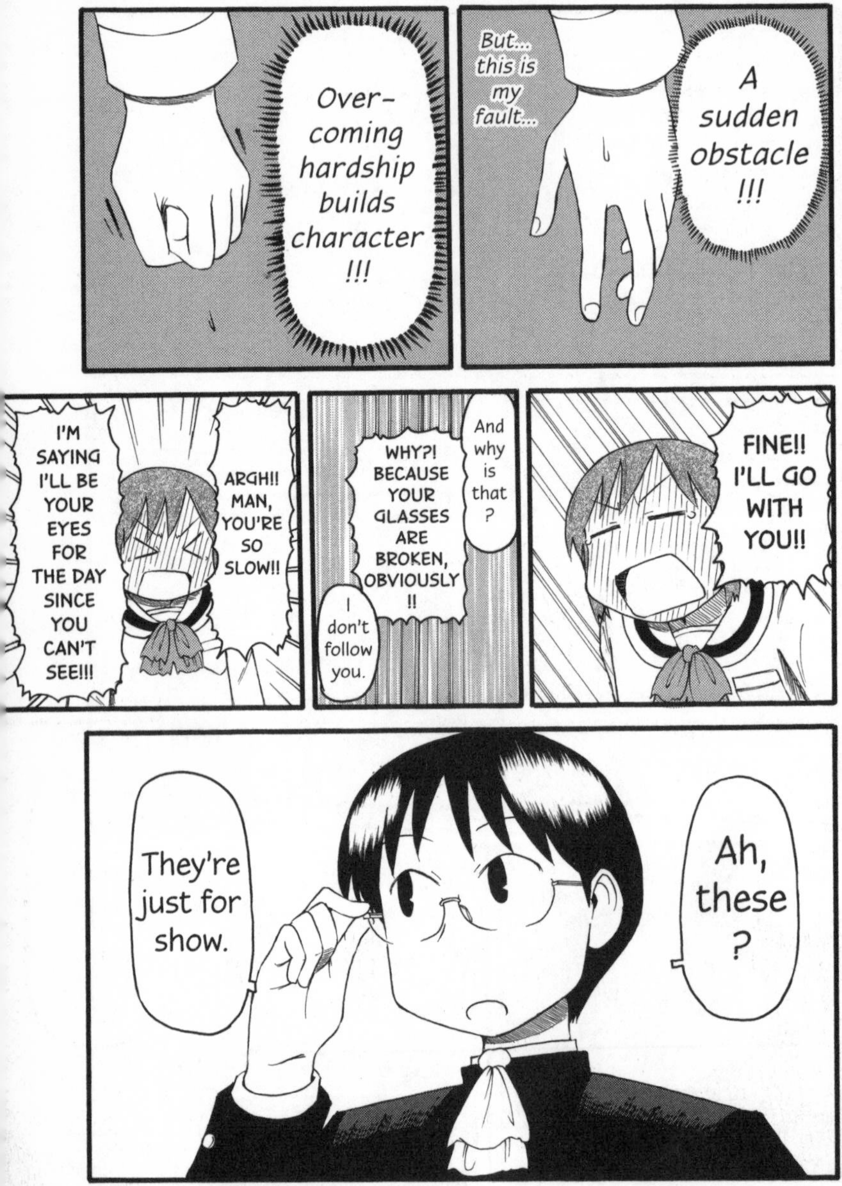
A sudden obstacle!!!
But... this is my fault...
Over-coming hardship builds character!!!
FINE!! I'LL GO WITH YOU!!
And why is that?
WHY?! BECAUSE YOUR GLASSES ARE BROKEN, OBVIOUSLY!!
I don't follow you.
ARGH!! MAN, YOU'RE SO SLOW!!
I'M SAYING I'LL BE YOUR EYES FOR THE DAY SINCE YOU CAN'T SEE!!!
Ah, these?
They're just for show.

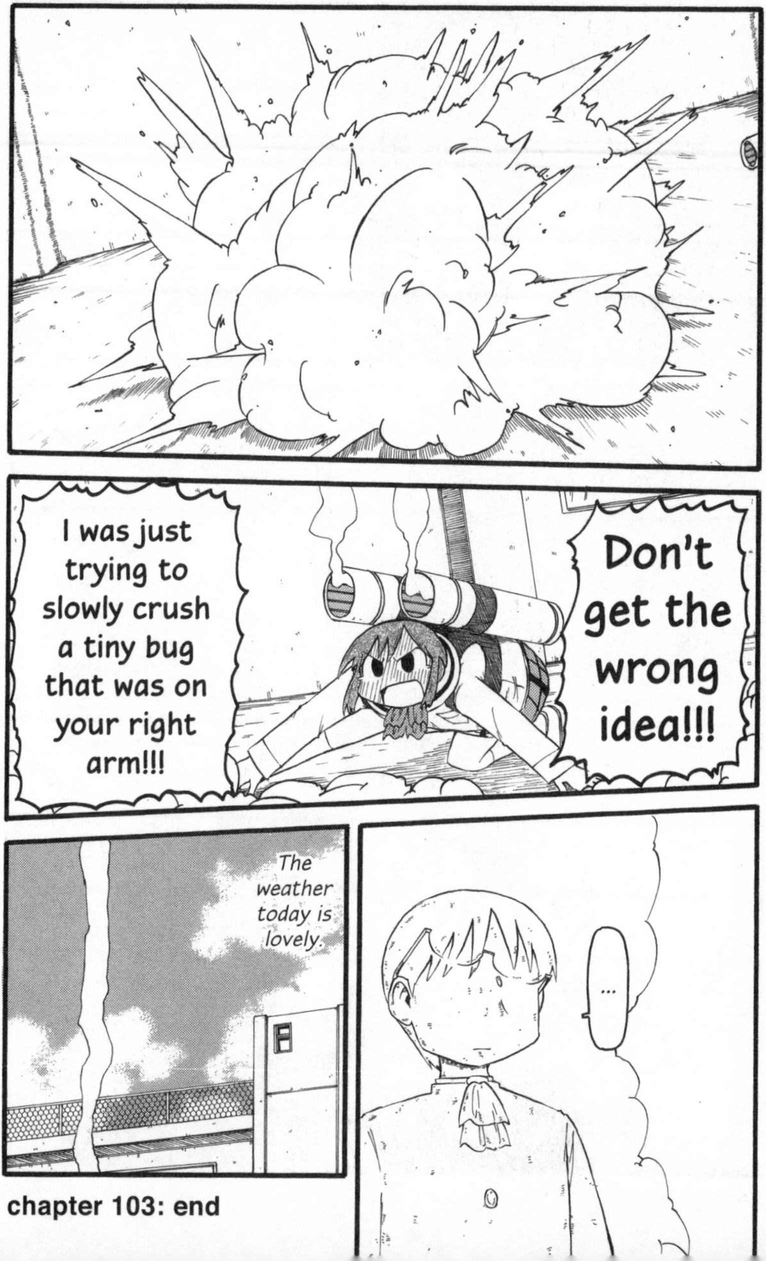
Don't get the wrong idea!!!
I was just trying to slowly crush a tiny bug that was on your right arm!!!
...
The weather today is lovely.

chapter 103: end

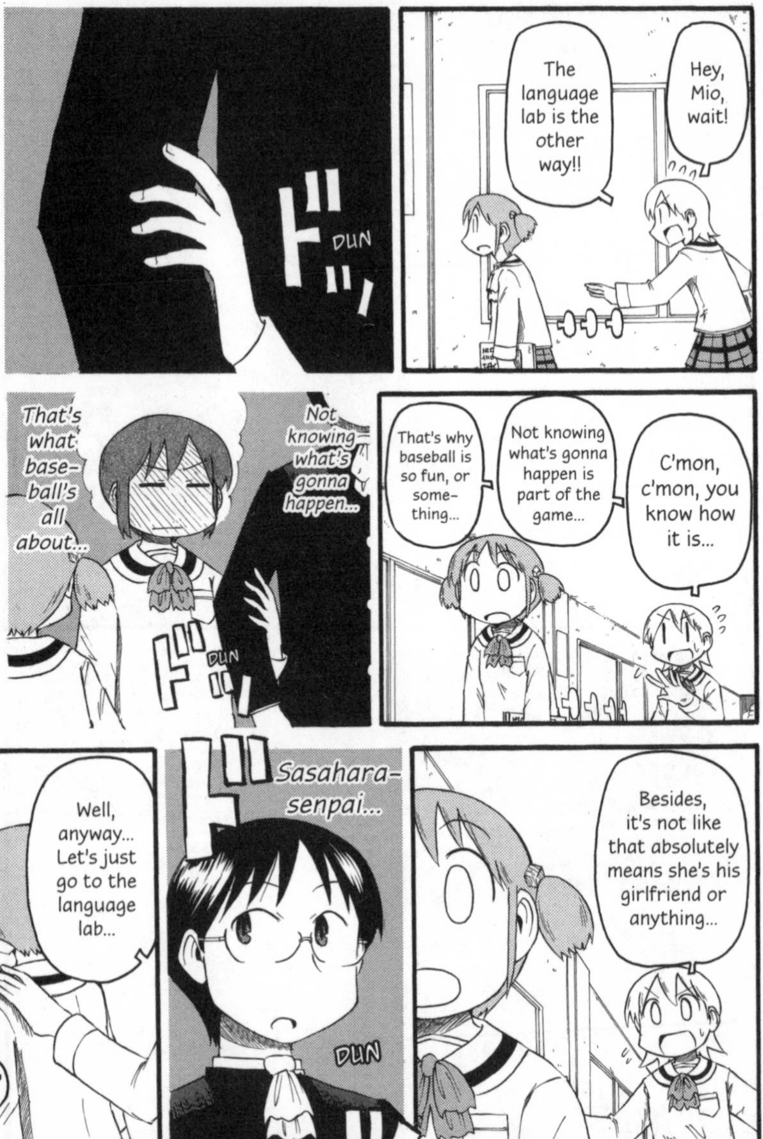
Hey, Mio, wait!
The language lab is the other way!!
DUN
C'mon, c'mon, you know how it is...
Not knowing what's gonna happen is part of the game...
That's why baseball is so fun, or some-thing...
Not knowing what's gonna happen...
That's what base-ball's all about...
DUN
Besides, it's not like that absolutely means she's his girlfriend or anything...
Sasahara-senpai...
DUN
Well, anyway... Let's just go to the language lab...
PAT

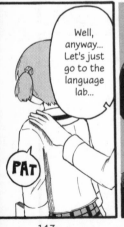

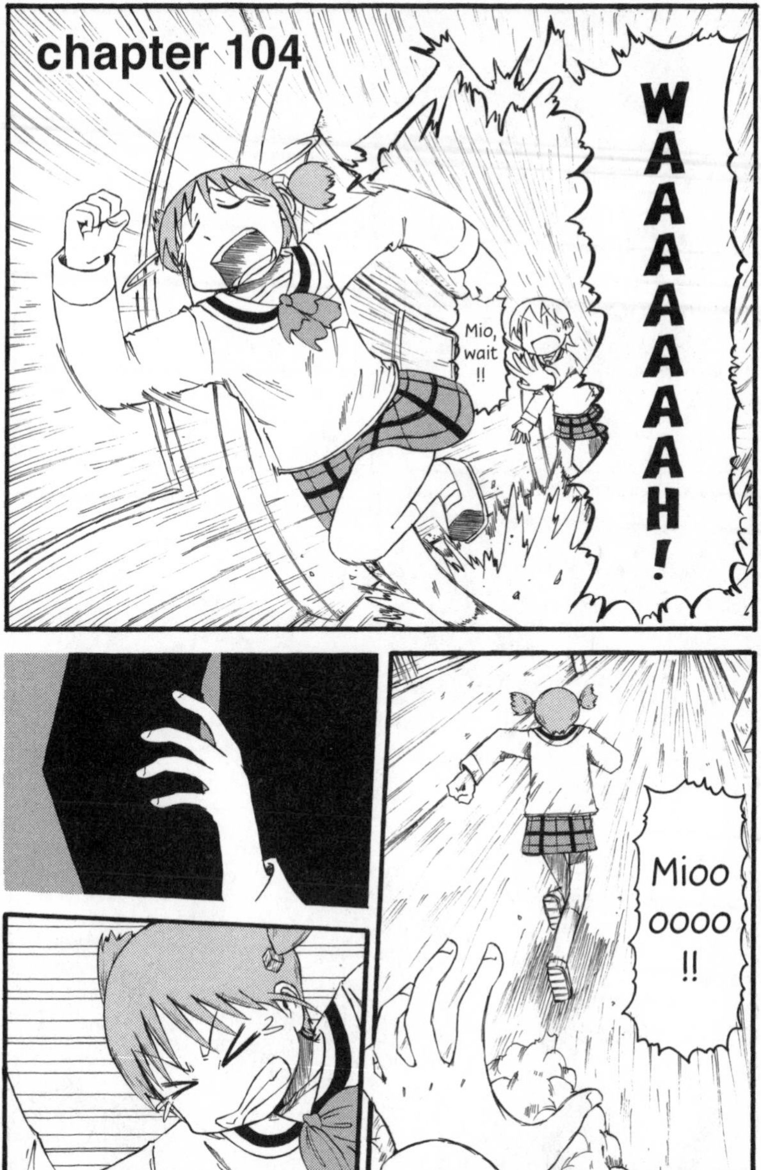
chapter 104
WAAAAAAAAH!
Mio, wait !!
Mioo oooo !!

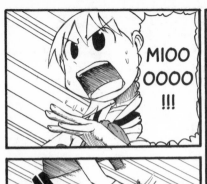

MIOO OOOO !!!

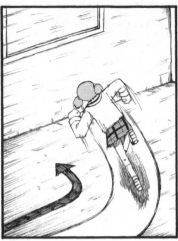

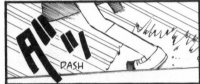

DASH

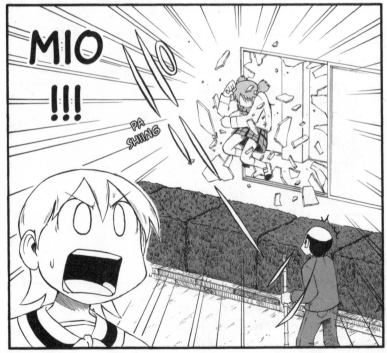

MIO !!!

PA SHING

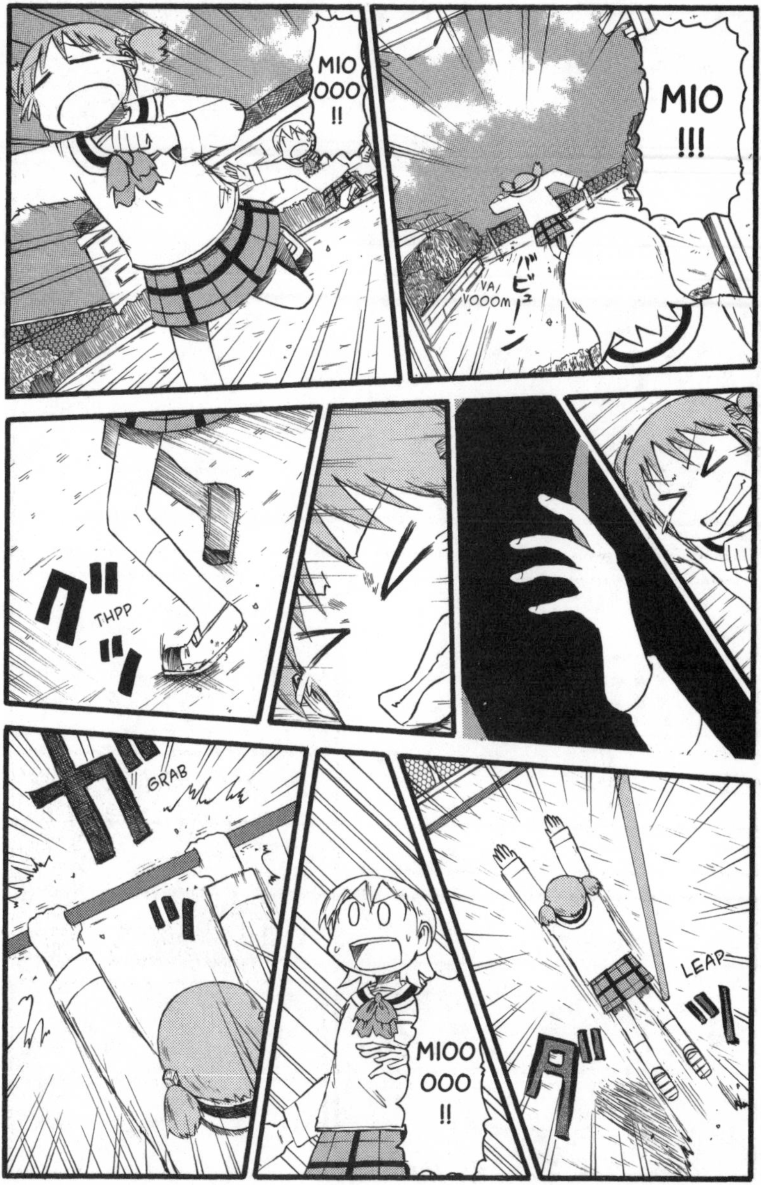
MIO !!!
VA VOOOM
MIO OOO !!
THPP
LEAP
MIOO OOO !!
GRAB

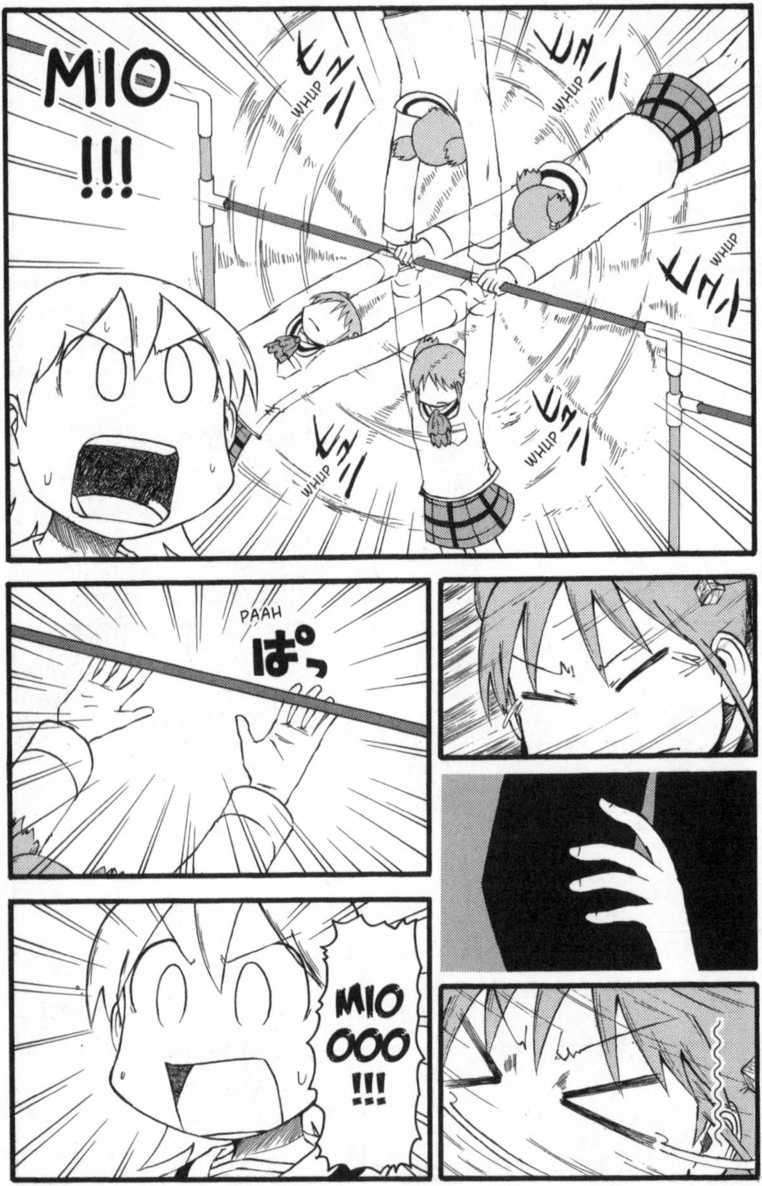
MIO
!!!
WHUP
WHUP
WHUP
WHUP
WHUP
PA'AH
ぱっ
MIO
OOO
!!!

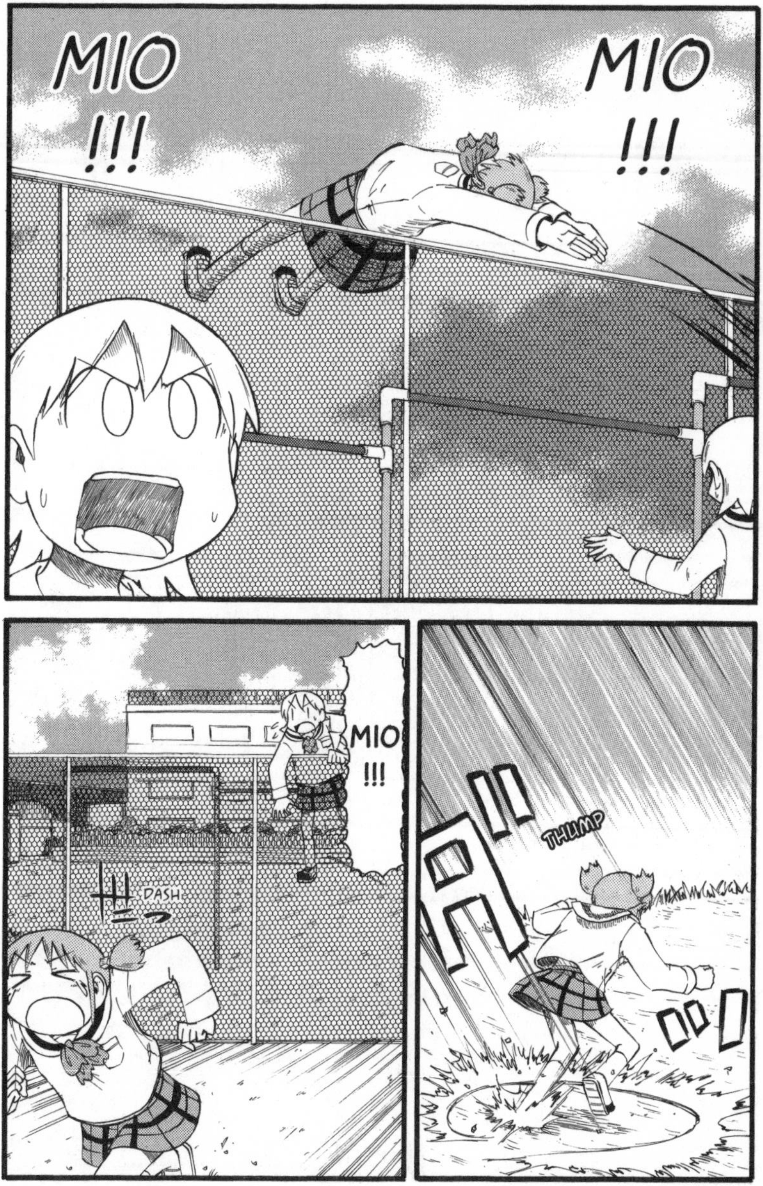
MIO !!!
MIO !!!
THUMP
MIO !!!
DASH

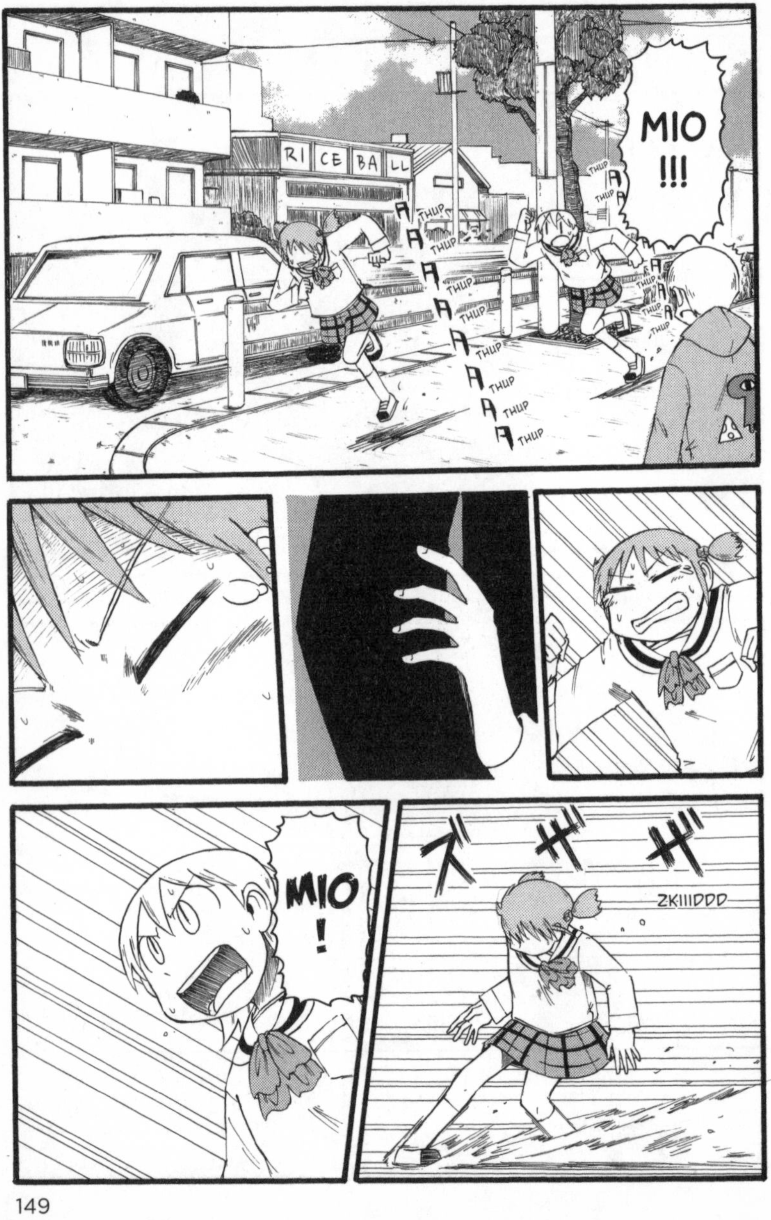
MIO !!!
THUP THUP THUP THUP THUP THUP THUP THUP THUP THUP THUP
RI CE BA LL
ズ ザ ザ
ZKIIIDDD
MIO !

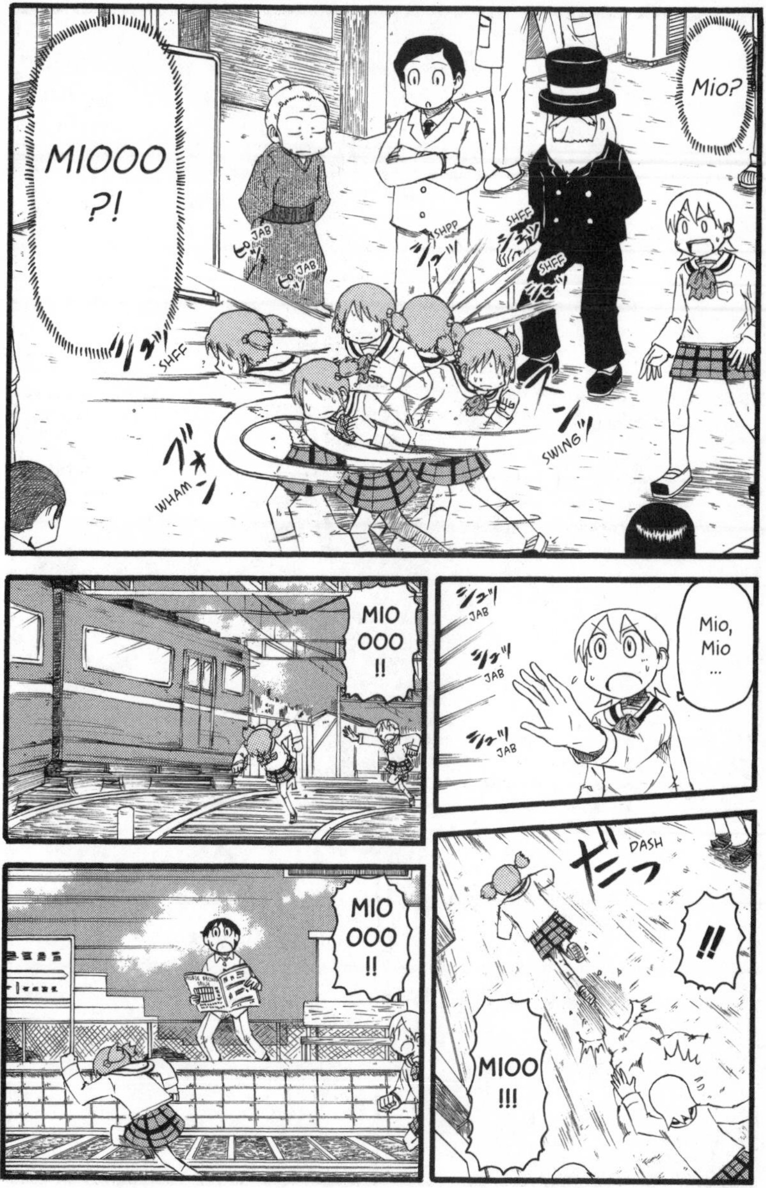
Mio?
SHFF
SHFF
SHPP
SWING
JAB
JAB
SHFF
WHAM
MIOOO ?!
JAB
JAB
JAB
Mio, Mio ...
MIO OOO !!
DASH
!!
MIOO !!!
MIO OOO !!

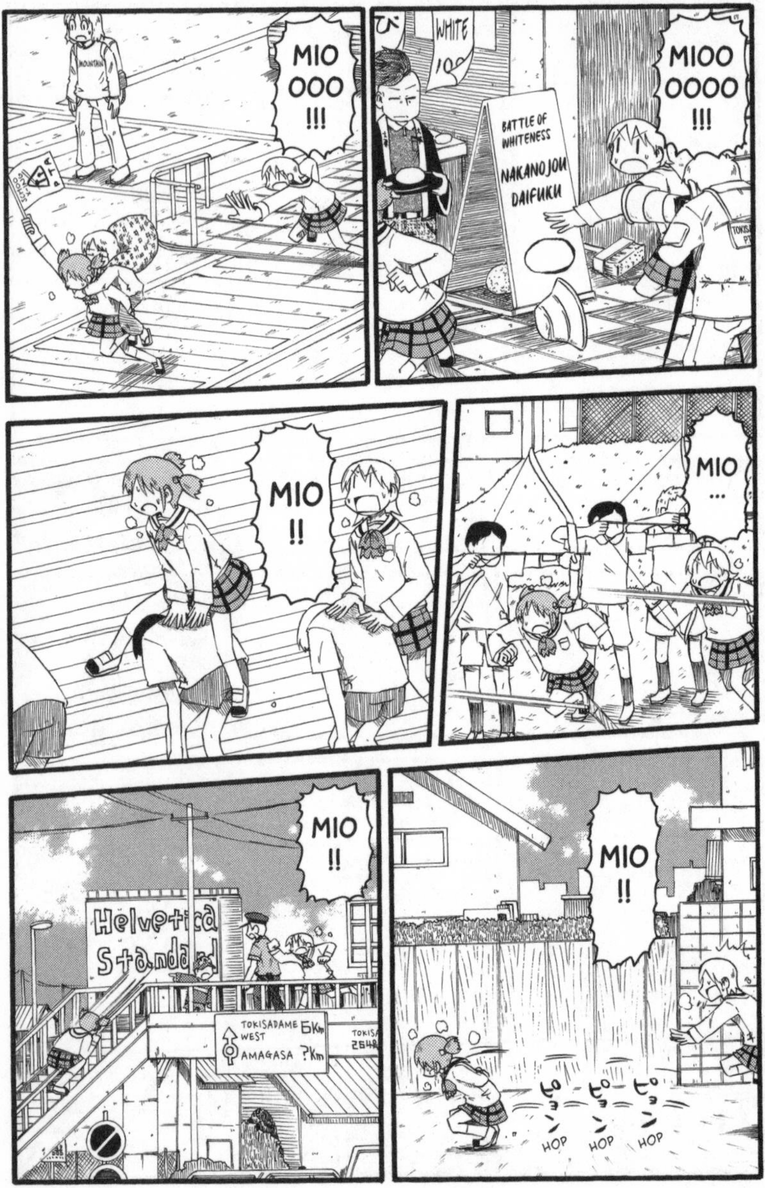
MIOO OOOO !!!
WHITE
BATTLE OF WHITENESS NAKANOJOU DAIFUKU
MIO OOO !!!
MIO ...
MIO !!
MIO !!
ピョン HOP
ピョン HOP
ピョン HOP
MIO !!
Helvetica Standard
TOKISADAME WEST 6Km
AMAGASA ?Km

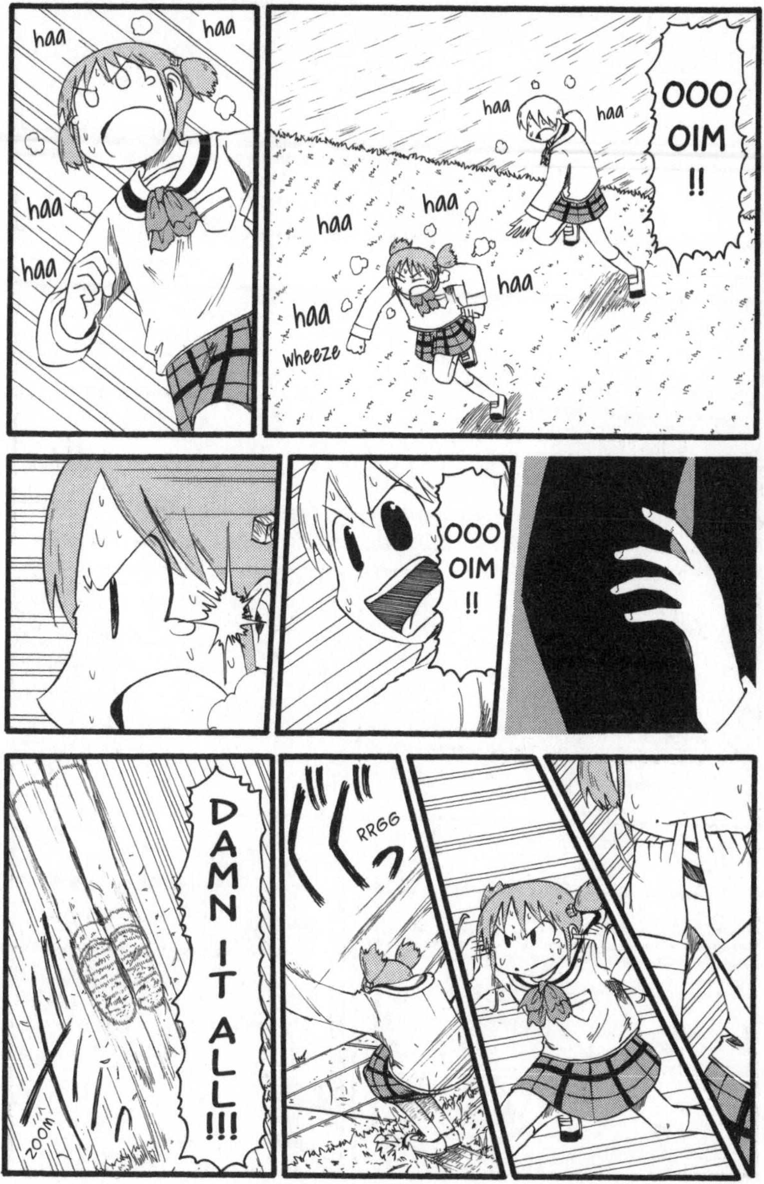
OOO OIM !!
haa
haa
haa
haa
haa
haa
wheeze
haa
haa
haa
haa
OOO OIM !!
RRGG
DAMN IT ALL!!!
ZOOM

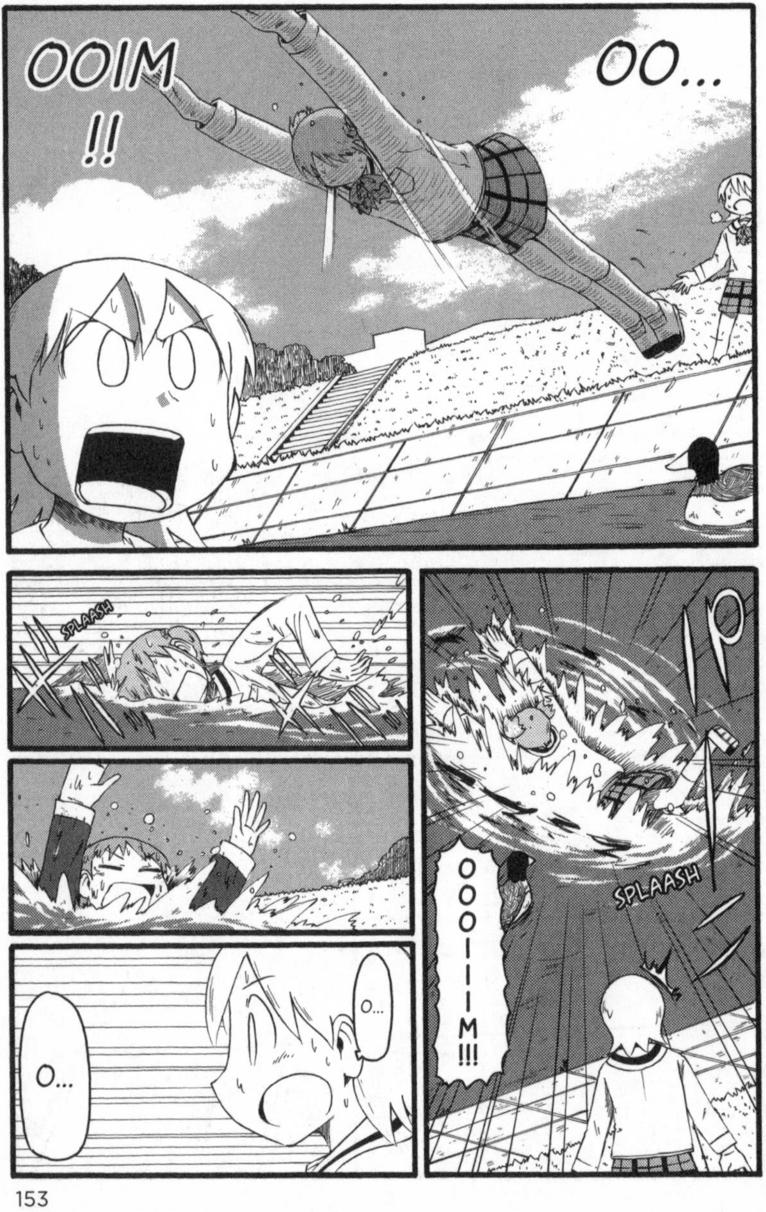
OO...
OOIM !!
OOOIIIIM!!!
SPLAASH
SPLAASH
O...
O...

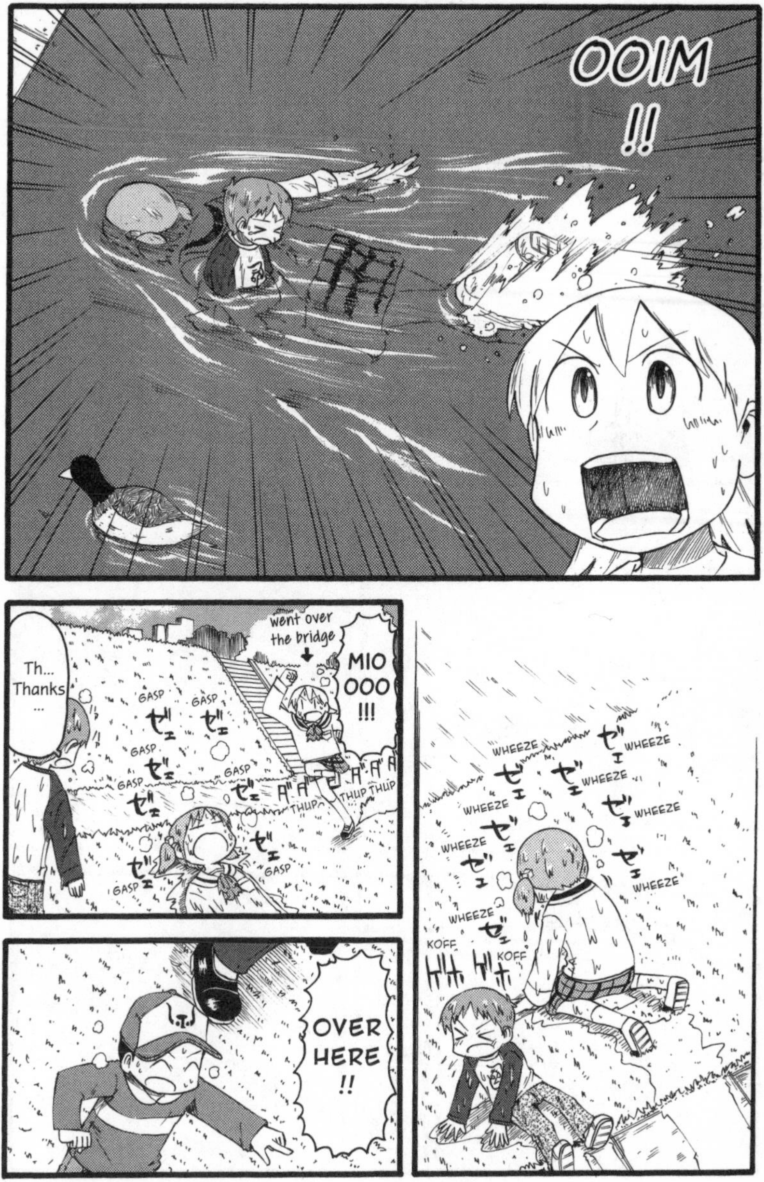
OOIM
!!
WHEEZE ゼェ
WHEEZE ゼェ
WHEEZE ゼェ
WHEEZE ゼェ
WHEEZE ゼェ
WHEEZE ゼェ
WHEEZE ゼェ
WHEEZE ゼェ
KOFF ゲホ
KOFF ゲホ
went over the bridge
MIO OOO !!!
THUP THUP
THUP
GASP ゼェ
GASP ゼェ
GASP ゼェ
GASP ゼェ
GASP ゼェ
GASP ゼェ
GASP ゼェ
Th... Thanks ...
OVER HERE !!

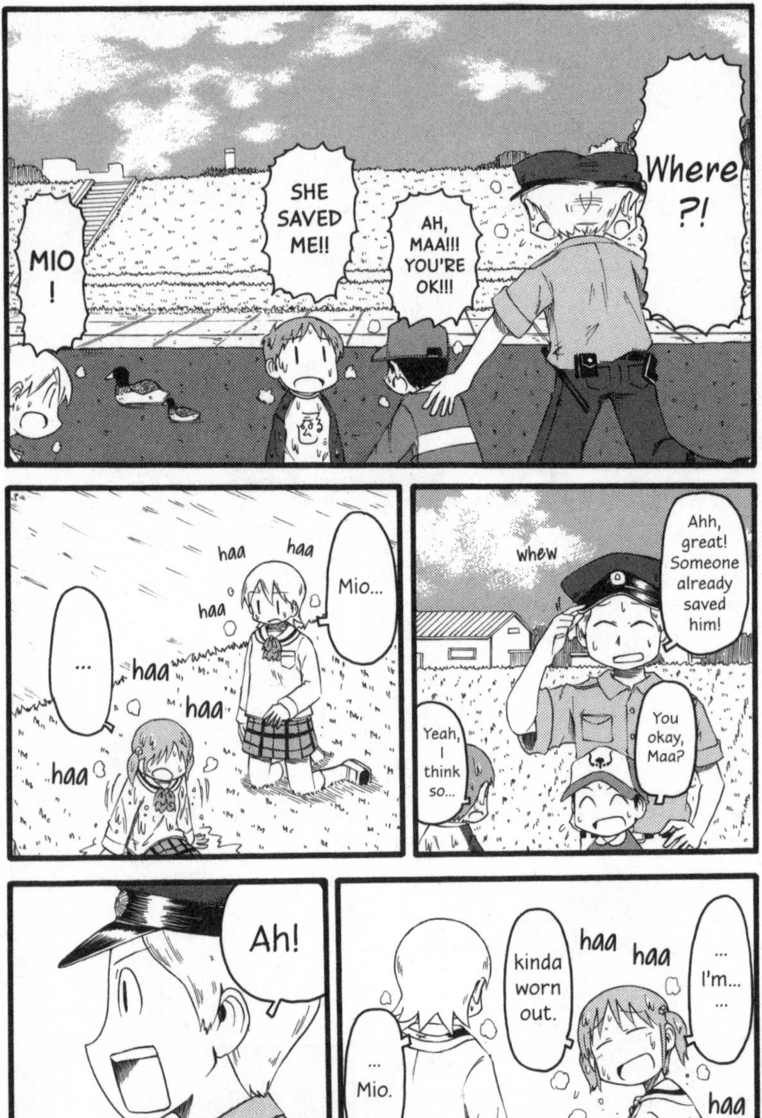
Where?!
AH, MAA!!! YOU'RE OK!!!
SHE SAVED ME!!
MIO!
Ahh, great! Someone already saved him!
whew
You okay, Maa?
Yeah, I think so...
Mio...
haa haa
haa
...
haa
haa
haa
... I'm... ...
haa haa
kinda worn out.
... Mio.
haa
Ah!

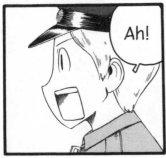

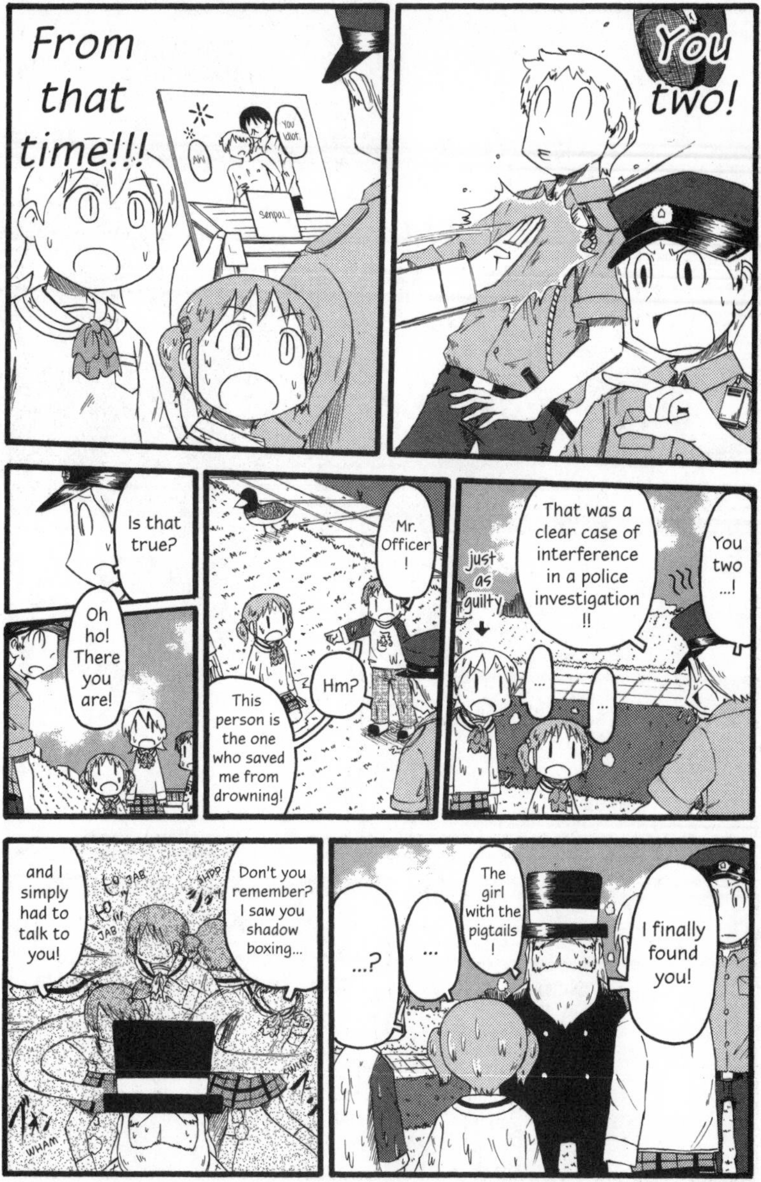
You two!
From that time!!!
You idiot.
Ah!
Senpai...
I...
You two ...!
That was a clear case of interference in a police investigation !!
just as guilty
...
...
Mr. Officer !
Hm?
This person is the one who saved me from drowning!
Is that true?
Oh ho! There you are!
I finally found you!
The girl with the pigtails !
...
...?
Don't you remember? I saw you shadow boxing...
and I simply had to talk to you!
JAB
SHPP
JAB
SWING
WHAM

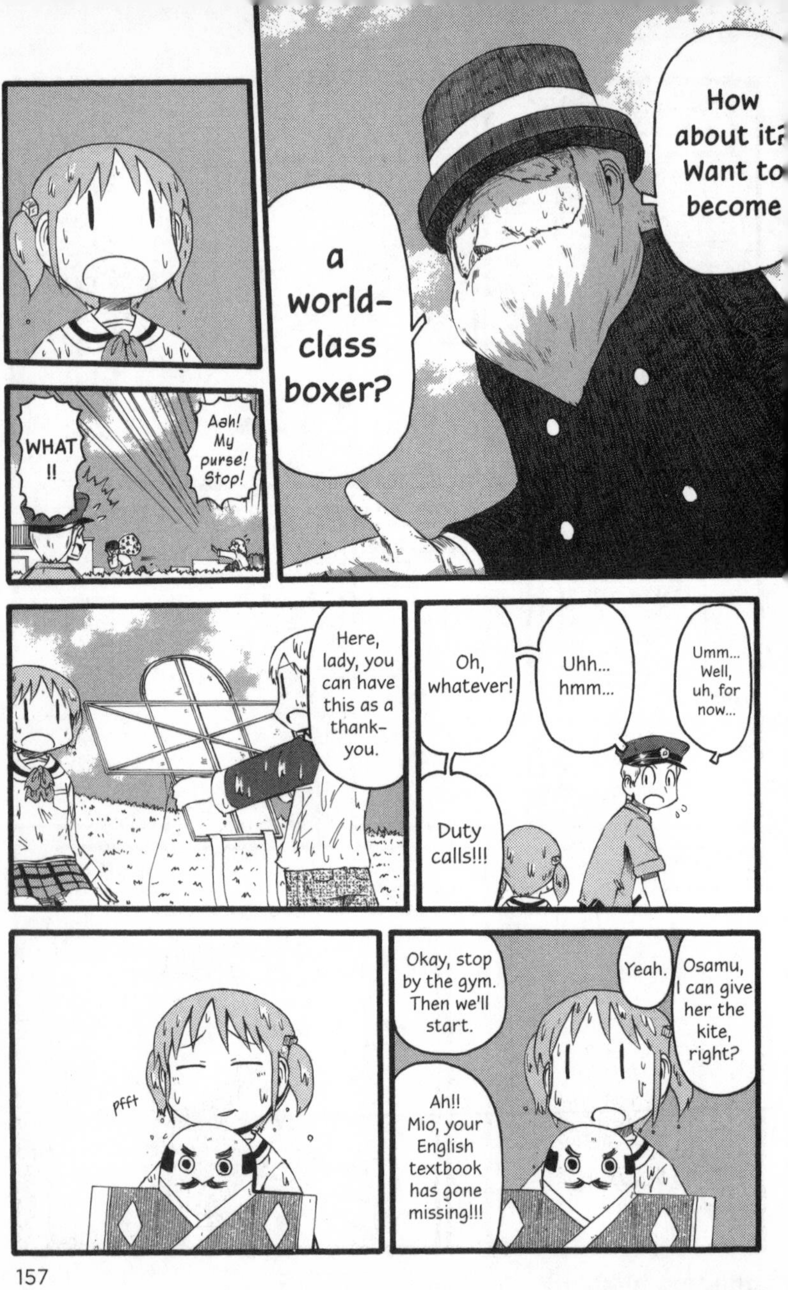
How about it? Want to become
a world-class boxer?
Aah! My purse! Stop!
WHAT !!
Umm... Well, uh, for now...
Uhh... hmm...
Oh, whatever!
Duty calls!!!
Here, lady, you can have this as a thank-you.
Osamu, I can give her the kite, right?
Yeah.
Okay, stop by the gym. Then we'll start.
Ah!! Mio, your English textbook has gone missing!!!
pfft

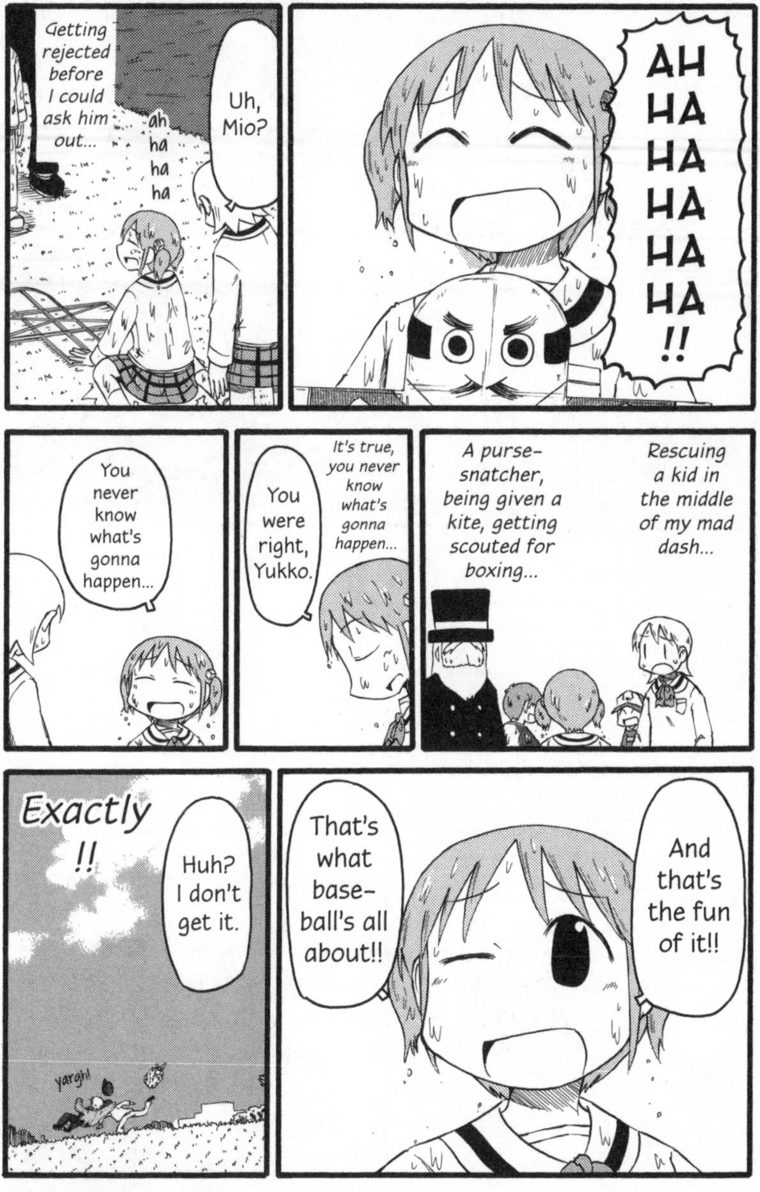
AH HA HA HA HA HA HA !!
Uh, Mio?
ah ha ha ha
Getting rejected before I could ask him out...
Rescuing a kid in the middle of my mad dash...
A purse-snatcher, being given a kite, getting scouted for boxing...
It's true, you never know what's gonna happen...
You were right, Yukko.
You never know what's gonna happen...
And that's the fun of it!!
That's what base-ball's all about!!
Huh? I don't get it.
Exactly !!
yargh!

chapter 104: end

chapter 105

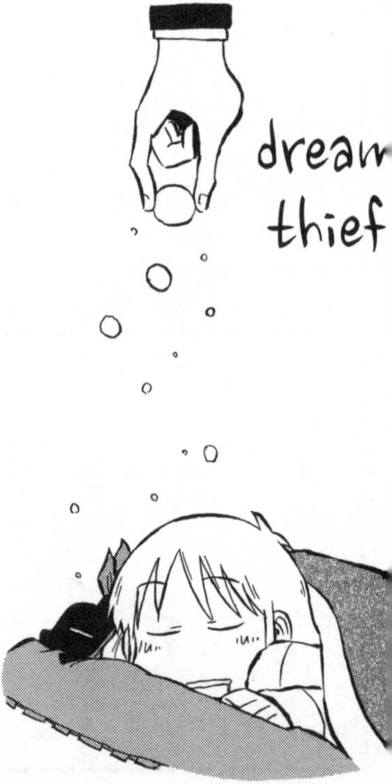
dream thief

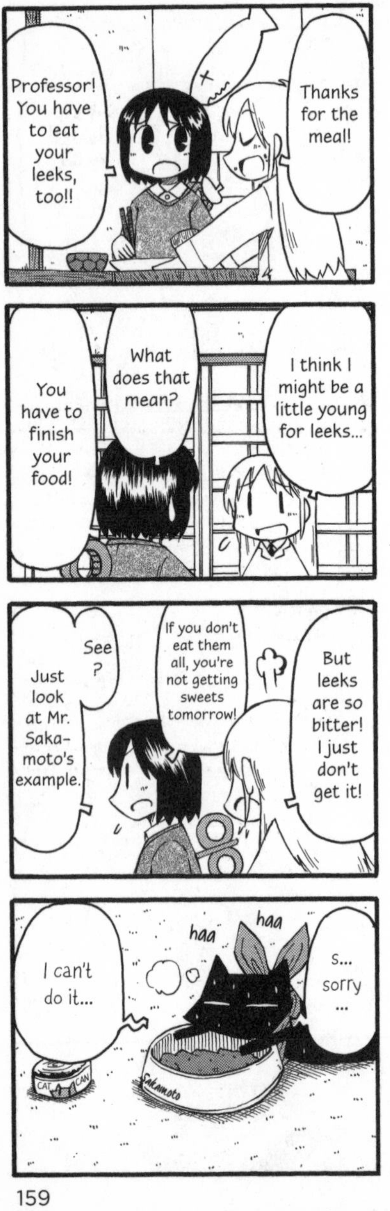
Thanks for the meal!
Professor! You have to eat your leeks, too!!
I think I might be a little young for leeks...
What does that mean?
You have to finish your food!
But leeks are so bitter! I just don't get it!
If you don't eat them all, you're not getting sweets tomorrow!
See?
Just look at Mr. Sakamoto's example.
haa
haa
S... sorry ...
I can't do it...
CAT CAN
Sakamoto

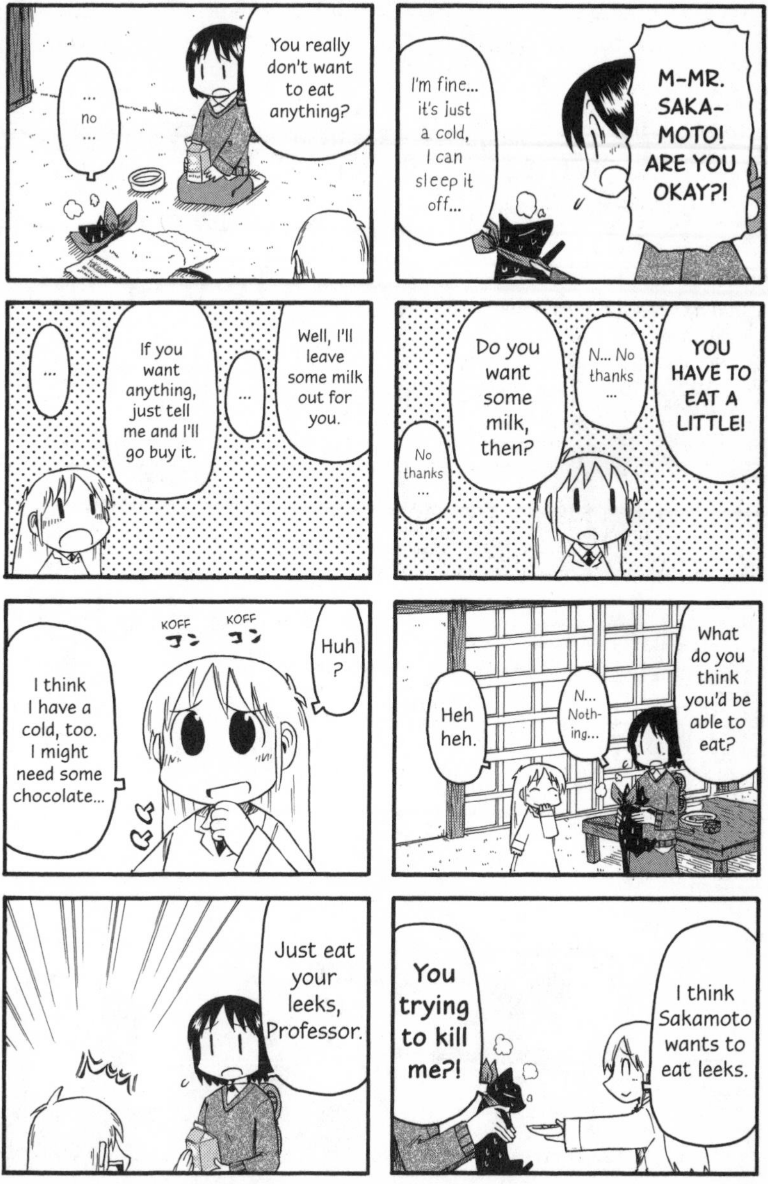
M-MR. SAKAMOTO! ARE YOU OKAY?!
I'm fine... it's just a cold, I can sleep it off...
You really don't want to eat anything?
... no ...
YOU HAVE TO EAT A LITTLE!
N... No thanks ...
Do you want some milk, then?
No thanks ...
Well, I'll leave some milk out for you.
...
If you want anything, just tell me and I'll go buy it.
...
What do you think you'd be able to eat?
N... Nothing...
Heh heh.
Huh?
KOFF コン KOFF コン
I think I have a cold, too. I might need some chocolate...
I think Sakamoto wants to eat leeks.
You trying to kill me?!
Just eat your leeks, Professor.

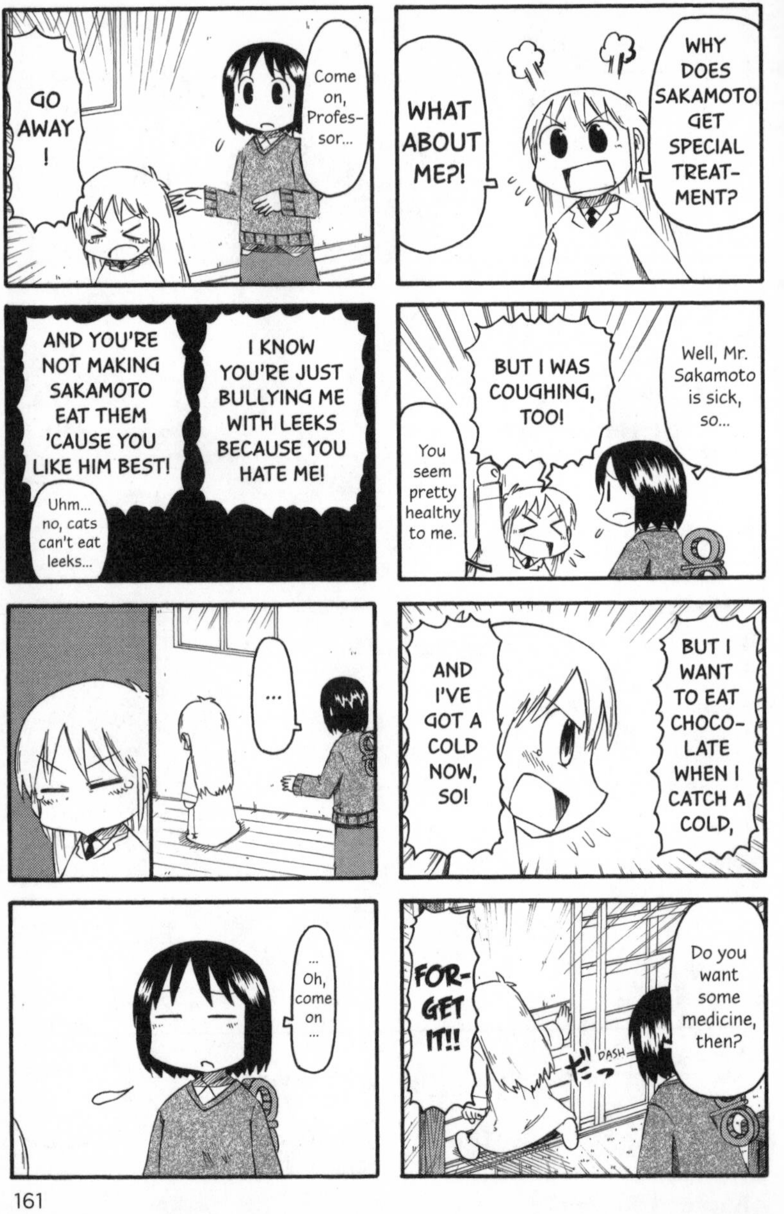
WHY DOES SAKAMOTO GET SPECIAL TREATMENT?
WHAT ABOUT ME?!
Well, Mr. Sakamoto is sick, so...
BUT I WAS COUGHING, TOO!
You seem pretty healthy to me.
BUT I WANT TO EAT CHOCOLATE WHEN I CATCH A COLD,
AND I'VE GOT A COLD NOW, SO!
Do you want some medicine, then?
FORGET IT!!
DASH
Come on, Professor...
GO AWAY!
I KNOW YOU'RE JUST BULLYING ME WITH LEEKS BECAUSE YOU HATE ME!
AND YOU'RE NOT MAKING SAKAMOTO EAT THEM 'CAUSE YOU LIKE HIM BEST!
Uhm... no, cats can't eat leeks...
...
... Oh, come on ...

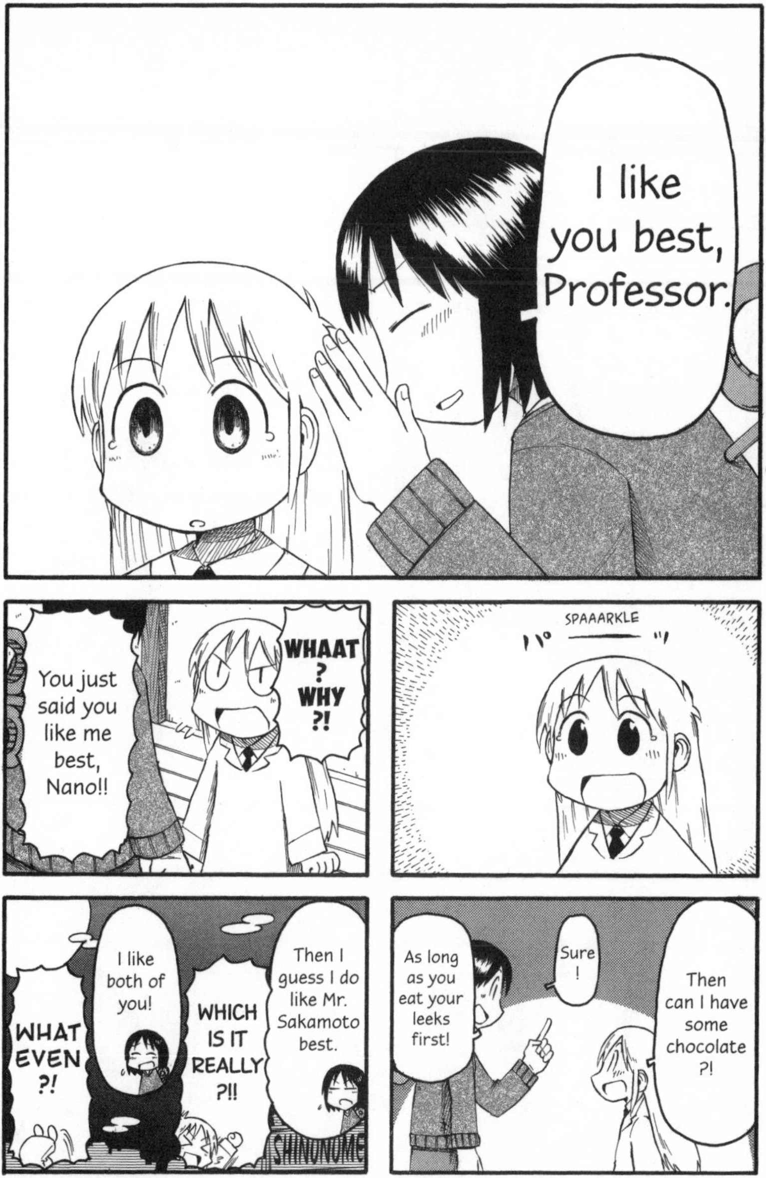
I like you best, Professor.
SPAAARKLE
WHAAT? WHY?!
You just said you like me best, Nano!!
Then can I have some chocolate?!
Sure!
As long as you eat your leeks first!
Then I guess I do like Mr. Sakamoto best.
WHICH IS IT REALLY?!!
I like both of you!
WHAT EVEN?!
SHINONOME

chapter 105: end

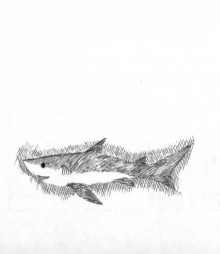

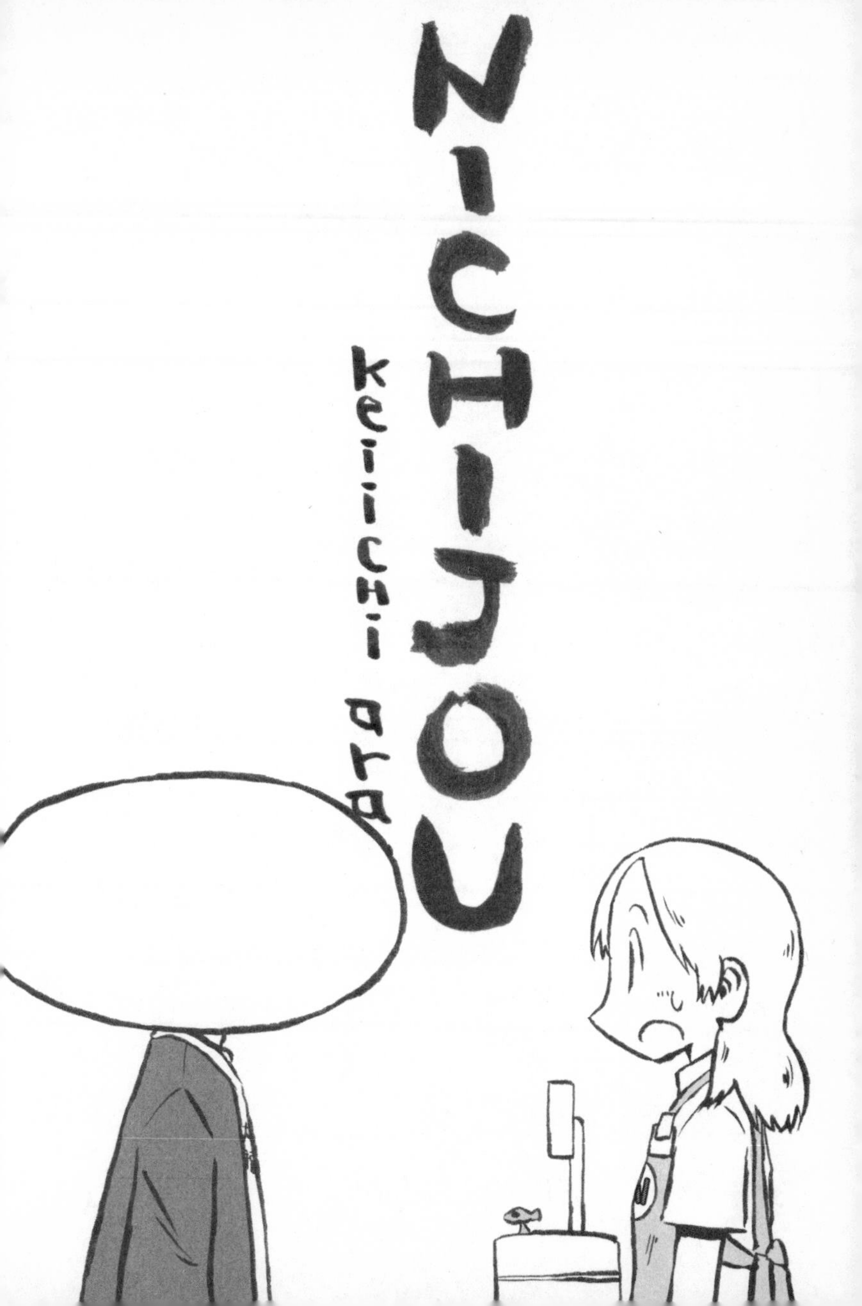
NICHIJOU
keiichi arai

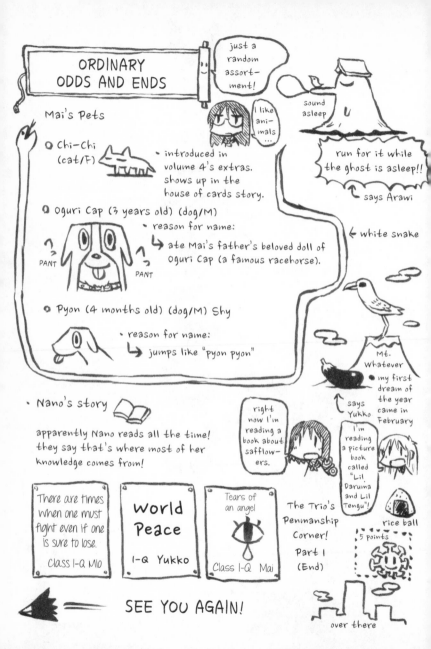

ORDINARY ODDS AND ENDS

just a random assortment!

I like animals...

sound asleep

run for it while the ghost is asleep!!

says Arawi

← white snake

Mai's Pets

O Chi-Chi (cat/F)
- introduced in volume 4's extras. shows up in the house of cards story.

O Oguri Cap (3 years old) (dog/M)
PANT   PANT
- reason for name:
  ↳ ate Mai's father's beloved doll of Oguri Cap (a famous racehorse).

O Pyon (4 months old) (dog/M) Shy
- reason for name:
  ↳ jumps like "pyon pyon"

Mt. Whatever
- my first dream of the year came in February
says Yukko

Nano's story
apparently Nano reads all the time! they say that's where most of her knowledge comes from!

right now I'm reading a book about safflowers.

I'm reading a picture book called "Lil Daruma and Lil Tengu"!

rice ball

There are times when one must fight even if one is sure to lose.
Class 1-Q Mio

World Peace
1-Q Yukko

Tears of an angel
Class 1-Q Mai

The Trio's Penmanship Corner! Part 1 (End)

5 points

SEE YOU AGAIN!

over there

NICHIJOU

keiichi arawi

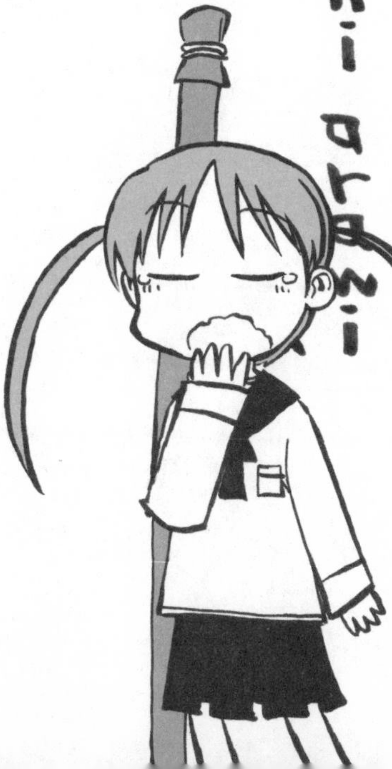

NICHIJOU (6)

this and that

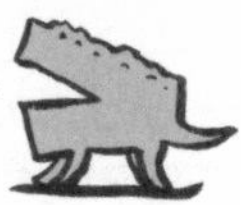

- **the river bank of youth**

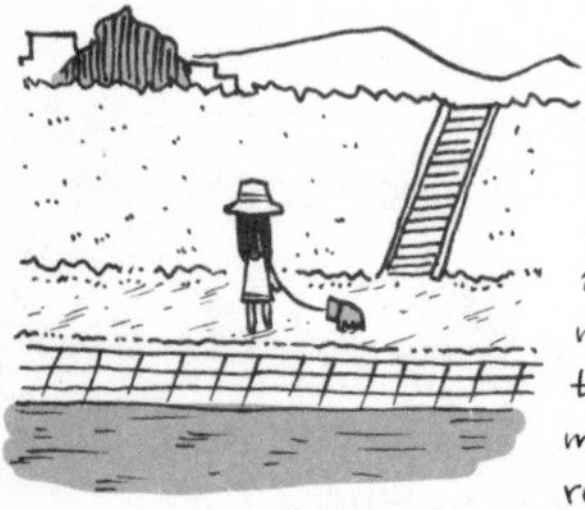

∘ a very nice river bank on the way home from school. many a student has created youthful memories there. in fact, not just students, but many men and women of all ages have made youthful memories there. yes, no matter how many years go by, our youth remains there for us.

- **Yamantaka Vidya-raja**

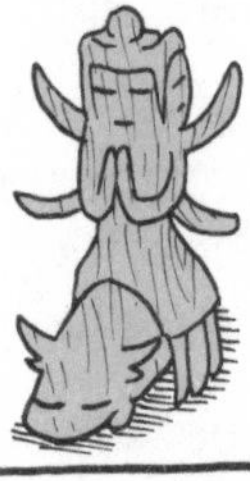

∘ one of the Five Wisdom Kings carved by Mai. seems she thinks it's cool that he's riding a cow. apparently this coolness is lost on the Professor. hopefully someday she'll understand.

- **"loser" ice cream**

daiku dairy industry's "n'ice cream"

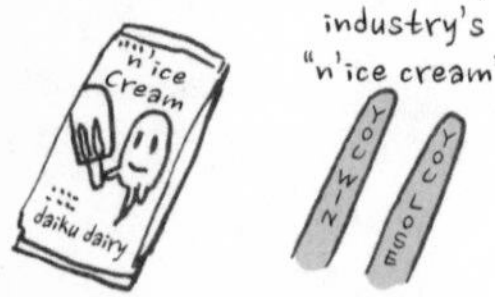
n'ice Cream
daiku dairy
YOU WIN
YOU LOSE

winners and losers both get text!

∘ a popsicle where winning sticks and losing sticks are both labelled. according to the daiku dairy CEO, "even if you lose, if there's something written there, you still feel like you've won!!"

- **duck**

the guardian of the river bank of youth. his ability to eat anything is one of his charms.

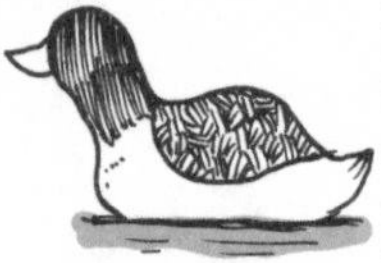

- **DVD vinyl**

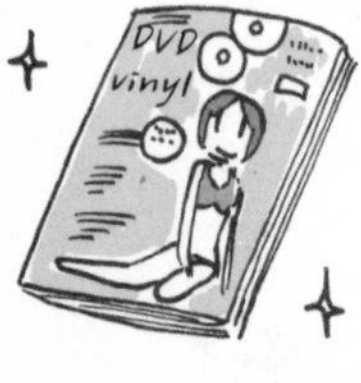
DVD
vinyl

fully loaded with dubiousness from the start!

an adult mag that Makoto is fond of reading. beneath the exterior of this magazine that covers every genre and gets right to the point, it contains hidden secrets that have been beloved for 65 years.

- **character eraser**

it smudges the words you're trying to erase.

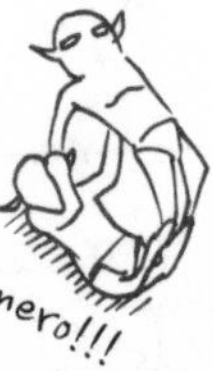

romero!!!

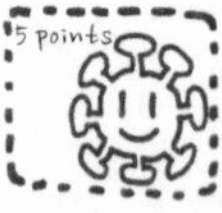
5 points

From the creator of *nichijou*, this surreal-slapstick series revolves around a penniless college student, Midori Nagumo, who lives in an ordinary city filled with not-quite-ordinary people. And as this reckless girl runs about, she sets the city in motion.

Midori is in a bit of a bind. She is in debt, and her landlady is trying to shake her down for unpaid rent. Her best friend refuses to a loan her cash since she's wised up to her tricks.

Maybe some bullying would help. Or a bit of petty theft? Neither is sustainable. Maybe getting a job would settle things... But working means less time for fun adventures in the big city...

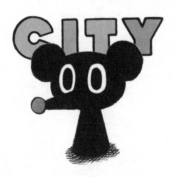

Coming March 2018!

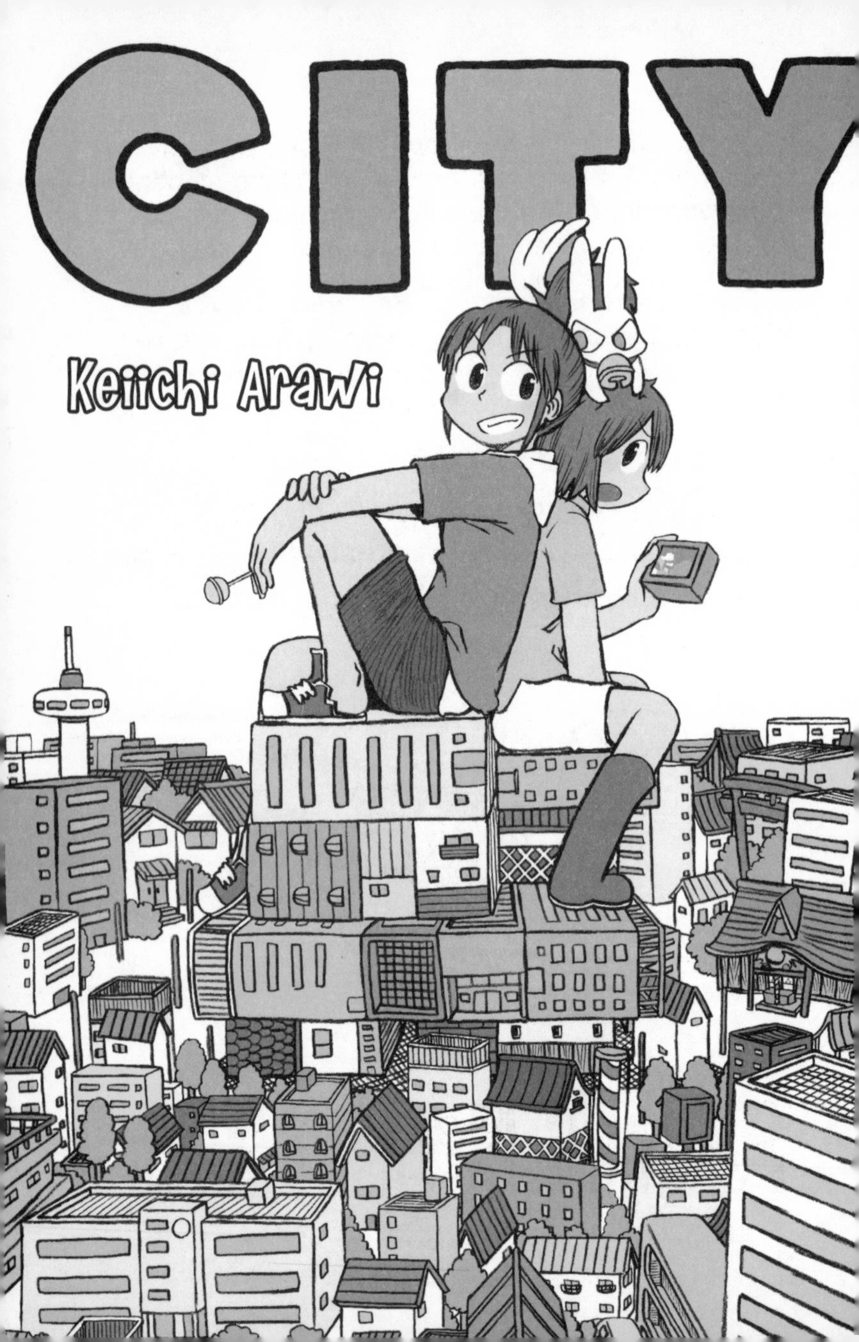
CITY
Keiichi Arawi

The follow up to the hit manga series ***nichijou***, ***Helvetica Standard*** is a full color anthology of Keiichi Arawi's comic art and design work. Funny and heartwarming, ***Helvetica Standard*** is a humorous look at modern day Japanese design in comic form.

Helvetica Standard is a deep dive into the artistic and creative world of Keiichi Arawi. Part comic, part diary, part art and design book, ***Helvetica Standard*** is a deconstruction of the world of ***nichijou***.

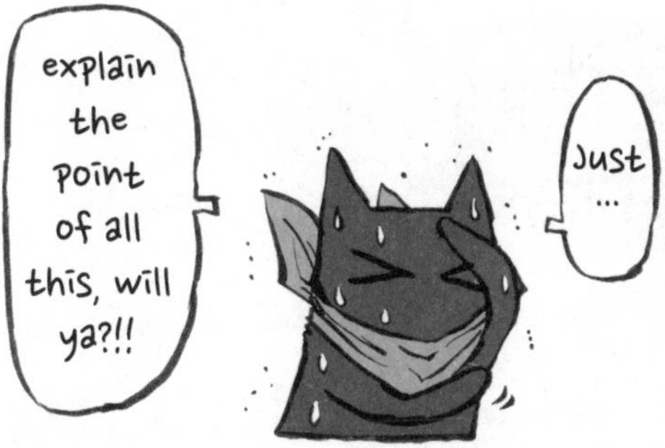
explain the point of all this, will ya?!!
Just ...

Both Parts Available Now!

keiichi
Arawi

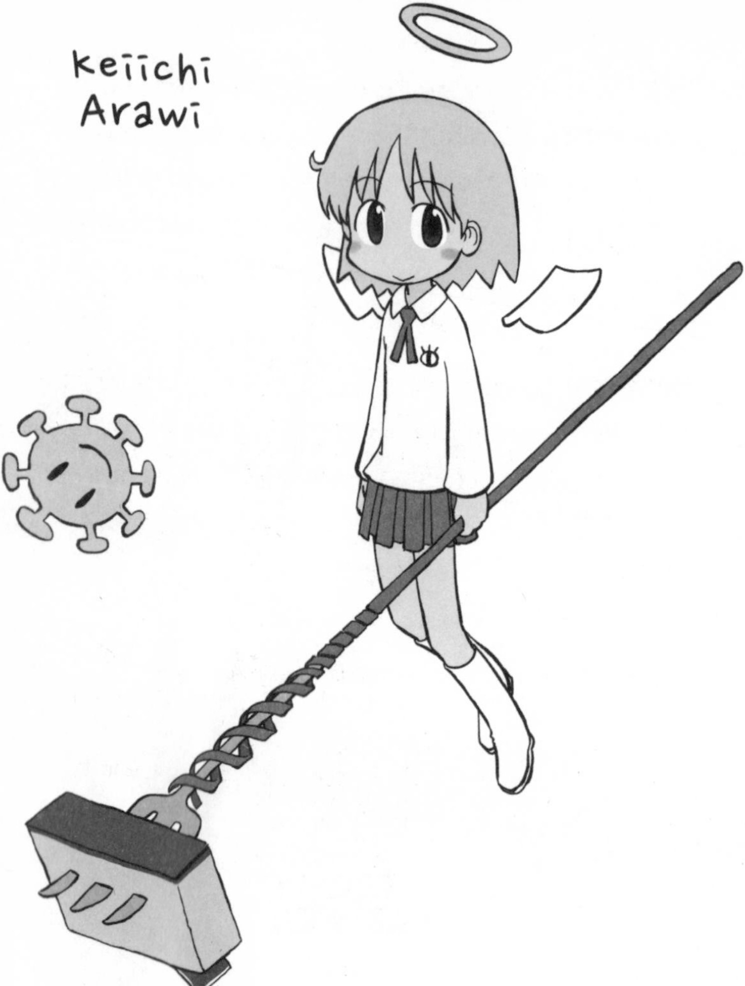

Helvetica Standard

nichijou 6

my ordinary life

A Vertical Comics Edition

Translation: Jenny McKeon
Production: Grace Lu
            Hiroko Mizuno
            Anthony Quintessenza

© Keiichi ARAWI 2011
First published in Japan in 2011 by KADOKAWA CORPORATION, Tokyo.
English translation rights arranged with KADOKAWA CORPORATION, Tokyo
through TUTTLE-MORI AGENCY, INC., Tokyo.

Published by Vertical Comics, an imprint of Vertical, Inc., New York

Originally published in Japanese as *nichijou 6* by Kadokawa Corporation, 2011
nichijou first serialized in *Monthly Shonen Ace,* Kadokawa Corporation, 2006-2015

This is a work of fiction.

ISBN: 978-1-942993-65-0

Manufactured in Canada

First Edition

Second Printing

Vertical, Inc.
451 Park Avenue South
7th Floor
New York, NY 10016
www.vertical-comics.com

Vertical books are distributed through Penguin-Random House Publisher